A RETURN TO INNOCENCE

. . . and there wrestled a man with him until the breaking of the day.

A RETURN TO INNOCENCE

PHILOSOPHICAL GUIDANCE
IN AN AGE OF CYNICISM

JEFFREY M. SCHWARTZ, M.D.
with Annie Gottlieb and Patrick Buckley

ReganBooks
An Imprint of HarperCollins*Publishers*

For Steve Wasserman
Requiescat In Pace

HarperCollins books may be purchased for educational, business, or sales promotional use. For information please write: Special Markets Department, HarperCollins Publishers, Inc., 10 East 53rd Street, New York, NY 10022.

Excerpts from "The Second Coming" and "A Prayer for my Daughter" by W. B. Yeats: Reprinted with permission of Simon & Schuster from *The Collected Works of W.B Yeats, Volume I: The Poems*, Revised and edited by Richard J. Finneran. Copyright © 1924 by Macmillan Publishing Company, renewed 1952 by Bertha Georgie Yeats.

Excerpts from *Mindfulness in Plain English* © Henepola Gunaratana 1992. Used by permission of Wisdom Publications, 199 Elm Street, Somerville, Massachusetts 02144.

FIRST EDITION

Designed by Nancy Field

ISBN 0-06-039240-1

98 99 00 01 02 10 9 8 7 6 5 4 3 2 1

CONTENTS

TRAINING YOUR MENTAL FORCE II: THE OWNER'S MANUAL FOR YOUR BRAIN   159

THE ROAD WARRIOR'S GUIDEBOOK   219

ACKNOWLEDGMENTS

As with everything I've accomplished in this decade, the generous support of the Charles and Lelah Hilton family gave me the opportunity to pursue these ideas to what I hope is a fruitful conclusion. My publisher, Judith Regan, first recognized the potential importance for a general audience of the ideas discussed in these letters to Patrick and urged me to make them into a book.

I have been very fortunate in the supportive and challenging input I have had from friends and colleagues while preparing these letters for publication. Marty Wax, Leslie Brothers, James Q. Wilson, John March, Mike Raleigh, Eric Reiman, Tom Brod, Mark Kampe, Dr. Khin Swe Win, and Donna Franks all provided very valuable, specific, insightful comments and recommendations that led to improvements in the text. I also had fruitful discussions with Ann Graybiel, Richard Gombrich, Dave Chalmers, Jim Leckman, Mike Jenike, and Scott Rauch about some of the deeper philosophical issues discussed here. Rabbi Harold Kushner helped teach me what a *mitzvah* is. My good friend Bhikkhu U Nandisena made helpful comments about some fine points of Buddhist philosophy, and my teacher, the Venerable U Silananda, provided insight and moral support and vetted the section on the Buddhist view of when life begins.

I have also been fortunate in getting some very valuable input from friends and colleagues who are closer to Patrick's age than to mine. Bryan Clark made numerous valuable comments. Matthew March, Renee Hamilton, Sara Wax, Maryela

Martinez, and David Reiman provided insightful information on their generation's perspective.

Annie Gottlieb contributed substantial skill and understanding to the task of turning these letters into a book. Above all, my friend Patrick not only gave me permission to publish my letters to him and his often very personal responses; by examining his life in the light of these ideas and by asking penetrating questions, he played an active and important role in shaping this book.

—*Jeffrey M. Schwartz*

I would like to thank Jacques Sandulescu and Barry Casselman, and to dedicate my participation in this book to the late Rabbi Jacob J. Weinstein and Sosai Masutatsu Oyama.

—*Annie Gottlieb*

I grew up during a time when absent fathers were the norm, but it has been my great fortune to have been guided and shaped by a few great men.

These are men who mean what they say, who care about people and who are always willing to take their time to help.

I am deeply grateful to everyone at Camp Keewaydin who instilled in me the camp motto, "*help the other fellow,*" something I first learned when I was eight. I especially want to thank Charlie Horner who was a figure of strength and wisdom and who saw a great day in every day.

I am forever thankful for a chance meeting at the Central Park Boat Pond with a gentleman who changed my life—and who taught me the art of model-boat building, Hal Wolf. He also taught me patience, dedication, how to have the courage to be better—and how the practice of boat building is the basis of all these things.

Jeff Schwartz changed my thinking about so many things. He took the time to teach me to respect others and he taught me how to face the world with my eyes open. Jeff was always there to answer my questions and to help me with any trouble I was having. I am eternally grateful for his wisdom.

I am grateful to my crew coach, Eric Houston, who taught me to push myself. More importantly, he taught me that fulfillment and success don't come from awards or even achievements. They come from inside and from the knowledge that you pushed yourself as hard as you could. He also taught me that you can't do everything by yourself, and that in order to fly down the race course, or excel at anything, you must learn to work with others.

Thank you Mr. Houston, Jeff Schwartz, Hal Wolf, and Charlie Horner for changing my life.

A special thanks to Susan Whitehead and Annie Gottleib for their quiet support. And to my grandmothers Rita and Jean for their devotion.

And thanks, Mom, for being so strong.

—*Patrick Buckley*

Though a thousand times a thousand men are conquered by one in battle, the one who conquers himself is truly the master of battle.

—GOTAMA BUDDHA, *Dhammapada 103*

Men are qualified for civil liberty, in exact proportion to their disposition to put moral chains upon their own appetites. . . . Society cannot exist unless a controlling power upon will and appetite be placed somewhere, and the less of it there is within, the more there must be without. It is ordained in the eternal constitution of things, that men of intemperate minds cannot be free. Their passions forge their fetters.

—EDMUND BURKE,
   A Letter to a Member of the National Assembly, 1791

May all beings' hearts rejoice.

—GOTAMA BUDDHA, *Mettā Sutta* (Loving-Kindness Discourse)

Dear Reader,

As I write this, a presidency hangs in the balance for want of the ideas, values, and methods you will find in this book.

The issue being hotly debated on every talk show and editorial page this year is whether a man is fit to govern the most powerful nation in the world if he can not or will not govern himself. But behind this urgent question, as serious as it is, loom far larger questions for all of us:

Why—and how—should *any* of us govern our own impulses, appetites, and emotions, when, for instance, a marriage grows overfamiliar or difficult and a new love beckons?

When self-gratification becomes a primary aim of life, what happens to intimacy, and loyalty, and private and public trust? What happens to our children? To our culture? To our freedom?

Are we humans primarily driven, or "drivers"? Are we the blameless puppets of our genes, our hormones, our childhoods, or do we have the power, and so the responsibility, to choose what we will do?

And if so, in a predominantly secular and materialistic culture, where should we look for guidance for our choices?

President Clinton's troubles are like a fever signaling an illness in our body politic. When we look at him, we see a magnified reflection of ourselves. It's no coincidence that both he and the young woman with whom he has been linked by scandal suffered early separation from their fathers (he by his father's accidental death and his stepfather's alcoholic violence, she by an angry divorce)—a condition now epidemic among America's youngsters, due to our runaway rates of divorce and unwed pregnancy. The fission of the nuclear family has become a self-perpetuating chain reaction, resulting in a massive explosion that has cast millions of young people emotionally and morally adrift. Values once protected families, families transmitted values—when either one breaks down, so does the other. Where will this vicious cycle stop? How many will remain who have the strength and courage to stand up and say, "It stops here"?

It was with questions like these very much on my mind that I began writing, to a young man of sixteen, the letters that have evolved into this book. Patrick is the son of a friend of mine, a single mother who was never married to his father. To be candid, I started writing to Patrick at her request—because, she told me, she was desperate that he get regular intellectual and spiritual input from a successful adult male. She didn't mince words—she told me he needed a father figure. His father, as you will see in our letters to each other, has been at best an intermittent and inconsistent presence in his life.

I'd known Patrick since he was eleven, but it was when he began to come of age that I felt it urgent to become a special kind of guardian to him—a philosophical guardian. He was reaching the age to make his own choices, but the path ahead of him bristled with dangerously deceptive road signs—false directions that could lure him right off a cliff. "Ideas have consequences," the southern essayist Richard M. Weaver declared, and he was right. We search in vain for the root causes of our social breakdown and emotional suffering when we look for them only in the material world, or even the psychotherapist's office. It is as a consequence of *bad ideas* about human nature and the proper balance between individual freedom and responsibility that Patrick and millions of his peers are growing up without their fathers. False, seductive, destructive ideas that appeal to the worst in us and flatter it as the best have led to epidemics of drug addiction, teenage pregnancy, sexually transmitted disease, crime, and violence. Modern society's refusal to acknowledge the vital role of faith in a functioning society has much to do with the pain in our hearts, the fear in our streets and schools, and the cynicism that has corroded our ideals.

JEFFREY M. SCHWARTZ

As a result of the destructive behavior unleashed by a mindless belief in bad ideas, we live in a society that has lost its innocence, and that is no longer able—or willing, if it involves any sacrifice of self-gratification—to protect the innocence of its young. In some circles, this corruption of innocence is actually regarded with pride, as a kind of growing up or wising up, a shedding of Victorian prudery and wide-eyed naïveté. For example, it's been stated in the media, with some satisfaction, that the American public's uneasy tolerance of immoral behavior by its public servants (as long as the economy is thriving) proves that we're finally becoming as mature and sophisticated as the French!

I'd like to direct anyone who believes such vicious nonsense to the original meaning of the word "innocence." It comes from the Latin prefix *in-* (not) + *nocere* (to harm). Innocence means *not harming*. Now, anyone who has ever been through a messy divorce, or been the victim of a crime, or had a child on drugs, or simply watches the evening news knows that it is extremely difficult—in fact it is a high art, and a lost art—for human beings simply *to refrain from doing harm* to each other and themselves! That is why, in my letters to Patrick, I state that *true* Innocence is actually the highest and most sophisticated of human achievements. To scorn innocence is to glamorize and promote suffering—and God knows (and so should we!) that life includes enough unavoidable pain without our recklessly causing more. Surely it is a challenge more worthy of our humanity to work to "love, honor, comfort, and keep" one another from harm, as the beautiful but battered words of the marriage vows say.

To protect ourselves, and to begin to repair the damage to our world, we urgently need to be armed with *good* ideas—ideas firmly based on true and accurate information about our human nature and the conditions that encourage the *best* in us to thrive. Patrick (like so many others) needed a guardian who could hand on to him these strength-giving, life-giving ideas—the living philosophical, moral, and spiritual guidance that our society no longer gives us "with our mother's milk," and that I, during my own growing up, largely had to search out for myself.

The places where I found it are hardly obscure. The Bible and the teachings of the Buddha are my primary sources. But great spiritual arteries such as these, feeding the human heart for over three millennia, have somehow been declared peripheral at best, and irrelevant at worst, to an age of unprecedented affluence, personal freedom, and scientific power. As a practicing psychiatrist and scientist, let me state this as forcefully as I can: *Nothing could be farther from the truth.* For everything that disgusts and grieves us about the way we live today has its antidote and cure in *the lost art of self-command* that waits to be rediscovered in those sources of spiritual empowerment. You will find the fundamentals of that art in this book, drawn from the timeless teachings of Moses, Jesus, and Buddha, but written in a language for the twenty-first century. The most exciting news I have to share is that science itself— the cutting edge of brain research—has begun to confirm the wisdom about human nature and its cultivation that was first declared by those great spiritual guides.

I believe that young people are more ready and eager for a return to this protective wisdom than we "mature" adults can possibly know. All too often we passively watch our culture break down around us and sadly shake our heads—but *they* feel the real brunt of the onslaught. As wave after wave of sordid scandals and salacious sitcoms breaks across their TV screens, as their classmates become potential sources of danger and their own families routinely come apart, our kids try to be tough and knowing, to shrug and say, "Whatever." But underneath the fragile sophistication, they are sending out unmistakable signals of distress. Everywhere I turn I hear unanswered cries for relief, for safety and security. The suicide rate in America is rising for only one age group—ten to nineteen—and in that group, it's *tripled* since 1960. Drug use in high schools, after declining throughout the '80s, has doubled since 1992—a sure sign of hopelessness and fear.

But a crisis is also an opportunity, and the catastrophic evidence that our fashionably value-free postmodern "values" *aren't working* has made many young people (and a lot of older ones too!) hunger to hear that yes, there's another way to live, and it's been there all along! ("To arrive where we started and know the place for the first time," as T. S. Eliot so eloquently put it.) That is why I decided, with Patrick's permission and cooperation, to expand my original letters to him into this book.

We often hear the phrase "Knowledge is power"—but nowhere is it truer than when it comes to knowledge of ourselves. And so I am inviting you on an inner journey, one my young friend Patrick has already embarked on and wants you to share. This book will show you a path to self-knowledge and the empowerment that it brings. But as the Buddha said, I can only show you the way. "The strenuous work must be done by you."

—JMS

A BIRTHDAY PRESENT

Happy Birthday, Patrick!

Presuming you followed the instructions on the back of the envelope—"Do Not Open Until April 12"—you're reading this on the morning of your sixteenth birthday. I wanted to be among the first to welcome you to adulthood.

Are you surprised that I'm saying that? We don't quite regard sixteen-year-olds as young adults—most people would draw that line where the law does, at eighteen or even twenty-one—and you may not feel quite ready to think of yourself as one. But tell me if I'm right: you *are* feeling a little bit different today, just a little bit new.

You've successfully run the rapids of puberty, so the physical changes that prepare you to be a grown man have already taken place. Let's face it, you'll never be a soprano again! And mentally, I'm sure you feel ready, even impatient, for new experiences and real challenges. Our society may still view you as a "kid," but in the Orthodox Jewish tradition I grew up in, you'd have been officially considered a grown man for three years now!

Today, I agree: thirteen is a bit young. When people only lived half as long, they had to grow up faster. But at sixteen, there are many good reasons for saying that you stand on the threshold of adulthood this morning, beginning the process of leaving your mother's and other adults' protection and taking charge of your own life. So, congratulations! Don't make light of this birthday. It's a genuinely important one.

In fact, in any traditional society anywhere in the world, you'd be having much more than just a birthday party today.

Like all the great passages of human life—birth, marriage, becoming a parent, and death—the transition to adulthood used to be an occasion not just for gathering, feasting, and gifts, but for solemn ceremony: Confirmation, Bar or Bat

Mitzvah, rites of initiation. (Echoes also linger in the Sweet Sixteen parties girls used to have when I was a kid, and the "Quinceañeras" parties fifteen-year-old Latino girls still have today.) In many ancient languages, the same word is used for "ceremony" and for "blessing." For example, a *mitzvah*, in Hebrew, is a divine commandment, of a moral and/or ritual nature, the performance of which brings blessings. *Mangala* in Sanskrit and Pāli,* a language of early Buddhism, means both "solemn ceremony" and "good-fortune-bringer." Even today, a majority of the world's people still believe that it brings good fortune to take serious things seriously by marking them with solemn ritual. And a new man or woman joining the community is a serious and joyous thing! To ensure a good start, to let you as a young person know just how much your future contribution matters, all the adults—but especially those of the same sex—gather around to formally bestow the new powers and privileges of adulthood, *and* the new responsibilities that come with them. As a boy, your father and other men of the community should be with you today to welcome and guide you, to show you by example and instruction how to be a good man.

And here a sadness starts to creep up on me, because your father is not an intimate presence in your life and never has been. I know he was never married to your mother (neither are the dads of over a fourth of the babies being born in this country right now), but even if he had been, with the divorce rate as high as it is, it's no guarantee that he'd be any more a part of your life today. It's because I know *you*, Patrick, that the scary statistics about American families—a third of kids currently living apart from their fathers, and more than half destined to for some part of their childhood—are so much more than just a bunch of numbers to me.

For five years, I've been a witness to your struggles to

*The long a, spelled ā, in Pāli words is pronounced like the a in "father."

grow up without a father and to forge a relationship with the distant and troubled man who played such a small role in your childhood. I've watched your mother struggle to fill that gap, to be all things to you. While she did everything she possibly could—including being a good provider (but at a sad price—you were in day care at age three months!), teaching you strong values, and making sure you had good men in your life—she couldn't fulfill your need for a father or make that need go away. She's told me how when she got married—you were six—you immediately started calling your new stepfather "Daddy." Those loving sentiments, sadly, were not mutual. That man didn't come to your holiday plays or swim meets ("Swimming isn't a *real* sport," he sniffed, not like the basketball his own sons played), and he was gone when your half-sister was only a year old. As a family friend, I can't make that up to you. What's done is done; no one can ever completely heal the wounds inflicted on your generation, the loneliness you've felt, the speed with which you've been forced to grow up, and the extent to which you've had to raise yourselves (with the questionable help of the entertainment industry).

What I *can* do, though, is the time-honored job of "the men of the community." I can stand by you, be there to try to answer your questions, and do my best to make sure you don't go out into life unprepared, unskilled, and unequipped. I can teach you what I know about how to be a good man and a strong, wise, and responsible human being—how to *be* the kind of man you wish your father had been. I can give you time-tested tools and skills that will enable you (if you use them!) to protect yourself and those you love against the destructive forces that are tearing our souls, families, and communities apart. And I can help you connect to the steadying, sheltering wisdom that's so desperately needed in a time when, as the great poet W. B. Yeats wrote, "Things fall apart, the center cannot hold. . . ."

A pretty bold claim, I know. But that's the birthday present I'm offering you. Are you interested? Before I say more, I want to make sure my words are falling on open ears! But I also want *you* to know that you can call *me* any time, and ask me any question. Our two generations haven't always communicated very well. Maybe you and I can start mending and reenergizing some of those broken promises—you know, the ones you still remember even after the people who make them seem to forget.

Happy birthday, Patrick, and many more.

Your friend,
Jeff

WRESTLING FOR MY SOUL

THANKS FOR THE DISCIPLINE

Dear Patrick,

It was good to talk to you on the phone last night. I'm sorry to hear that "broken promises" is such an ongoing theme in your relationship with your dad—that time and again, as you put it, "he says he's going to do something, and then he doesn't do it." But I'm very glad he called you on your birthday—that much ceremony, at least, he can still get it together to observe. Most of all, I'm glad you're taking me up on my birthday offer.

By beginning this conversation, we're actually resuming, in a whole new way, a transmission of ideas from generation to generation that was held sacred until just one or two generations ago. (It's no coincidence that that's also when our families and communities really started falling apart.) The ideas we'll be talking about—which are nothing less than the operating instructions for human nature—are timeless, but for their eternal relevance to shine forth, they need to be freshly applied to the new circumstances of each generation. (Showing that these great ideas are still the main source of spiritual power, even in an age of science and technology, is the only way to restore them to their rightful place as life's true foundation.) That's why your part in this dialogue is so important. I can reconnect you to the power source of three thousand years of wisdom, but you're the one who's going to have to ground it in the urgent concerns of a young person living right now, at the beginning of a new millennium.

If that sounds like a setup—like I'm going to expect long letters from *you*—don't worry. I know how busy you are, with swimming, football, and now crew, too, on top of all your classes. I also know you and letter-writing—I've gotten a few of your one-liners over the years! It's not a problem. There's a gem of a line in Shakespeare's play *Hamlet:* "Brevity is the soul of wit." So it's fine with me if you weigh in now and then by phone, post card, or E-mail, in twenty-five words or less!

Meanwhile, I'll start by telling you how I found my way, as much out of sheer desperation as anything else, to the sources of wise guidance that I'll be sharing with you. The story begins when I was almost exactly your age, and—this might surprise you—athletics play an important part in it.

You expressed some concern last night over whether all your sports will leave you enough time for studying. So far, you seem to be handling it, according to your mom. Your rowing coach, who's also your biology teacher, says you're doing great at both. To my mind, that's probably no coincidence. Academics provide the content of education, but good athletic training builds a strong and capable container! Your passion for athletics will actually make my job easier, because your experience of training your body will give you a head start in understanding what I have to say about training your mind and character.

I was a wrestler in high school, and what I learned from it has served me all my life. When my coach, Bill Linkner, retired two years ago, over thirty years' worth of former wrestlers and football players gave him a big testimonial dinner. One of the gifts was a poster-size picture of him, which we all signed. What I wrote on that picture was, *"Thanks for the discipline."* Because that discipline formed the foundation for everything I've accomplished since. To this day, everything I do contains some element of what I learned as a wrestler.

Near the end of that evening, when we were presenting our coach the gifts we'd gotten for him, one of my old teammates said to me, "You know, if Coach Linkner had asked you to die for the team back then, you wouldn't be here to see this." And I said, "You know, you're right." It's well understood now that that's how soldiers fight, how they can face death in combat without batting an eye. They do it for each other, and their common goal. It's about identity and connectedness with your buddies, your platoon, doing well for them, earning their respect and esteem. Clearly, Patrick, you're experiencing that right now—from what you tell me, especially on the rowing team. And I'm proud to say that's what my teammates most remembered about me. They used to joke that if Coach Linkner told me, "Go run through that brick wall," I'd try. There were definitely better wrestlers than me on the team, but no one was more dedicated. I'm not exaggerating when I say that when I was your age wrestling was more important to me than life itself. I may not have been too wise, but no one who was there would deny that I was brave.

Most adolescents devote themselves to *something* with that kind of life-or-death intensity, and for a good reason. You are, in reality, dying as a child and being reborn as a young adult. If society doesn't assist that passage with a rigorous, transforming challenge—and outside of the military, athletics is almost the last one we've got left—kids will often act it out in tragically self-destructive ways, like drinking and driving, gangs, or drugs. I vividly remember saying something back then that sums up in one line how much wrestling meant to me. A friend from another school had told me that his football coach liked to say that soccer (which I also played) was only a game, but football was a *sport*. (Americans have acquired more respect for soccer since then!) I replied, "Well, you tell your coach that maybe soccer is only a game, and football is a sport, but *wrestling* is a *religion!*"

On that note, I'll send you back to the sacred rites of rowing and continue this story tomorrow!

Your friend,
Jeff

. . . and there wrestled a man with him until the breaking of the day.

JEFFREY M. SCHWARTZ

YOU'RE ON YOUR OWN

Dear Patrick,

When I said "Wrestling is a religion," and I said it more than once in high school, I was saying something all dedicated athletes come to know, something I'm sure you've already had a taste of: the all-out physical and mental effort that you make when you strive for excellence can lift you beyond your ordinary self, into a clarity and freedom that partakes of the spiritual realm. But I suspect it goes even deeper than that—I was probably also remembering (at least subconsciously) one of the most powerful and mysterious initiation images of the Jewish faith I was born into—an image in which *religion* is *wrestling!*

This is how the Book of Genesis tells it:

> *And Jacob was left alone, and there wrestled a man with him until the breaking of the day.*
>
> *And when he saw that he prevailed not against him, he touched the hollow of his thigh; and the hollow of Jacob's thigh was out of joint, as he wrestled with him.*
>
> *And he said, Let me go, for the day breaketh. And [Jacob] said, I will not let thee go, except thou bless me.*
>
> *And he said unto him, What is thy name? And he said, Jacob.*
>
> *And he said, Thy name shall be called no more Jacob, but Israel, for thou hast striven with God and with men, and hast prevailed.*

When I was very young, I read that story of a man who grapples with God, and who wins his name and a name for his whole people, in my grandfather's big Old Testament. (I can still see that big Bible, which sat on a little table next to his easy chair.) And maybe it planted a seed that would take root in my mind when I was sixteen and wrestling for my own identity and blessing. "Jacob was left alone": I sure could relate to *that* at sixteen. Outside the gym, I was very alienated and lonely. Socially I didn't know how to play the game, and refused to learn. (If this rumor that you've got a girlfriend is true, you're way ahead of me. At your age, I had had zero dates.) And as far as having a role model for learning that kind of thing—well, for whatever reason, I just didn't seem to make contact with anyone on that level. Mostly I just felt very alone.

Emotionally, it sometimes felt like I never had a father—even though, like most fathers of the World War II generation, mine was *there* physically during my childhood. (He left my mother when I was not much older than you.) And there's no denying that he worked like hell to support us with all the material benefits he never had. In a very real sense that made it much harder to understand what was missing. He certainly wasn't a deadbeat, a drunk, or a bum. His attitude was "Hey, I'm really there for you, you can always count on me," and in the material realm, it was definitely true. But he believed—he still believes—that if a father fulfills the material-provider role, he has done everything a father needs to do.

It was the classic mistake of his generation, the World War II generation. Now, I hesitate to say *anything* critical about a generation that survived the Depression, defeated Hitler, and gave my own postwar baby-boom generation a life of security, affluence, and education never before seen on Planet Earth. For any of *us* to talk about *their* mistakes (much less to rant and scream about them, as many college kids did in the 1960s) is in bad taste, because in the things that turn out to matter most—like sticking by your loved ones and keeping your word—their record is so much better than ours. Or at least, it *was* until we reached adolescence, launched our so-called "cultural revolution," and started corrupting *them!*

It's one of the saddest ironies of recent history, and one you don't hear too much about, that quite a few members of that heroic generation wound up envying and imitating the orgy of self-gratification their own labors had made possible for their children. By the time the "Me Generation" of the '70s rolled around, it seemed like everybody and their uncle (especially *my* uncle, as you'll see!) wanted to "get it on" with the "Free Love" thing. There was more than a little gray hair hanging over collars onto love beads in those days, and a sudden rash of midlife "liberation" divorces among people who had once said "Till death do us part" and meant it. If the moral flabbiness and general sense of entitlement that has infected this country since the late '60s had been half as prevalent in the early '40s, we'd probably all be speaking German and Japanese today!

Fortunately, when the world hung in the balance, the vast majority of my parents' generation were the original "promise keepers." They did not hesitate to sacrifice their own personal gratification for the sake of family and country—sacrifices, paradoxically, that often brought them a deeper and more lasting gratification than today's "self-fulfillment" seekers will probably ever know. And plenty of them, beyond a shadow of a doubt, have kept the faith. Your mom gave me a copy of the eulogy she wrote for her late uncle Eddie, your great-uncle and her godfather, Edward Imprescia. Her description of him holds true for many members of an amazing generation. There are millions for whom this eulogy could be recited:

"By his own example he taught me, and all of us, everything we needed to know to live a life of goodness and generosity—as a loving and dutiful husband for fifty years, as a committed and loving father, as a courageous warrior in World War II, as a thoughtful and generous neighbor. . . . This was a man who knew how to give and he gave with no conditions. This was a man with supreme humility."

That said, however, and Uncle Eddie aside, I believe something crucial had already been lost from the heart of the World War II generation's giving and promise-keeping, and that was *the ultimate reason why*—what it's really all *for.* The words "generation gap" weren't coined until the '60s, but a very significant gap had already opened up between the World War II generation and *their* parents, which set the stage for all the trouble that was to come. In many families, tradition—the inseparable weave of religious belief and social custom that had always given human life its form and meaning—had suddenly lost its hold. This was easiest to see in immigrant families like mine, where the first American-born generation, eager to be "modern" and not to seem "foreign," jettisoned, and sometimes even scorned, many of their parents' "Old World" ways. My mother has confided to me how embarrassed she was, when she was growing up, by my grandmother's broken English and Eastern European customs—a reaction that, while very understandable, is also quite sad. So interwoven was dying custom with life-giving faith that the baby was often thrown out with the bathwater, and many children of devout immigrants became proudly secular, generic Americans.

But they weren't the only ones. For in a very real sense, *every* American, and perhaps every Westerner, in the first half of the twentieth century *was* an immigrant—from an "Old World" shaped by tradition to a new one shaped by science and technology; from a world ruled by God's power to one dominated by man's rapidly growing power; from a world infused with potent Spirit to one made of readily manipulated matter. As the nineteenth century ended, the philosopher Friedrich Nietzsche declared "God is dead." Humanity, beginning to take charge of its own destiny, felt it no longer needed a Father to guide it. (Freud, in what I consider to be the stupidest thing he ever did, actually dared to call God the Father an "illusion"!)

Material progress became the new god, the motivating engine at the center of modern life. So the momentum of the old promises continued to shape the World War II generation's conduct—and they dutifully and devotedly cared for their families. But they did so not as their elders had, to perpetuate the service of God, or to honor and be blessed by the eternal order of the universe, but *to give their children a better, more comfortable life.*

It was a goal that the baby boomers, even as we arrogantly took it as our due, correctly sensed to be spiritually void. (It would be comic, if it weren't so tragic, to watch a substantial segment of my generation try to revive spirituality without displacing themselves from the center of the universe.) Without any transcendent purpose, our parents' self-sacrifice for our sake seemed somehow hollow and pointless—and perhaps, by 1970, some of *them* thought so, too.

My father spent his whole life in New York City's garment center, a hard place where most people get "wised up," not wise. He worked like a dog (and the garment center being what it is, he also got treated like one!), all to fulfill the material-provider role up to the call of duty and beyond. Like so many parents of today, his mind was almost totally focused on "making a buck" (as he called it)—which always was justified, and sincerely so, by "giving the kids a better life." It was more than just the necessities: whatever desires I had, he fulfilled. If I needed money—even money he thought shouldn't be spent—hey, no problem. (He had a genuinely morbid fear of being accused of denying me!) What had somehow gotten lost in the accelerating "progress" of American culture was that there are huge aspects of a "better life" that "making a buck" simply can't provide. When I needed the guidance that comes from genuine wisdom, or the kind of support that can only be grounded in personal honor and moral courage—my father didn't have it to give.

His older brother, Aaron, on the other hand, was all too eager to provide guidance, albeit of a somewhat different kind. My uncle was a charming con man and bunko artist. (He used to travel under the alias Al Grace—what a joke!) However, truth be told, he was also my father's idol and role model, the one person on earth he most wanted to please. Would you like to hear the "timeless wisdom" my Uncle Aaron imparted to me around the time of *my* sixteenth birthday?

"Kid," he said, "listen good, because I'm going to tell you something you better remember for the rest of your life." (I assure you he got my full attention with *that* intro!)

If you find a friend
That's true and blue,
Make sure you screw him
Before he screws you.

I remember the feeling of simultaneous confusion and disgust that he elicited with that little rhyme. If you can relate to my feeling like I'd been sucker-punched in the stomach, you'll begin to understand why, when I thought about wrestling with the great questions on the threshold of adulthood, a little voice inside me said, "Face it, sonny boy, you're on your own." No coach, no seconds. I faced those big challenges like Jacob did, alone.

And yet, somewhere deep in my consciousness was that vivid and saving memory of reading the Old Testament with my grandfather, my mother's father. Tomorrow, I'll write you about him.

Your friend,
Jeff

STRENGTHENING YOUR BRAIN

Dear Patrick,

Grandfathers, like your mom's Sicilian one, who I know she was close to, are often our only link to the lost world that had fathers as its backbone.

My maternal grandfather was in many ways the exact opposite of my father: a gentle and devout man who had suffered terrible losses in his life. I wish he'd been a stronger counterforce to the brash hollow men on my father's side, but he was the one close relative I made real emotional contact with, and the only one who gave me any kind of spiritual foundation. My grandfather had had a formal Jewish education in Europe, and he could have become a rabbi, but he immigrated here, giving up that dream for the American dream of safety and security. Instead, he became an upholsterer. He lived above his shop on Ditmars Boulevard in Astoria, Queens. I used to sit up there and study the Bible with him. That was my first exposure to words of power and wisdom, to the force of truth that transcends the merely human.

It must have been very important to my grandfather to pass his heritage on to me. I am named after his youngest brother, whom he really loved and admired. (Our Hebrew names are both Yaacov—Jacob—just like that Jewish wrestler in Genesis!) When my grandfather came to America with one brother and one sister, that young brother and five others were left behind, and they all perished. They kept up a close correspondence until just before Hitler marched into Poland. The last letter, my mother remembers, arrived just before Labor Day weekend, 1939. She vividly recalls how upset and worried my grandfather became the instant the news of the Nazi invasion of Poland flashed on the radio. "I told them not to stay. I told them to get out of there," he said. Then the letters stopped, and none of them was ever seen again. There is no record of what happened to them. They probably were shot; before the death factories were built, many thousands of Jews were simply rounded up and shot execution style, then thrown into mass graves.

All that unspoken memory, and all of his unfulfilled rabbinical calling, my grandfather poured into preparing me for my Orthodox Bar Mitzvah when I was thirteen. He trained me in the traditional way, and he performed the first half of the service. I memorized and recited the entire second half, in Hebrew. It all took a lot of effort and concentration, but going through that formal training in the years leading up to age thirteen gave me lifelong discipline of the mind. A year or two later wrestling would begin to add discipline of the body. Those two initiatory challenges—one cerebral, the other athletic—shaped my character, and became the twin foundations of my life.

Both disciplines would be a great advantage to me later on, in my twenties, when I began the serious study of Buddhism and Yoga that I continue to this day. The flexibility and pain tolerance I had developed as a wrestler would make it possible (though not easy at first) for me to do meditation sitting in the full lotus position—legs fully crossed, each foot on the opposite thigh. I have done that for at least an hour every morning for over twenty years. And by memorizing and reciting the Hebrew for my Bar Mitzvah, it turns out, I had wired my own brain to be able to memorize and chant entire sermons of the Buddha in *their* ancient language, Pāli.

Now, you might ask, why wasn't I just wiring my brain for more Hebrew? If all the great religious traditions refer to the same ultimate truth (and I am convinced that they do, though they use different approaches), why did I feel the need to seek outside my own heritage, especially when I was my grandfather's hope for continuity? That is a very fair

That's me, doing meditation in full lotus position.

question—one often asked of American Jews and Christians who have been drawn to Buddhism (and for that matter, of Jews who admire the teachings of Jesus Christ, among whom I also count myself). I can only give you my own answers, which go back to that biblical image of Jacob alone in the desert, wrestling for his spiritual life.

First of all, I have never left my heritage. I consider myself a Jew who practices Buddhist mindfulness meditation and studies Buddhist and Christian philosophy from their original sources. In all the years I have visited and meditated in Buddhist monasteries and temples, I have never once bowed before a statue of the Buddha, even when deeply observant Burmese laymen and Buddhist monks all around me were doing so. Why? Because Jews are commanded not to bow down before idols. It's just as simple as that.

Within a year or two of my Bar Mitzvah, though, I felt increasingly unfulfilled by the practice of Orthodox Judaism—enough so that I would eventually decide to seek beyond it. The modern world's biggest challenge, Patrick, which so far we've flunked miserably, is continuity in change—how the eternal truths that stand guard over human souls and societies can speak with full authority to new generations seduced by the flattering promises of science and technology. Most religions have either softened their message and compromised their authority in order to be hip or "relevant," or they've preserved their traditions down to the smallest detail, at the risk of falling out of touch. To me, the powerful truths at the core of Orthodox Judaism seemed cloaked by the rituals of another time and place, one that had been tragically destroyed and could not be recreated. My grandfather's approach to religion, as much as I admire it, didn't seem to confront the terrifying realities of living—and dying—in the twentieth century. In the face of the Holocaust, saying Kaddish, the prayer for the dead, was certainly necessary. But for me it was not enough.

And that brings me to my other difficulty with my own tradition. When I started reading the English translation printed opposite the Hebrew, I found that it was all about being God's children, trusting in God and beseeching Him to take care of things. That struck me as putting my fate too much in another's hands, even if those hands were God's! It was too passive; the religion didn't give me enough sense of active participation in and responsibility for my own life. I needed something more along the lines of "God helps those who help themselves," the way my grandfather had helped himself by coming to America, while his brother, whom I was named for, had been murdered in spite of God. It seemed to me that God's power for good had to work *through* us, and that since there is evil both around us and within us, it was going to be a struggle. That was fine with me: I was a wrestler!

In the men of my family, strength and wisdom—the two qualities you would hope for in a father—were divided: strength without enough wisdom on the one hand, wisdom without enough strength on the other. Neither side could provide all the protection I needed when I was a child, or the means to fully protect myself when I got older. I had to discover that for myself. I am writing to you so you won't have to wander so long in the desert—but, Patrick, you're still going to face your own struggle. I loved that story of Jacob wrestling with God, which says that you need strength and guts and endurance to be wise. And I reacted with immediate recognition the first time I read Gotama Buddha's words: *"You* must do the strenuous work. Enlightened ones are only teachers."

Well, I hope I've left you enough time for your training *and* your studying! Now at least you know a lot more about me, and where *I'm* coming from. They say a picture is worth a thousand words, so I'm going to leave you with one.

That's the same kid who was a maniacal warrior on the wrestling mat. There's no contradiction: it would take every bit of that warrior spirit to protect that sincerity and innocence. And make no mistake about it—it's been a battle! But I can look at that picture today, and know that same boy remains alive in me—a little war-weary perhaps, but still untouched. I swore I would protect him, and I did.

I'll bet if you look around at most of your friends, though, Patrick, you'll see that purity of heart (which exists in almost every young person) already disappearing, being either destroyed or covered up. Nobody likes getting hurt, and the simplest way not to get hurt is not to care too much. That's why few adults have all that much of a sense of continuity with their younger self. To hold on to that, you have to be *tough*. Not fake-tough like my Uncle Aaron, whose sneering worldliness was, at bottom, based on craving and fear. You must dare to stay open and vulnerable in a world where there is evil. Cheap cynicism can't give you that caliber of protection. It only comes from cultivating real mental strength.

That same boy remains alive in me.

A few years ago I went to the hospital to see my uncle, not long before his death. He joked around, like always. For good or for bad he always joked around; nothing was ever too serious with him. "It's all a lot of happy horseshit"—that was always his favorite saying. But at a certain point, after I humorously parried the last one of his pointed barbs I would ever hear, he looked at me and he said, "No one's ever really gotten to you, have they?"

Coming from Uncle Aaron, that was quite a compliment.

Your friend,
Jeff

RECOVERING INNOCENCE IN A CYNICAL AGE

Be not be conformed to this age, but be transformed by the renewing of your mind, so that you may discern what is the will of God, the good and well-pleasing and perfect.

—The Epistle of St. Paul to the Romans, 12:2

Dear Jeff,
OK, so, how do you "cultivate real mental strength?" Because I feel like people get to me, a lot!

See you later,
Patrick

REGIMEN FOR A STRONG MIND

Dear Patrick,

You hit the nail right on the head: how to cultivate real mental strength is a big part of what this conversation between us is all about. But I can't tell you how in so many words. I will have to show you, step by step, through your own everyday experiences. One of the things I respect most about the teaching of the Buddha is that it is a "come and see" teaching. He didn't just "tell it like it is" and then expect you to take his word for it. He wanted you to find out for yourself, and so do those of us who have benefited from his teaching.

I *can* give you a preview, though. For an athlete like you, it should be easy to understand. To become strong and stay strong, minds, like bodies, need good nutrition, proper training, and regular, vigorous exercise.

In the case of a mind, good *nutrition* would be exposure to wise, true, and kind words and ideas (not enough of *those* in the air these days!), and avoidance of mental "junk food" and toxins. Of course, this is influenced to a great extent by the culture that surrounds you, but it depends even more on what influences *you* choose to take into your mind or guard yourself against. *Training,* to be effective, has to be based on a correct and profound understanding of what a mind *is* and how it works. In that regard, I believe Freud and all his heirs can only supplement, never replace, Moses, Jesus, and Buddha (and I'm a psychiatrist!). Finally, the best training in the world won't make your mind strong unless you *exercise* it hard and regularly. But without a healthy "diet" and correct training techniques, your best-intentioned efforts may be misspent. (That's why I'm here to be your "nutritionist" and coach!)

It was this stark, simple regimen for a strong mind that was—and is—the common core of the great religions. Buddhism, Judaism, and Christianity (and Islam, too—I won't discuss it simply because I don't know enough about it) tell different dramatic stories about how human beings wrestled for or were blessed with the Truth. They differ in their accounts of this remarkable universe we inhabit: the Bible says in no uncertain terms that God created it and watches over it; the Buddha takes no particular stand on how the universe came to be—in fact, he says we human beings cannot know that—and confines himself to an elegant dissection of the lawful way it works. (That's why Buddhist philosophy can coexist so comfortably with both Western religion and science.) The religions even differ on the nature of our spiritual essence and what happens to it after death. For Christianity, we have a soul that goes to Heaven or Hell. For Buddhism, we are a momentum of past and present actions that is reborn into circumstances that reflect the quality of those actions. It shouldn't escape your notice, however, that a strong common thread links these two very different doctrines. Make a note of it, because it is all-important: **ACTIONS HAVE CONSEQUENCES**—and those consequences are directly linked to the moral quality, wholesome or unwholesome, of your actions.

Whatever these differences might be, though, beneath them is a foundation of practical wisdom in which the great traditions hardly differ *at all*. And that foundation is the rigorous discipline they require for human beings to become fully human, to do ourselves and each other good instead of harm and evil, and to claim our spiritual birthright. This discipline is spelled out by each tradition in simple, unmistakable, and nearly identical terms. It includes codes of speech and conduct—such as "Thou shalt not steal," which is both the Eighth Commandment God gave to Moses and the Second Buddhist Precept, "not to take what is not given"—as well as practices to control and purify the mind. These rules and methods have appeared in widely separated times and places, not only because they come from the same source (which I believe transcends the merely human), but because they are addressing the same phenomenon: the human animal—and the human spirit that inhabits and can master it.

One of the most damaging myths of our time is that technology and trends are changing our lives so rapidly and totally that no ancient tradition could ever encompass our unprecedented situation or have anything useful to say to

From a source which I believe transcends the merely human

us. Well, I'll tell you something, Patrick: technology has changed a lot of things—but it hasn't changed the main thing: human nature. That's the same as it has always been. That's why, when you read Homer's *Odyssey*, or the stories in the Bible, or Shakespeare's plays, you can't help noticing that only the ships and shoes and weapons are different; the motives and emotions are just the same as today. (Have you ever read *Othello?* He was a sixteenth-century O. J.!) Here we are venturing into cyberspace and outer space, discovering how to clone ourselves—and yet we still have the same exact battles with each other and with our own inner urges and runaway thoughts! Battles just as mighty and as tough to win as they've ever been. And yet, the best ways to train and guide this nature of ours—which still remains the only way to win those battles—are almost exactly the same as they have been for over two thousand years. If we want to have lives of self-mastery and poise instead of fear, greed, and violence, we still have to pay the same price to earn that victory that people have had to pay since time immemorial.

Today, many so-called "sophisticated" people have contempt for "traditional values" (like the two-parent family!). They think traditional means stuffy, repressive, old-fashioned, and uptight. Yet you may be surprised to learn that the "traditional values" that made civilization possible were thought to be outrageously radical and daring when they were first introduced by revolutionaries like Moses, Buddha, Jesus, and Mohammed. People then said (just like they're saying again today), *"You mean, it's a person's* conduct *that matters, not their wealth, power, and connections? You mean there are reasons to control* sexuality? *Gimme a break!"* Yet those codes of behavior became "traditional"—that is, they got handed down from generation to generation to generation—for one simple reason: *they work.* And they work because they're based on a highly sophisticated and deeply wise understanding of human nature.

To put it in computer-era language: if you think of the human body and brain as our hardware, "traditional values" are the only operating system proven to get superior performance out of it safely and consistently. Running any other software means taking a serious risk of having the entire system crash and irreversibly damaging the hard drive. That makes the "TradVal" package totally up-to-date. What's more, it's in no way clear that any of the "more sophisticated" software packages under development are even compatible with human components over the long haul. In fact, there's already plenty of evidence to the contrary!

With all my psychiatric training and experience, it's clear to me that *the moral codes of the great religions haven't been approached, much less surpassed, as practical guides to human psychology.* And now, at the turn of the millennium, confirmation is starting to come from an unexpected source: the

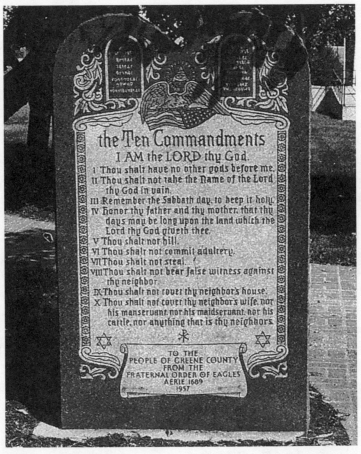

Handed down for one simple reason: they work.

most high-tech, cutting-edge research on the brain—some of it being done by my colleagues and me at UCLA. By using sophisticated machines to compare the brain activity of people with trained and untrained minds, we can actually begin to *see* the relationship between human biology and the human spirit that was taught by the great spiritual masters. I'll be telling you a lot more about this work, because I think it provides support for the relevance of the wisdom of generations past to the goal of directing your mental force both today and in the future.

But I find these developments so exciting (they're what I based my professional career on, after all!) that I'm getting ahead of myself and not following the Buddha's advice to show, not tell. The fact is, you don't need to come to my lab or anyone else's to see vivid proof that the moral codes of the great religions work. All you have to do is look around you, and see what happens when people abandon their faith.

There is a direct cause-and-effect relationship between the abandoning of this very basic spiritual discipline (which, to be sure, is not easy to maintain) and the rapid disintegration of individuals and societies. It *always* happens. For example, if you read the Old Testament prophets Isaiah and Jeremiah, besides some amazing poetry, you'll find detailed descriptions of societies that had forgotten God and His commandments and were riddled with adultery, promiscuity, sexual perversion, lying, stealing, murder, ill-gotten riches, vanity and luxury, exploitation of the defenseless, and lack of concern for the fatherless and the needy. Sounds a lot like New York or L.A. to me.

But we need to focus down even closer, on things you see with your own eyes and hear with your own ears every day, but probably just take for granted as "the way things are." Unlike your parents, you and your peers have never *seen,* and can hardly imagine, a world where it's just "the way things are" for most people to actually try to honor the

The prophet Isaiah in meditation

basic moral precepts. And yet I am going to tell you that your generation has the opportunity, and the awesome responsibility, to recreate such a world. But before you can take on such a major task, you must really understand *why*.

I'll start with words and ideas, our "soul food," because in that realm, toxic junk has a particularly overwhelming and addictive effect on untrained minds . . . and too many of the minds you see around you today are woefully untrained.

With the media turned up full blast, you and your contemporaries are exposed to an incredible deluge of raw information, mere entertainment, and just plain noise. How long does it take you to think of something you *don't* like out of all the words you hear around you—either from your friends, in movies, music, or on TV? (By the way, my questions aren't always that easy. . . .)

Your friend,
Jeff

Dear Jeff,

The first thing that comes to my mind is the way a lot of guys talk about girls. I'm in the room sometimes when they're doing it, and I'm like, you guys, why do you do that? They don't see anything bad about it. They think it's normal.

Patrick

TRASH TALK

Dear Patrick,

The fact that you have a kind of "gag reflex" when you hear guys speaking in derogatory ways about girls (like my reaction to my uncle's "screw or get screwed" advice) is a good sign. It shows that despite all the junk that surrounds you, you still clearly know the difference between wholesome and toxic talk. You don't have to go into detail for me to know the kind of rank crudity you're referring to: take any fifteen-second sample from those endless sessions in which men talk about women as the sum total of their body parts, as *stuff to get*. I've overheard more than enough of that "locker-room" talk myself (it's why I'm not overly fond of locker rooms). There isn't a male outside a monastery who hasn't heard that soul-damaging talk, and there are probably few who haven't participated to some extent. It actually has quite a lot in common with my uncle's way of talking about friendship: a view of life that's crudely reduced to "getting yours," an ugly bravado that masks a morbid fear of failure and rejection.

I'm impressed by your honesty, Patrick. Not too many males your age (or *any* age) have the courage to admit that anything bothers them about that kind of talk. As you say, it's considered normal—today more than ever, and at younger ages than ever. You've already noticed how if you're in a room where it's going on and you don't join in, you rather quickly come to feel like an outsider looking in. In my experience, that's no particular problem. Simply remaining clear-minded and observant at such times is a character-building experience. On top of that, by observing you can learn quite a bit about the moral fiber of your peers—how insecure they are, what they think impresses other people, how much they're willing to sell out to do so, who they most fear being rejected by—all valuable information to know about people you have to live and interact with. But here's a piece of practical advice: don't be reckless about openly showing your disapproval. Fear of rejection being the profoundly powerful force it is, people always tend to feel vulnerable and defensive when they're running their mouths like that. It's an easy time to make needless enemies. Discretion may not be the *better* part of valor, but it is *a* part of it.

Gotama Buddha had a fair amount to say about that kind of crude speech. He called it "animal talk," or as it's sometimes referred to today, "trash talk," and he warned against the degrading effects of indulging in it. (By the way, Gotama was his family name, and "Buddha" means "the Awakened," in much the same way that Jesus is a given name and "Christ" means "the Anointed.") Wherever the great religions agree, at that point, like the X on a treasure map, you'll find something that is real, and both Buddhism and our own Old Testament took *the power of words* very seriously—seriously enough to forbid certain uses of them.

Two of the Ten Commandments Moses brought down from Mount Sinai dealt with the restraint of speech: "Thou shalt not take the name of the Lord thy God in vain" (i.e., don't be frivolous in the face of mystery and majesty), and "Thou shalt not bear false witness against thy neighbor" (don't lie with deliberate intent to harm). Gotama named *four* kinds of unwholesome speech to refrain from: false speech or lying, malicious speech (talk that stirs up trouble between people), harsh speech (obscene, vulgar, crude, or cruel), and frivolous chitchat, or "small talk." See how many of *those* you can detect the next time you hear a bunch of guys talking rudely and crudely about girls or women. And when you do, try to mentally note them by their names: "false speech," "harsh speech." (With that simple act of labeling your observations, the training of your mind has already begun!)

Of course, the airwaves of our media today are choked

with all four. Think, for example, of exploitative advertising (drink this and you'll get that), confrontational talk shows (which have led to blows and even murder), action-movie dialogue (every other word the F-word, spat out with supreme hostility), or tabloid-style celebrity gossip. Think (heaven help us) of Jerry Springer's mind-bending and mind-corrupting show. This nonstop torrent of "trash talk" would have shocked and disgusted most *adult* Americans not that long ago. To your generation. sadly, it's just normal, the familiar background noise of American life.

The dismantling of boundaries over the intervening years—those agreed-on, invisible lines that used to separate adulthood and childhood, good and bad taste, public and private, forbidden and allowed—has made our culture "promiscuous" in the original sense of that word. It comes from the Latin *misceo* (to mix) and *pro-* (forth or forward), and it implies an aggressive disregard for the protective function of boundaries, a denial that there's anything (like the purity of a young person's spirit) that needs or is worth protecting. The opinion makers who are responsible for throwing open the floodgates, who shouted down all restraints on "trash talk" as "Puritanism," "repression," and "censorship,"

Lying, malicious speech, harsh speech, and frivolous chit-chat

would like you to believe it hasn't hurt you. It's "just talk," they say, an insignificant price to pay for freedom of speech: tasteless, sure, but harmless.

Gotama would say otherwise.

In his teaching, there is no such thing as "just" talk. Speech is powerful, and its quality is all-important, because like breathing, it's a two-way interchange across the boundary between our inner and outer worlds. How we talk is highly symptomatic of the wholesome or unwholesome state of our own minds, and it's also highly contagious: "sick" speech can infect a whole population of other minds, and even a healthy mind can get infected if you're not both strong and careful. (A different nephew might have "come down with" my Uncle Aaron's harsh attitude—like my father did, to an unfortunate degree—instead of becoming fervently determined to resist it.)

What's more, there's no leakproof barrier safely separating talk from bodily action—as you know if you've ever watched a fight escalate from words to fists! What we say not only has its own power to hurt or heal, but it also tends to set the tone and blaze the trail for what we *do*. (Within the brain, this may be almost literally true. Very recent research indicates that repeated thoughts and words may form nervous-system interconnections that actually "lay down tracks" for likely action.) Does anyone in their right mind really imagine that there's no connection between the lyrics of "gangsta" rap and acts of violence? And do you really think guys can "talk trash" about girls with no effect on their own motives and behavior? Do you think, when they're alone with a girl (or anyone else, for that matter), they're still capable of being completely trustworthy, open, and sincere?

And who even *talks* that way anymore? "Trustworthy, open and sincere"—when was the last time you heard words like that uttered with a straight face? Who still believes that *being* like that is even a possibility, much less a goal and an ideal? Well, I know at least one person, Patrick: I do. And I've got more of those words for you: "innocence," "virtue" and "beauty"; "custom" and "ceremony"; "wisdom" and "courage" . . . but first, we'll have to completely retune our ears. Those are actually words of great strength. If they sound laughably naive and prissy now, it's a sign of how attuned to harsh, discordant, and trivial speech we've become. And the state of our language reveals the state of our souls. The way we talk, and the talk we choose to hear, is the way we are. Gotama was totally explicit about this—he taught that speech is a form of action. Thought, too, for that matter.

Do you personally know anyone who tries *not* to "take the name of the Lord in vain"? For a lot of educated urban and suburban Americans, that's an extremely quaint notion. In fact, the issue probably never even crosses their minds, even when they stub a toe and every name in the Book crosses their lips. Only when they notice that someone has bothered to bleep every "Goddamn" out of the popular movies edited for prime-time TV do they faintly sense the presence of the millions of evangelical Christians and other Americans for whom God is still a living part of day-to-day reality. Those for whom He is not have long since moved on to taking their own bodily functions in vain, particularly the act which—when done with care and respect—has the genuinely awesome power to transmit love and create life. (I sometimes think *nothing* is sacred in this culture, except perhaps "the Self" and the "esteem" to which it supposedly has a "right.")

No one gives much thought anymore to the indiscriminate and proudly aggressive use of "the F-word." It seems, as speech, to have lost all meaning, and therefore to be harmless. But wait a minute. Why is it that so many people seem to be committing the act with the *same* crude lust, fearful antagonism, and callous indifference with which they use the word? Could it be because, as a culture, the way we say it *is* the way we do it? And that has bred a fear, contempt, and mistrust at the very core of life that has spread to contaminate *all* relationships. Not only between boys and girls, men and women, but between parents and kids, students and teachers, bosses and employees, businesses and customers—you name it—there festers the fear of getting "screwed" . . . figuratively, if not literally.

Do you see Gotama's point about speech? If you talk like an animal . . . you start to *act* like an animal. And speaking of animals, I sometimes think some of the "greener" members of my generation care more about protecting wild owls, wolves, and bears than about protecting their own children's minds and souls. How can they be so concerned about the condition of our planet's physical resources—and yet so apparently blasé about the deterioration of our moral and spiritual resources? They act as if they think Nature is limited to what we can experience with our five senses. But Nature must include our inner lives, too.

The fact is, we don't only live in an "ecosphere," a shared realm of air and woods and water. We also live in an "ethosphere," a shared realm of attitudes, behavior, and ethics. Yet people seem oblivious to the fact that bad thoughts, harsh words, and irresponsible actions are every bit as real and damaging as toxic fumes or nuclear waste—and that good thoughts, kind words, and responsible actions are as protective as the ozone layer. Over the last thirty years, while the quality of our rivers, lakes, and air has greatly improved, the character and conduct of our lives has gotten much worse. Inescapable violence, lewdness, and just plain *rudeness*—the sick notion that it's hip to have "attitude" and be "in your face"—now hang like a thick, noxious smog over our lives. So wretchedly polluted and exploited is our ethosphere, I can hardly describe its condition without using the F-word! But to show you how hard I've worked on my self-control, I'll dispense with crude adjectives and simply say "It's a mess!"

A young man is coming for an appointment in a few minutes, so I'll stop now and continue tomorrow. In the meantime, Patrick, I hope you're listening to the talk around you with new ears and a clear mind.

Your friend,
Jeff

JEFFREY M. SCHWARTZ

THE OTHER F-WORD

Th' expense of spirit in a waste of shame
Is lust in action. . . .

— Shakespeare, Sonnet 129

Dear Patrick,

As I was starting to say to you yesterday, that *other* F-word—
sexual "freedom," in talk and action—has turned out to be
neither a lovely nor a loving thing. This has come as quite
an unpleasant surprise to those who imagined that "letting
nature take its course" would lead straight to an Eden of
innocent pleasure. But it would not have surprised Gotama,
Moses, or Jesus at all.

Like restraint of speech, restraint of sexuality is another
one of those "power points" where the great religions of East
and West meet. "Excellent is restraint with body, speech and
mind. Restraint everywhere is excellent," said the Buddha.
Our Seventh Commandment, "Thou shalt not commit adultery," is envisioned more broadly by the Third Buddhist
Precept, "to abstain from sexual misconduct," which explicitly includes, among other things, adultery and sex with
minors. When Jesus counseled forgiveness, shielding a
woman adulterer from a rock-brandishing mob with the
words "Let him who is without sin cast the first stone," he
acknowledged that these rules are hard for all humans to follow. But he never remotely suggested that the solution was
to relax or abolish the rules! On the contrary, he said to try
harder, and to ask God for spiritual help.

In fact, both Gotama and Jesus considered sexual misconduct so harmful, and yet so difficult to resist, that they
traced it back to its roots deep in the mind and said, *"Here's*
where you've got to start." Gotama said, "Just as rain penetrates an ill-thatched house,/So lust penetrates an undevel-

Jesus shielding a woman adulterer

oped mind./ Just as rain does not penetrate a well-thatched house/So lust does not penetrate a well-developed mind." Jesus warned that "whosoever looketh on a woman to lust after her hath committed adultery with her already in his heart." (You weren't born yet when Jimmy Carter, a faithful husband and openly religious president, was ridiculed back in the "swinging" '70s for admitting in an interview that "I have lusted in my heart.")

As a '70s swinger might have put it, what was these guys'

problem? Were the great spiritual teachers pleasure-hating prudes or what? Not exactly. The Jewish tradition, in particular, considers sex between a husband and wife to be a holy joy, a blessing from God. You're *supposed* to do it if you're Jewish—and married. And you're supposed to get married. For Christians, too, marriage is a holy sacrament, sex and all. Gotama Buddha taught that *any* pleasant sensation is the result of a prior wholesome action—if you feel good now, it is because you did good before! Not exactly a condemnation of pleasure. Gotama said all sensations are morally neutral; it's in how we *respond* to them that good and evil begin. (When a girl's beauty moves you, what do you think, say, and *do?*) Gotama's main problem with sensual pleasure (of which sexuality is such a potent example) was that, since it can lead so rapidly to craving and clinging, it is one of the strongest forces that gives rise to suffering. On a mundane level, you can easily observe this: lust doesn't help most people choose their partners wisely, as so many lust-driven couples in Hollywood have proven.

The consensus of the great traditions is simple and unequivocal: when sex is used lovingly to create and bond families, it is a force for good; when it's used primarily for self-gratification, it destroys families, and it becomes a force for evil. It's a lot like fire: kept in the hearth, it can warm a whole household; turned loose, it can burn down not just the house but the whole neighborhood! And in your own life, depending on how well you control and direct it, sex can be an internal combustion engine powering you to your chosen goals, or a treacherous explosive that blows all your plans sky-high. You and I will be talking about how to make it empowering and not destructive when we come to the "training" part of this regimen for a strong mind.

Maybe you can see now that rules to restrain and guide sexuality have nothing to do with being mean or prudish; rather, they are about being practical and compassionate.

They're to prevent exactly what happened to *you*, Patrick—growing up without a father! They're to prevent the kinds of suffering that have multiplied all around us in the thirty or so years since the rules were called off in the name of "freedom": the devastating emotional and economic impact of divorce on both adults and kids (another thing you're an expert on, having lived through it with your mom and sister); your generation's resultant deep doubts and fears about ever finding someone to trust and love; girls' anxious obsession with their bodies, and boys' with their sexual prowess, at an age when you need to focus on your calling and prepare for your future; the anguish of teenage pregnancy, no matter what "choice" is made; and the spread of AIDS and other STDs. Our romantic landscape looks more like a bloody battlefield! And as on all the battlefields that have ever been, it's young people who suffer the most casualties.

In the face of this incontrovertible evidence, it's frightening how many people continue to insist that sexual "freedom" is a basically good thing, and that more sex education, more condoms, and higher self-esteem in girls will clear up the remaining problems. As if early, loveless sex weren't one of the major *causes* of low self-esteem in girls! One recent study showed that high-achieving high-school girls who are already having sex are *twice* as likely as their virgin peers to be depressed or even to think about suicide.

As a matter of fact, those who *are* honest enough to acknowledge this obvious cause and effect tend to assume that it's girls and women who are suffering most. *They're* the ones, the argument goes, who have always needed the lost protections of chastity and chivalry; boys, biologically wired like other male animals to sow their seed widely, are much more in their element today, and have much less to gain from a return to meaningful sexual standards (so they'll have to be tricked or trapped into it). Well, Patrick, I'd like someone to try and tell that to the young man who had an appointment with me yesterday. He's been in treatment with me now for several months.

I'll call him Jaime. He's twenty-three now, and he's *still* suffering from the trauma of a first sexual experience that came too early—eight years ago. As I tell you his story—just the way he told it to me—take note of the major role that "trash talk" played. Notice, also, the sad (and far from uncommon) spectacle of a young girl who thinks the only way to protect herself is to act as tough and experienced as the boys think *they're* supposed to act.

When Jaime's parents went out of town (somehow in these stories the parents are always out of town), a girl he'd known since the eighth grade invited herself over. Jamie just knew they were going to "mess around." It had happened before with her—the first time when they were only twelve, after she rode her bike over one day, and then the year before, at fourteen, when they'd dated for a while and almost, but not quite, had sex. (That time, Jamie had stopped because he was afraid of hurting her—a sign of his real capacity for connection and caring . . . a capacity that was about to sustain serious damage.) Jaime had the feeling tonight was going to be the night. They had the apartment all to themselves. The girl expected him to "make love" to her.

There was just one problem.

Jaime was a virgin. He had no idea what he was "supposed" to do.

But then, why should he? Jaime was only fifteen! His inexperience was normal, natural, and appropriate for his age and deserved to be protected, not pressured and rushed. But Jaime, like most of your generation, had grown up immersed in a peer and media culture that drowns out the harried—and often solo—voices of parents who now, perhaps for the first time ever, get no backing from the society as a whole. And it's a pop culture that leeringly urges "sexual prowess and sexual performance" (Jaime's words) on kids too young even to know what that really means. As early as the sixth grade, the boys in Jaime's school, imitating older kids and TV, were taunting each other about sex on the playground. (I've heard of even much younger elementary-school kids playing such "games.") In eighth grade, the girl on the bike had invited him to kiss and touch. And at fifteen, "I felt this need to be experienced and cool," Jaime says sadly. "I could have been totally honest with her. Instead, I lied the whole time, because of this cool hierarchy I was in." (How many of the Buddha's four kinds of unwholesome speech—lying, troublemaking, harsh speech, and sheer trivia—have you spotted so far?)

Patrick, I want you to take note of the total lack of tenderness and loving kindness that dominates the following exchange. It's an interaction ruled by fear and hostility. Two frightened people in over their heads, totally out of their depth: friends before the interaction started. No longer friends, even adversaries, when it was over.

"I want to do this," the girl said, "but I don't want you to think I'm a slut."

"Oh, of course not," Jaime reassured her. He admits now that "had everything worked out, I probably would've!" However, everything did not work out.

"Are you a virgin?" the girl asked him.

"Of course not," Jaime lied, fearing she'd go out and tell everyone.

"And so, of course, she expected me to know what I was doing. It was pitch black in my room. I couldn't even see anything. And she said, 'You're doing it wrong.' She'd already condemned me. My heart was beating really fast. There was so much pressure on me, so much pressure—I just neutralized." Jaime's body knew only one way to get him out of this mess: it quit. He lost his erection and so wasn't able to have sex.

"I blamed her. I said, 'This has never happened before. It worked with all the other girls.' She goes, 'No, you're abnormal.'" This from a fifteen-year-old girl whose own worldly experience, Jaime later learned, amounted to exactly one night—she'd had sex with her date after the prom!

That first time was so mortifying that the memory has been "a cloud" over Jaime's relationships with women ever since. "On three separate occasions, women have been interested in me and I was the one saying no," he told me, "because I still have this fear of a humiliating experience." One of those women Jaime had dated long enough to start thinking the relationship could become a profoundly meaningful one. She had evidently thought so, too—judging by how upset she was when Jaime abruptly and quite clumsily broke it off. Now all he's left with is a gnawing feeling about "what might have been." Jaime really understands—too late—the wisdom contained in that saying "True love waits."

What sad and senseless damage to a young man's psyche and his life! As a psychiatrist, I can tell you that a persistent fear of being humiliated is one of the most vicious and painful feelings anyone can suffer. Jaime sought help to overcome his difficult feelings, but it has not been easy. He still struggles with them today. He found out the hard way that treating another person as an object—or letting someone treat *you* like one—leaves scars on your soul. Engaging in loveless sex dulls the spirit and can damage or even kill your capacity to love. And that is equally true whether you are male or female.

People who believe evolution has preprogrammed human sexual behavior would like to deny that you, Patrick, are anything more than just a male animal with a big brain. But you *are* more—and that "more" is the most valuable part of you. As a human being, you have an *inner life,* one that can register emotional joy and pain, both your own and another's. You have the potential for deep intimacy. You have a will that can transcend and master your animal heritage—if you so choose. I will prove it to you. And most important, you have the capacity to choose—and the responsibility that goes with it. And that is what maturity really amounts to—taking responsibility. To waste all that on meaningless "conquests" or vain attempts to prove you're cool and hip is something plain common sense tells you you'll regret.

Unfortunately, Jaime's experience is far from unusual. Just to show you how much and how fast things have changed, when I was a kid there was a saying that went "Sweet sixteen and never been kissed." Even then, I must admit that it was mostly our parents who said it! Yet I still remember the sense that a first *kiss* was a big deal, something really momentous, especially for girls. Today, *30 percent* of the fifteen-year-olds in America have already had intercourse! How many of those do you think did it out of real readiness and true love, or even true friendship? How about loneliness and craving for status and acceptance? That tells me that there are a lot of young people walking around out there with scarred souls. And it's not even as if they don't know it. In a survey of sexually active teens, *81 percent* of the girls said they wish they'd waited longer—and so did *60 percent* of the boys!

Maybe, Patrick, it's time to take another look at innocence.

Your friend,
Jeff

Dear Jeff,

My mom said I should tell you my condom story.

In junior high, eighth grade, we had an assignment to go and buy condoms for our sex education class. I was fourteen. Everyone, including the girls, had to buy condoms and bring them to class. I was actually too embarrassed to go into the store. So I called up the deli down the street and had them delivered!! Ice cream, soda—and condoms! When they delivered everything but the condoms, I had to call back. "You forgot something in the delivery. . . ." I had to ask for them again!

"Oh, what kind of condoms do you want?"

"I don't know," I said. I didn't know what to say. For some reason they ended up sending two boxes!

In sex ed they talked about AIDS, and putting condoms on, and puberty, and they taught us that if you had strange or different feelings, that was normal. We never talked about relationships, caring, commitment, or anything. My mom was the total opposite. "Don't have sex, don't have sex! I want you to have a loving, committed marriage. Don't waste yourself and don't treat women with such disrespect."

"OK, Mom, whatever." I didn't think much about it. I figured, "I don't have to deal with that right now."

But late in eighth grade, I found out some of my friends were. It was a big surprise. I didn't know the girls, just the guys. They were nonchalant about it, like it was a normal thing, like "Oh, I went for a smoke" or something. It wasn't a big deal for them. But I was definitely shocked.

So that's it. Talk to you soon,

Patrick

IN PRAISE OF EMBARRASSMENT

Dear Patrick,

That's definitely the longest letter I've ever received from you!

Your writing is so much better, even since last year—spelling, handwriting, the way you express yourself. I know what a battle it's been to improve your reading and writing skills, ever since that car hit you when you were, how old? Four or five? You were in a coma for days! That left you with a hell of a struggle to catch up to your classmates, and a fair amount of frustration, on top of everything else that was going on in your life. But you showed real courage and never gave up. And now look at you, getting an A+ in biology! (We won't talk about Latin. You could ace that, too, if you didn't hate it. Just remember, you can't become pope without it. . . .)

So much in life is *not giving up.* I suspect when I start telling you more about my favorite subject—how you can reprogram your own brain—you'll already be familiar with that concept. I mean, hey, you've done it! (Been there . . . done that . . .) But in fact, success in every facet of life involves much the same process of practice and perseverance, whether you're working on your learning skills, your athletic performance, or your character.

Patrick, as you look back on it, you don't really think there's anything wrong with being embarrassed to buy condoms at age fourteen, do you? Does anyone really doubt (hip platitudes aside) that it's your *school* that should have been embarrassed to force such an assignment on you? Your embarrassment was a natural, self-protective recoil from the coercion, abuse, and violation you were subjected to. It was sending you a clear message that, in your words, "I don't have to deal with that right now"—and you *shouldn't* have to. Your mom was right. Fourteen-year-olds are not ready, either to be sexually active or to discuss sex clinically (by which I mean like a surgeon discusses anatomy or a plumber discusses pipes) in what used to be called "mixed company." By fourteen you certainly needed to know the "facts of life," but it's that missing father who should have been telling them to you, in privacy and with a stress on their *emotional significance, power,* and *mystery* (as opposed to their urological significance). Educators on a crusade to "demystify" sex end up stripping all inner meaning from it, and what's left is mechanical and ugly. In my opinion, they should be spending that time working to demystify algebra (still a bit of a mystery to me . . .).

When sex-ed classes like yours rip away kids' natural protective covering of embarrassment, which is a gentle yet effective guardian and guide, their first response, often to please a teacher with a sex-manual mentality, may well be to lie about the discomfort, even terror, they feel. Eventually, they tend to put on a hard armor of irony and cynicism which, because it is extremely difficult to remove in situations of genuine intimacy, ends up being much more like a prison cell for solitary confinement. While on the surface it looks like they can discuss and even flaunt their sexuality "freely"—they do so only at the price of damaging one of life's most deeply felt experiences.

The Buddha had a very clear message when it came to the subject of embarrassment and shame. He explicitly stated that "to be embarrassed by embarrassing things" (like buying condoms when you're fourteen!) is one of the signs of a good person. And "to feel no shame when encountering unwholesome things" is the sure sign of a fool!

It's a fact that the word *shame* is closely associated with sex in languages all over the world. For example, in both Latin and German, the words for the genitals literally mean "shame-parts." Halfway around the world, in Pāli, the language of the oldest Buddhist scriptures, the loincloth that

covers them is called a "cloth that covers shame" because, as
the ancient texts explain, "when the member is exposed, one
becomes agitated by appropriate shame" *(hiri* is the Pāli word
for this kind of shame). To modern sex educators, such feelings of shame are relics of "cruel" superstition that has no

The moment when we became truly human

JEFFREY M. SCHWARTZ

place in an "enlightened" society. They've made it their mission to remove any trace of shame from sex, to make it just another "bodily function," as straightforward to talk about and to do as eating or brushing your teeth. But, lo and behold, that last bit of embarrassment just doesn't quite seem to come out—and if and when it ever does, sex will become "shameless" in the worst sense of the word—just a physical act by two animals responding to an urge.

When it comes to understanding human nature, old words often contain more wisdom than new policies. Sex ed class tells you to "get over" your embarrassment. The old words help you understand the reasons why it's so important that the embarrassment is there—because sex is not just another act between two animals.

Of course crippling, mortifying shame, such as Jaime experienced, is unhealthy. But there is a *healthy* kind of shame that exists precisely to protect us from what happened to Jaime. *(That's* the kind that the Pāli word *hiri* specifically refers to.) Another name it goes by is *modesty*—the feeling that makes you blush and cover yourself when someone walks in on you naked or when you're answering "nature's call." Try *not* doing that! It's essentially a reflex, and it is as old as our humanity. In fact, in the Old Testament Book of Genesis, it's that gesture that marks the moment when we became truly human:

> And when the woman saw that the tree [of the knowledge of good and evil] was good . . . and a tree to be desired to make one wise, she took of the fruit thereof, and did eat, and gave also unto her husband with her; and he did eat.
> And the eyes of them both were opened, and they knew that they were naked; and they sewed fig leaves together, and made themselves aprons.

The very *first* manifestation of wisdom—the knowledge of good and evil—is that "they knew that they were naked," and they covered themselves! Later on, the Book of Genesis goes on to tell the story of a particular tribe of humans, but *this* story is about the origin of humanity itself. And there is a profound truth to it, for to the best of my knowledge, anthropologists have never documented a human society whose members, once past puberty, did not cover their sexual parts.

There are many things to ponder about this story, but one of them is that it's your embarrassment that makes you human, different from all other animals. Feeling shy about sex doesn't mean you're an inhibited nerd, it means that you recognize and respect the power of sex, both for good and for evil. *That* kind of "shame" is very closely related to reverence and awe—wise attitudes that our culture has abandoned to an alarming extent. Instead, the prevailing view of sex is the one expressed by your eighth-grade friends (though I'm willing to bet they were faking it): "It's no big deal."

Let's face it—despite all the people who get hurt by it every day (many far worse than Jaime), our society doesn't take sexuality half as seriously as . . . driving! (That reminds me, Patrick: congratulations on fulfilling the age requirement for getting your driver's license. When are you planning to undergo *that* grand initiation into adulthood? Are you taking drivers ed?) We'd never casually hand a fourteen-year-old the keys to the car—he's not even considered old enough for a learner's permit—but we push condoms on him. Do you think it's a complete coincidence that within months of that sex-ed class, some of your friends were having sex? They'd basically been given the "official" signal to fire up a far more powerful and dangerous machine than any car. It's more like a nuclear reactor! And when you start fooling around with life's glowing fuel core, don't kid yourself: a thin piece of rubber isn't enough to protect you. (Even if all you're talking about is preventing disease and pregnancy, the failure rate of condoms, especially in teens, is very far from negligible.)

The human body can not only generate great joy and great suffering; it can create life—and it can bring death. And I'm not only talking about AIDS. Consider this: two fifteen-year-olds can kindle a new life before they ever think about what it all means. And what do they do then? Give it to Grandma? Go on welfare? Give up their own life plans to do a barely adequate job of supporting it? According to social scientists William Galston and James Q. Wilson, avoiding choices like these is also the simplest way to avoid sentencing your children to poverty. Just follow three rules: finish high school, produce no child before marriage and no child before age twenty. Only 8 percent of families who follow all three will have children who live in poverty—compared to *almost 80* percent of those who don't!

And yet, Wilson reports, over half of all Americans, and 70 percent of those under thirty-five, now think *no shame* should attach to having children out of wedlock, even though a mere thirty-five years ago, it was one of the greatest disgraces a young person could bring upon his or her family.

But today, there's another alternative readily available for dealing with that inconvenient by-product of uncommitted sex. How about just "terminating" it? Did you know that that's the solution most often chosen by teens in higher socioeconomic brackets? Poor kids are much more likely to keep their babies—and perpetuate their poverty. Better-off kids keep their options open, but at what price in poverty of spirit?

Do you know anyone who's had to make this decision, Patrick? Have you and your friends ever talked about what you'd do if you were faced with it? Tell me what your contemporaries at school think about pregnancy and abortion, and then I'll tell you what Gotama Buddha said about it.

Your friend,
Jeff

Dear Jeff,

I don't really know anybody close to me that's ever gotten pregnant. But my friends' point of view on abortion is they pretty much accept it. Everybody I know is mostly pro-choice—and they think it's the decision of the woman. Since it affects the mother's life so much, they think it's more her choice, and pro-life people shouldn't take away that choice. But it's a very tough choice, or at least I think it should be. I don't think people should use it as a tool to evade responsibility. And I totally see that the guy is in some instances even more *responsible. Sometimes guys pressure girls into having sex.*

I don't think I'd ever get myself into that situation. If I did, I don't know what I'd do. It's one reason why I realize that sex is a really serious thing. I don't think I'm ready for it at all—not even close.

Yours,
Patrick

A MATTER OF LIFE AND DEATH

Dear Patrick,

You're right: the best way to deal with that choice is to never have to make it. It's almost impossible to overstress how extremely high the stakes really are. And I'm quite concerned that most of your "pro-choice" friends haven't stopped to think about it with the utmost seriousness it requires. No matter how you try to get around it by focusing all your attention on "the woman's right to choose," you cannot be honest about this issue without confronting the very nasty subject of killing.

Killing, of course, is another of those things that the great religious traditions unanimously forbid. The sixth of our Ten Commandments, "Thou shalt not kill," is identical to the first of the Buddhist Five Precepts: "to abstain from taking life." Obviously, this vitally important commandment and precept has too often been, as the old saying goes, "more honored in the breach than in the observance"—but without it, we might not be here at all! Witness the fact that in the twentieth century, when humans began feeling too powerful to submit to commandments and precepts, the Law against killing has been broken on a horrific scale never before imagined.

And yet, it is probably one that you can't imagine yourself or your close friends ever breaking. If you were an inner-city kid, worried about needing a gun to be safe in school, it might be a different story. But unless, God forbid, there were some unforeseeable circumstance involving a war, there are only two situations in which you, Patrick, face any significant risk of being party to a serious violation of the Sixth Commandment/First Precept. One is reckless or drunken driving. The other, and this is just plain unavoidable reality, is if you get someone pregnant.

Let me tell you something about Gotama Buddha's teaching that most of his new legions of American followers have been rather quiet about. The Buddha taught that three conditions are required for conception to occur: (1) the parents come together in union during (2) the woman's fertile period and (3) a spirit must be present. Buddhist teaching clearly states that at the moment of conception, a human life enters into existence on Planet Earth; a conscious being has just arisen, a new destiny has just begun. An abortion destroys that life, aborts that destiny. From a Buddhist perspective, this is entirely straightforward. There are no two ways about it.

People often think of that as the conservative Christian position, but the fact is, it is also Gotama Buddha's position, and any honest Buddhist has to admit it. The world's preeminent Buddhist, the Dalai Lama, certainly does. He was asked, in an interview at Harvard in 1988, "How do Buddhists feel about abortion?" His answer: "Abortion is considered an ill deed of killing a living being." In fact, he said, one of the four worst violations of Buddhist vows is "to kill a human being or something forming as a human being."

But let me be very clear about this: I'm not discussing legal questions right now—I think the legal issues are extremely complicated. I'm discussing a *moral* issue, and to be precise, the issue of what the Buddha taught about when human life begins. On that, as on so many moral issues, Gotama was totally clear. What the legal implications of that might be is something we can talk about another time. But what are the *practical* implications for you, Patrick?

The law today gives you a choice, but if you seriously consider Gotama Buddha's teaching, I think it will further strengthen your resolve to avoid that choice. That means things like conscientiously using birth control, and, because birth control isn't perfect, being mentally prepared to either raise a child or to put any child who might be conceived up for adoption. Of course, what it *ultimately* should mean is not having intercourse with any woman with whom you

For conception to occur, a spirit must be present.

aren't willing and able to raise a child—which is really just another way of saying someone you're ready to marry (not to mention already married to!).

Rather than place such "drastic" limits on their sexual and

emotional "freedom"—limits honored by human civilization for thousands of years—many people today prefer not to believe that a spirit is present at conception. But do you think they're fully aware of the implications of *that* "choice?" It essentially means believing that what we call the human spirit or the conscious mind, your own included, is merely a by-product of the workings of the brain—and so will die, and totally cease to be, when the brain dies. (Since a newborn infant's brain isn't yet developed enough to generate a very "sophisticated" consciousness, the logical next step is a breakdown of the prohibitions against infanticide—as we've already begun to see in gruesome news stories about perfectly "nice" teenagers giving birth and killing their babies.) And it means believing that there's nothing intrinsically special or meaningful about *any* human life—your own included.

In a world like that, all human relationships come to be viewed as self-serving and disposable "options" rather than sacred bonds. For if your relationship to a child of your own body can be so lightly dismissed, what relationship can't? If starting a new, potentially eighty-year life, and then stopping it, can be rationalized away in the name of "choice," then "choice" itself becomes the most sacred thing there is—more sacred than any vow or commitment or promise a person may have previously happened to make.

Please note, Patrick, that all these "modern" beliefs are just that—*beliefs*, not *facts*. There is no more hard evidence for them than there is for the traditional religious view (and in fact, as you'll see, there are grounds to believe there is *less)*. They happen to be the beliefs that are "in the air" of our culture right now, but that doesn't give them any special status as truth. So which ideas would you rather take to heart: the ones that are proven to make life more meaningful, or the ones that are advertised as making it more fun? Which, of course, is false advertising anyway, since "free" sex rather quickly turns out not even to be fun! The invention of the Pill in 1960 and the legalization of abortion in 1973 fooled people into believing that something as powerful as the sexual act could be enjoyed without consequences. But as it turns out, believing that actions have *no* consequences simply brings *bad* consequences!

By contrast, the great traditions are in complete accord that the belief that actions have no consequences is the gravest of mistakes—in Buddhist philosophy it's pretty much the most foolish mistake you can possibly make! And so awareness of the Truth means realizing that breaking the precepts and commandments, and harming others, is going to bring *you* painful consequences. That's one thing you *can* count on. You simply cannot "get away" with an act as grave as taking life, and that includes taking life by abortion; the man-made law may not hold you culpable, but the inner Law will. In ways that you may or may not recognize as causally connected, there will come a time when you will suffer for the life you have taken. This is the part of all the traditional moral codes that modern people are most anxious to laugh off, because it interferes with their pleasure and convenience. Yet if you just look, you can *see* the pain and emptiness right under the surface of lives devoted to self-gratification. (Tell me, Patrick, is your father a happy man?)

I will have a lot more to tell you about this Law of Consequences that is the very heart of timeless wisdom, and the key to a truly fulfilling life. But there's one consequence that you can see for yourself right now, and that is the kind of person you would have to become to say, "If the condom breaks, no problem—we'll just have an abortion." (Or, down the line, "If we fall out of love, no problem—we'll just get a divorce.") You have to coarsen and desensitize your soul. You have to deny the sacred trust implicit in the most intimate human relationships. You have to become someone to whom matters of life and death don't much matter and don't even seem real. You have to learn to believe the lie I've spent my whole life fighting against: "It's all a lot of happy horseshit."

Plenty of people take that course, trading off life's deepest meaning, bit by bit, for their personal agendas and desires. It would certainly have been the easier course of action for your mother. She wasn't married, and she must have seen the handwriting on the wall about your dad. She was ambitious, too, and being a single mom was bound to complicate the course of her career. If she hadn't held to the Sixth Commandment and First Precept, just as fiercely as she now insists you guard your innocence, just think, Patrick: you wouldn't be here at all.

Your friend,
Jeff

P.S. I'm arriving in New York next Thursday night. If you have any time on Sunday I'd like to visit with you and see your school.

Dear Jeff,

Sunday's good. We get out of chapel at 12. The team has a meeting at 1. So I'll be around, either at the boathouse or back in my room.

Your letters are intense. I feel like I want to share this information with my friends but I don't know how. I know they would benefit from it.

About my license, driver's ed is a big deal here. It's a whole term course where you have to read a book, pass tests, and you get your learner's permit, and you get your license at the end. But it's so expensive, it's ridiculous. So when I go visit my dad in Florida, I think I'm going to get my learner's permit down there. You have to take a drug and alcohol course and a traffic rules course, so it's somewhat like basic driver's ed.

See you Sunday,

Patrick

THE INTOXICATED SOCIETY

Dear Patrick,

It was really good to see you last weekend, and to see with my own eyes how well you're doing. I enjoyed meeting your close friends—they make a very good impression, both the guys and the girls—and if things work out with the one you've been paying special attention to, that would be nice. But most important is to keep a clear mind and take each day as it comes.

That you've been chosen to be captain of the team next year is *major* news. (It's just like you not to say a word about it on the phone.) When your coach told me, it made me real happy to realize what a great opportunity you have—and I'm sure you'll make the most of it, because I know how dedicated you can be when you focus your mind on a goal.

I'm no expert on rowing, but I know it's a sport that requires tremendous stamina and pain tolerance in order to excel—i.e., it's serious business. And after watching you and your teammates pushing and exhorting each other to max out on the training equipment, I can see that you guys have a pretty clear focus on what it takes to make the grade. A sport like this, that strengthens the mind through tremendous effort and discipline, could well become as pivotal in your life as wrestling has been in mine. You've chosen rigorous challenge over easy comfort, and it's one of the wisest decisions you'll ever make. May you apply the same courage in the kinds of choices you make in your personal life—and always choose the challenge of doing what is right over the comfort of fitting in with the crowd.

Speaking of which, I'm sorry about that friend of yours I *didn't* get to meet because he'd been kicked out of school for smoking pot. But I'm proud of you for not getting sucked in. (One clue to the difference may be your description of your friend's parents: "They're very nice people, but they don't really give him direction, or expect anything from him. They're not a real presence in his life." *Your* mother certainly does—loudly, at times—and is.) I was tremendously saddened when you told me that you first found out a lot of your friends were smoking pot in the seventh grade—age *twelve!* Here, too, what are just scary statistics to me are your everyday reality: high school drug use has doubled since 1992, after declining during the '80s, and binge drinking in colleges has gotten so far out of hand that at least three young men have died of alcohol poisoning in just this past fall term alone.

Listen to a lot of popular songs, look around in the malls, and you'd almost conclude that "youth culture" *is* drug culture—another vicious trend I'm ashamed to say was kicked off by my generation. It used to be the troubled kids, who were obviously suffering from a variety of problems, who did drugs or drank themselves sick. Today that kind of self-destructive behavior is "in," glamorized by the antics of actors, models, and rock stars. *Refusing* to do it can make you feel like *you're* the one with the problem! To resist that feeling with very little social support takes a mental strength that's rare enough in an adult, and a tremendous challenge for any teenager. (That's why it's so important to train your mind!) But drugs aren't a problem that can be blamed solely on "those young people." At a deeper level, it reflects our whole culture: its addiction to sensual pleasures and excitements, and to quick material fixes for getting them ("thrills," "highs," "stuff"); its ignorance of our *inner* resources, and of our power—using nothing but mental force—to control our own states of mind. In a real sense, we live in an intoxicated society.

I've been telling you about all the places on the map of human conduct where the great wisdom traditions agree. Now I'm going to tell you about one point where Buddhist philosophy (and Islam, too) is even more demanding than our own Judeo-Christian tradition. As I've already mentioned, the core of moral behavior, for Buddhists, is contained in Gotama's Five Precepts. The first four are essentially identical with four of our own Ten Commandments: don't kill, steal, commit sexual misconduct, or lie. But Gotama Buddha added a fifth Precept, one that was left out of the Western commandments: *don't take intoxicants.*

Not that the Bible doesn't warn against the dangers of intoxicants. "Wine is a mocker, strong drink is raging: and whosoever is deceived thereby is not wise," says Proverbs 20:1. But perhaps because Jews and Christians make ritual and sacramental use of wine, that's only a mild finger-shaking compared to Gotama's (and Mohammed's) very explicit "Just Say No." And while the Bible tucks it away in a grab bag of folk wisdom, Gotama placed sobriety right at the very heart of his teaching.

One reason is simple: he knew that people who are drunk or on drugs are far more likely to kill, steal, lie, commit sexual misconduct, and do all kinds of other unkind, impulsive, unwholesome, and destructive things. Our society has finally figured this out when it comes to drunk *driving,* the cause of over 40 percent of the deaths in traffic accidents. Drug and alcohol courses, like the one you might be taking in Florida, are now a required part of every driver's-ed course, and stiffer penalties for "driving under the influence" have been enacted into law across the nation. Public-service ad campaigns have done their job, too: my sixteen-year-old friend Sara in St. Louis tells me, "I know if one of my friends had too much to drink they would let someone else drive their car." In other words, we've gained some insight into the wisdom of the Fifth Precept, but only in the special case of operating a motor vehicle!

However, we don't seem to maintain that insight when we're engaged in another life-and-death activity, involving a powerful drive, where impaired judgment makes it virtually certain that people will get hurt: drunk *dating*. Where is the SADD or MADD to raise our consciousness about *this* issue? Despite the clear physical and psychological dangers of heedless sex, *60 percent of teen sexual encounters are initiated under the influence of alcohol or drugs*—probably because that's the only way to knock out the natural shyness and inhibition that are trying to protect you! Obviously, Patrick, being intoxicated impairs your judgment and self-control, greatly multiplying the risks of "messing around" (a telling choice of words!) with a girl. But does our society consider this as serious a threat to life and health as drunk driving? Or is it shrugged off as "harmless fun?"

In February 1997, three young men, an eighteen-year-old high-school graduate and two of his younger friends still in school, were arrested in New Jersey, accused of raping a girl while she was passed out from drinking. Even as local newspapers were filled with alarm and outrage over this crime, as columnists deplored society's moral decline and wondered what young people are coming to, the *TV Guide* for that *very same week* featured the following description of a popular TV show (ironically enough, on its "Guidelines" page):

> *Drunken debauchery. Promiscuity. Fisticuffs. It's all part of an uproarious* Friends *that finds Chandler blanking out after getting inebriated and having an encounter with one of Joey's sisters.*

Alarming and enraging, or uproarious? This culture can't have it both ways.

Clearly, then, the Buddhist Precept to "just say no to drugs" is designed, in part, to help us keep the other four. But Gotama's reasons for it go deeper still. For the Buddha, the ultimate secret of a strong mind is simply this: *Wake up!* Indeed, that's what the word "Buddha" literally means: *awake* or *awakened*. The purity of clear awareness is the source, the very heart, of moral behavior. To be a skillful, kind, and responsible human being, in Gotama's view, it's not enough just to obey the precepts and commandments (though it's not a bad start, that's for sure!); you must also *understand* them. And above all, you must strive *to see things as they truly are*—yourself and your own intentions, as well as the feelings of others.

Acting according to this principle, your dad couldn't just make you an impulsive promise at a moment when he was feeling generous. He'd have to take an honest look at his own ability and commitment to follow through, and he'd have to realize how breaking his word would affect *you*. It's hard enough to achieve that kind of clarity and objectivity when you're sober (but I'm going to show you some tools Gotama gave us to do it). *It's essentially impossible when you're drunk or drugged.* Just as Proverbs says, drugs are deceivers. If you've ever had even a few beers too many, you know how they make you feel invulnerable and invincible, elated and fearless, just when you're really dullest, dumbest, and most at risk!

The word "intoxicate" contains the word "toxic" in its very core: it means to poison the mind. We've talked about health food vs. junk food for the mind, but poison isn't just poor nourishment—it's the deadly opposite. Drugs are literally a poison which can physically damage—meaning cause cell death in—an adult's brain, with resultant irreversible deterioration of the workings of the mind. What do you figure that says about the harm they can do to the still-developing brain of a sixteen-year-old—or a *twelve*-year-old?

Right now, you are laying the all-important foundations of your future, and the place where that groundwork is literally, physically being laid is *in your brain*. As a neuroscientist and physician, I want to stress this with special intensity: we know now that at sixteen your brain is still busily forming the connections it needs to reach full potential. That process can be stunted and warped by drugs, especially in the areas of memory, learning, and motivation—functions you'll need to squeeze every bit of capacity out of if you're to access your full intelligence and creativity (not to mention your full earning power!). And the younger you are, the more vulnerable the brain is. For an adult to sustain significant damage to intellect and creativity requires really chronic drug and/or alcohol abuse. For a teen, the risks of long-term damage are much higher. Your brain deserves *special* protection, and a chance to get all its circuits in place!

But I know here I'm preaching to the converted—thank God! You had a one-liner that your mother really liked. You were discussing the fact that your friend is in drug counseling now, and you're hoping he'll be allowed back into school next year. If he is, you plan to room with him, and you said, "Mom, he's not gonna get *me* to smoke marijuana, I'm gonna get *him* to realize that he *shouldn't* smoke marijuana." Well, Patrick, feel free to use this letter (and to ask whatever questions come up!) as a means of empowering you to achieve that goal!

Your friend,
Jeff

THIS, TOO, SHALL PASS

Dear Patrick,

Gotama Buddha was such a megafan of sobriety that he devoted his last words on earth to it. This was his final exhortation to his followers before his body stopped living: *"Succeed by using clear-mindedness!"* And the word he used for "clear-mindedness" literally means "nonintoxication." So I feel justified in devoting one more letter to the subject while you're soberly studying for your exams!

You could say that the Buddhist tradition is a 2,500-year campaign against "drunk living," while our society is reeling from the results of a 30-year campaign to *promote* "drunk living"—and in far more than just the literal smoking, snorting, shooting, swigging sense. For Gotama keenly observed that you don't have to imbibe, ingest, or inhale any substance to get "drunk." He identified the human passions—lust, anger, fear—as toxins that cloud awareness and distort judgment every bit as surely and strongly as alcohol, cocaine, or marijuana.

In this Gotama was way ahead of his time, for modern neurobiology has discovered that, in fact, each of these basic emotions floods your body with hormones, released in response to bursts of activity in the brain. The hormones then work in concert with, and intensify, further changes in the brain and throughout the body. The result is alterations in your consciousness that prime you for automatic, almost robotlike actions: copulation, acquisition, aggression, fight or flight. (I'll have a lot more to tell you about that!) The heart of Buddhist teachings is a set of practical methods for "sobering up": learning to cool, tame, and master your passions so you aren't driven through life drunk on them, creating disturbances wherever you go, but rather can steer your own way alertly, calmly, and wisely.

Our society does exactly the opposite! Think about it:

nearly everything in our popular culture is designed to inflame, not tame, the passions. Rock videos, movies, and advertising assail us from all sides with provocative images. The lyrics and heavy beat of a lot of rap and rock music are deliberately designed to arouse, incite, and intimidate. Blockbuster movies are loaded with explosions and disasters, sex and gore. We move through an environment that aims to keep us excited and distracted, stimulated and saturated with hormonal levels which are psychically toxic. As a result we become, in essence, drunk out of our minds. And that's *before* alcohol and who knows what else is stirred into the mix! This is what passes today for entertainment.

And then there's our culture's obsession with youth, which really began when the huge numbers of the baby-boom generation were young (but has continued, to our chagrin, now that *we're* middle-aged!). This might surprise you, Patrick, but in Gotama's view, you're already a little bit "drunk" just by virtue of being young! He spoke of the "intoxication of youth," a state which, if you're careless, will cloud your judgment and result in you doing bad things. It's not just that all your hormones and feelings are flowing full force. It's that your health and strength can give you the illusion that you're invulnerable, almost immortal—and that can make you arrogant, conceited, even cruel. For instance, you may not have much patience with old people, or much empathy for someone who is suffering.

Gotama thought it was so important to "sober up" those who were drunk on their youth (after all, two-thirds of the criminals in our own prisons are under thirty-five!) that he prescribed a daily dose of the truth: reflecting on the unavoidable fact that you, too, will one day grow old, get sick, and die. He instructed every woman and every man to reflect on five things every day. The first three of them are:

- It is my nature to grow old (literally, to decay), it is unavoidable that I will grow old

- It is my nature to get sick, it is unavoidable that I will get sick.
- It is my nature to die, it is unavoidable that I will die.

Can you imagine if Gotama had gone on today's talk radio with this message? He would have been deluged with call-ins: "Eww, *morbid!*" "What a bummer." "Don't bring me down!" Yet bringing you "down" is exactly what he meant to do—from the dangerous "high" of illusion and delusion to the firm bedrock of Truth. Gotama would have fully agreed with these words of Jesus: "And ye shall know the truth, and the truth shall make you free." [John 8:32]

In the Buddha's teaching, there are Four Noble Truths, and the First Noble Truth is *dukkha* (a Pāli word meaning unpleasant or difficult): the essential nature of reality is

It is my nature to grow old.

It is my nature to get sick.

It is my nature to die.

unsatisfactory to such a degree that life is inevitably plagued by suffering. Everything that arises changes and passes away, and that includes not only ourselves but all the people and things we love. (That's the *fourth* thing Gotama said you should reflect on every day: "Everything I like and cherish will change and become separated from me." You begin to discover *this* truth very early on, perhaps the first time you break one of your toys!) This fact is painful to us. But Gotama said that the root cause of our pain is not just the nature of the universe but our craving for it to conform to and fulfill all our desires. That's the Second Noble Truth: it's craving that causes suffering. The Third Noble Truth is that this craving, and the suffering it causes, can end, and the Fourth Noble Truth is the Buddha's way to end it: a detailed plan for facing reality and living your life in harmony with it, called the Noble Eightfold Path.

So reminding yourself daily (yes, even at age sixteen!) that you will someday age, get sick, and die, and that all your favorite things will change, is a kind of detox from delusion, a surefire way to stay in touch with reality. It's not some uniquely Buddhist insight. It's just the truth, and is noted in our Western tradition as well. My favorite pre-Socratic philosopher, Heraclitus, who lived at almost exactly the same time as Gotama, stressed in his philosophy that all things are constantly changing, that everything is in perpetual flux. And the Jewish tradition has a wonderful rabbinical tale that makes much the same point:

> A king who collected the most precious jewels in the world dreamed one night of a magical ring, more valuable than his entire collection. A ring with such power that when he was sad, it would make him happy; when he was drunk with power or passion, it would clear his mind and bring him to himself; and when he was truly joyful, it would deepen his joy.
>
> The king offered all his advisors a magnificent reward and sent them out to scour the world for the magic ring. Years passed, and one by one they came home empty-handed. The king's humblest, most devoted servant was the last to give up. As he was trudging back to the palace to admit defeat, he made one last stop at a small, dusty shop. When he sadly told the

*proprietor what he had been seeking for so long, the old man
smiled and said, "I have the ring." Taking a little box down
from a high shelf, he refused payment. "Your king needs it," he
said. "Take it as a gift."*

*The king tore open the box with trembling fingers. Inside was
a plain metal ring! Was this the treasure he had gone to so
much trouble for? Astonished and angry, the king was about to
throw the box across the room when he noticed that there were
Hebrew letters engraved around the ring. He looked more closely.*

"Gam zeh ya-avor," it said. "This, too, shall pass."

*The king wore the ring for the rest of his life. Whenever he was
sad, or intoxicated, or joyful, he would read those words—and it
worked exactly as he had dreamed.*

The wisdom of this story, which has the special warm,
poignant flavor of the Jewish tradition, is that being aware of
the transitoriness of all things—and all moods—immediately
puts them into true perspective. It helps you to endure what
is bad (because it will pass), resist losing yourself in some
intoxicating passion (which will pass), and truly cherish
what is good (because this, too, shall pass).

If sixteen-year-olds were routinely taught to reflect on
transitoriness every day, Patrick, we'd have a lot less reason

This, too, shall pass.

to say that "youth is wasted on the young." Don't take your clear, fresh senses, your quick mind, and your strong muscles for granted. Savor every moment, because believe me—this, too, shall pass! I remember a time when I could easily have stayed up all night to finish this letter! I'm not sure whether the reason why I don't generally do things like that anymore is because I have more wisdom or less energy . . . probably some combination of the two!

In the morning, I'll tell you the fifth, and most important, thing Gotama said we should reflect on daily.

BY THEIR FRUITS YE SHALL
KNOW THEM

OK. I've washed my face, eaten my nutrition bar and done my daily meditation and chanting. I'm ready to go. (Later I'll go work out. . . .)

The fifth thing the Buddha said every one of us should reflect on each and every day is our *karma,* which means we should reflect on what we *do. Karma* is a word American popular culture misuses to mean something with a mystical flavor, almost like "fate," that kind of falls on you from the sky. This is a serious misunderstanding.

In fact, *karma* is just the Sanskrit word for an action or a deed. Your karma is what you *do!* Further, the Buddha explained that by *karma* he meant the kind of intentions you have, wholesome or unwholesome, good or evil, when you act. One simple but accurate way to think about karma is that your wholesome and unwholesome actions are like good and bad seeds—they tend to ripen into sweet or bitter fruits. Or, in other words, **ACTIONS HAVE CONSEQUENCES**—the *other* fact of life people are most reluctant to face.

This is tough stuff, Patrick! Some people might hear the word "wisdom" and think of inspiring, soothing advice from some old guy with a long beard. You're beginning to know that it's something much starker than that, and something no one else can do for you: *seeing things as they are.* Wisdom is not for wimps. (One of the greatest poets of the twentieth century, and one of my favorites, T. S. Eliot, observed wistfully, "Humankind cannot bear very much reality.") It's also not just for older people. As you know from the saying "There's no fool like an old fool"—and from a glance at the adults around you—the aging process doesn't automatically confer wisdom. (The only thing it *automatically* confers is decrepitude.) And young people don't *have* to be "intoxicated." Ultimately, wisdom doesn't come from experience, it comes from close observation, courage, and honesty—which are available to anyone with sufficient fortitude at any age.

Nonetheless, a wise culture respects aging people, and even finds a certain beauty in them, because they embody the capacity to endure and accept the harsh facts of reality. (The school of Buddhism I study and practice in is called *Theravāda*, which means "Doctrine of the Elders.") Our society, by contrast—addicted to the "drug" of youth and the superficial pleasures it represents—sees very little that's pleasing or admirable in a wrinkled face or a wise, dispassionate attitude. People will do almost anything not to sober up in this sense: swallow powerful hormones with unknown long-term side effects, pay many thousands of dollars for plastic surgery, seek out and virtually deify false prophets of various kinds—all in a frantic attempt to hang on to their youthful appearance and sexual allure as they move into their forties, fifties, and sixties. Of course, there's nothing wrong with "trying to look your best." It's the morbid fear of facing the realities of aging and inescapable death that causes problems. Not only is the dignity of age foolishly denigrated, the benefits of youth are idealized to an almost insane degree.

What's more, it's not just physical youth this society worships. The *psychological* traits of youth, formerly called immaturity, have also been elevated to an "ideal" worth striving for. Who really wants their parents acting the way their flakier friends do?? But, Patrick, don't you know parents who do almost exactly that? It's hardly surprising, since that kind of behavior gets so much indulgence, even approval, from the culture.

Today, "acceptable" models for adult character and behavior include an impulsiveness and irresponsibility more characteristic of youth at its most intoxicated and self-indulgent. A forty-year-old who dumps his family for some passionate new attraction can be viewed as bravely pursuing "authenticity" and "growth." He's being "true to himself," maybe even to his "inner child." But impulsive acts like that are profound examples of reckless disregard for your karma: you're not reflecting on what you're doing! This inevitably means that you're acting with unwholesome intentions. How do we know people doing things like that are acting with bad intent? By the results—the pain they cause, the emotional wreckage they leave behind them. As Jesus Christ said: "By their fruits ye shall know them." A spouse and children left forsaken in the dust—is this just the price of "personal freedom"?

It may be hard to believe, but I actually know of "psychotherapists" who spout this kind of trash about "freedom and authenticity" to balding men with abandoned kids your age and a lot younger! But then I live near Hollywood and Beverly Hills. These days it seems like the whole country lives near Hollywood and Beverly Hills.

But I have a lot of confidence that you, and those friends of yours I've been fortunate enough to meet, have the desire and capacity to do better than that. Much better, in fact.

Your friend,
Jeff

Dear Jeff,

I have a friend (you didn't meet him) who I think is drunk on youth. He used to be even a closer friend. We had a big discussion, sort of about how you should live your life. I'd gotten these letters, and I was saying how "actions have consequences"—really important, major point, which I think a lot of people my age don't realize. Don't just go out and have a good time and not think about what you're doing, because you're going to hurt somebody. This guy got really defensive, because he thought that I was attacking the way he lives. He's out all night, he's the biggest womanizer I know. He said, "Well, I'm young. I'm gonna hook up with as many girls as I can, and I'm gonna live life, and come up with my own way of living."

One more thing—a couple of times you talked about rap music being violent. It's not always like that. There's a good group that I listen to, called A Tribe Called Quest. They're rap music, or hip hop, and I like the way they sound, but I'm also aware of what they're saying. They talk about sex and drugs and stuff in their music, but they also talk about religion and spirituality. I think there's some wisdom in there.

I should have played it for you when you were up here, but I guess we were too busy playing the Wallflowers.

Patrick

RAPPERS, POETS, AND PROPHETS

Dear Patrick,

Too busy playing the Wallflowers? You mean there was something *else* you wanted to play? How could that be possible? Well, OK—next time *you* pick the album.

By the way, you're right about your friend—he *is* drunk on youth. Just watch as he speeds and swerves through life as dangerously as any drunk driver. It will be useful for you to observe not only how his hit-and-run sex life hurts others, but also the damage it does to *him*—to his self-respect, for example—perhaps more subtle in the short run, but just as real.

Our society may have repealed the unwritten moral law against what your friend is doing, but there's still no escaping the underlying Law of Consequences. You just can't hurt other people, regularly using them for your own narrow interests, and not have it take its toll on your insides. That's as basic to the way this universe works as the law of gravity. In this sense, you can no more "come up with your own way of living" than you can step off a cliff and fly! When you hurt other people, you also hurt yourself—especially on the inside. This is universal moral law.

Indeed, we could even speak of "the laws of moral physics." Do you remember learning in physics class that "For every action, there is an equal and opposite reaction"? The corresponding law in the moral realm can be expressed as a twist on the Golden Rule: "What you do unto others, you also do unto yourself." (With prayer and meditation—as I will show you—you can observe this through your own experience.) It's equally true that any harm you do yourself—by using drugs, for example—also harms others. These fundamental Laws of Reality help to explain why harm and damage have spread so far and fast through a society of individualists who claim merely to be "doing their own thing."

The laws of moral physics

I believe you, though, when you tell me that not all rap music is harmful—I guess it's like anything else, you just have to know where to look to find what's worthwhile. Why do you think it's so hard for each generation to hear the wisdom in the next generation's music? I certainly remember how my parents thought I was going off the deep end back when I was singing Bob Dylan's songs over and *over* and **over**. But it kept me alive. Come to think of it, some have said that "Subterranean Homesick Blues" is the original rap song! If you like Jakob Dylan, Patrick, try listening to his old man sometime.

I will never forget the first time I heard "Positively 4th Street," in 1965. It was a major epiphany. I remember so clearly the feeling that "This is exactly how I feel!" By 1967 or '68, I knew every word and note of every song Bob Dylan had ever written. In fact, in '68, when I was a junior in high school, my English teacher, Mr. Hartman, actually let me write three term papers on Dylan!—he actually appreciated how intensely dedicated I was to learning every nuance of it. And to think that a lot of the students were really scared of him because of how strict he was! He trusted my sincerity about Dylan, though. . . . I really appreciated that.

That experience learning about Dylan gave me my first taste of what it feels like to really know something, to thoroughly master it. And you know, it's still with me. Until just a few years ago I still used to say, "If they ever put on the song 'Like a Rolling Stone' and I can't sing every word perfectly, bury me, 'cause I'm dead." So don't think the stuff you get into now won't stick with you—because if you're really into it, it will.

As I think back on it, I would have to say that the most important thing Dylan's songs did for me was to open up the world of great poetry—some of the most nutritious "soul food" there is. I wouldn't have started reading poetry myself—coming from a totally uncultured background, with respect to literature, anyway—if it weren't for Dylan. And so I would not have encountered two of my greatest teachers, W. B. Yeats (1865–1939) and T. S. Eliot (1888–1965)—who were also two of the greatest prophets of the spiritual crisis you and I have been talking about. A prophet's job has always been to "Wake up!" a people gone astray, warn them of the disaster they're heading for, and call them home to the right path before it's too late. And as one of the main tools of their trade, prophets have always used poetry, because of the tremendous power of words, when they are well used, to awaken the mind and rouse the spirit.

Bob Dylan certainly played a prophetic role in the '60s. You might even manage to convince me that the best rappers do today. But right after the First World War, a mind-boggling slaughter that shocked and sobered everyone who had believed scientific progress would bring heaven on earth, it was the poets, and particularly Yeats and Eliot, who prophesied.

In 1922, Eliot published "The Waste Land," a long, difficult poem about the shattering of traditions and the spiritual deadness at the heart of modern life. (It's difficult because it "samples"—to use a rap term!—several thousand years of liturgy and literature, from Sanskrit and Greek on down.) In the third section is the following grim scene of what we would now call "casual" sex between a typist and her dinner guest, a "young man carbuncular":

> The time is now propitious, as he guesses,
> The meal is ended, she is bored and tired,
> Endeavors to engage her in caresses
> Which still are unreproved, if undesired.
> Flushed and decided, he assaults at once;
> Exploring hands encounter no defense;
> His vanity requires no response,
> And makes a welcome of indifference. . . .

Having had his way, without making the slightest emotional contact, the young man (who may remind you of your "womanizing" friend)

> Bestows one final patronizing kiss,
> And gropes his way, finding the stairs unlit . . .
> She turns and looks a moment in the glass,

Hardly aware of her departed lover;
Her brain allows one half-formed thought to pass:
"Well now that's done: and I'm glad it's over."

Eliot called this the central scene of the poem! He was saying, I believe, that it's one of the chief symptoms of spiritual sickness to treat the life-force itself, as expressed in sexual desire, as "no big deal," and other people as objects for our self-gratification. Near the poem's end, he contrasts the life-transforming power of real intimacy:

. . . what have we given?
My friend, blood shaking my heart
The awful daring of a moment's surrender
Which an age of prudence can never retract,
By this, and this only, we have existed. . . .

Eliot's sense that twentieth-century life had become a spiritual "Waste Land" led him to a profound interest in Buddhism, as well as leading to his conversion to Anglo-Catholicism at the age of thirty-nine. He became convinced that only the wisdom contained in the world's great traditions has enough power to shelter and protect all that's meaningful in human life from the destructive tendencies in human nature.

In 1921, the year before "The Waste Land" appeared, the Irish poet William Butler Yeats, probably the greatest master of English poetry in this century, published a famous poem called "The Second Coming." I've already told you one of its lines: "Things fall apart; the center cannot hold." This is what follows—a prophecy, written well before Hitler and Hiroshima, of what was yet to come as humanity, in a "widening gyre," strayed further and further from its moral center:

Mere anarchy is loosed upon the world,
The blood-dimmed tide is loosed, and everywhere
The ceremony of innocence is drowned . . .

And what rough beast, its hour come round at last,
Slouches toward Bethlehem to be born?

"The ceremony of innocence!" Patrick, I think you can feel those words enriching your mind, even if you're unsure of exactly what Yeats meant. But let the words sink into your brain, like rain to the roots of a tree. They'll prepare you to consider "innocence" in a new light, and to understand what "ceremony" has to do with preparing to battle the rough beast steadily slouching toward us.

Your friend,
Jeff

A FATHER'S PRAYER

Dear Patrick,

In our day and age, who really wants to be "innocent"? The word has come to mean everything your peers are so eager to shed: inexperience (especially in matters sexual), childishness, protectedness, vulnerability, maybe even foolishness and naïveté. Everyone wants to be, or at least appear to be, street-wise, experienced, cool, cynical, and in the know. To sum up the current attitude: "Innocence is for babies," or even worse, for "losers"!

But what most people *don't* know is that the source of the word "innocent" is a place of great power. It originally comes from the Latin words for "not" *(in)* and "to harm" *(nocere,* from which "noxious" also comes). The Hippocratic oath that has bound all of us who practice medicine for twenty-five hundred years begins *"Primum non nocere":* First, do no harm. "Innocence," then, literally means "not harming" or "not harmful."

Now if that still doesn't sound like much to you, Patrick, take a look at the evening news. Better yet, go read a good news-paper. Think about your mother's struggles to form a lasting relationship with a man. Look around you at the sheer amount of pain and suffering people cause each other and themselves every day.

For human beings, it seems, "not harming" is anything but easy!

Like all authentic spirituality, Buddhist morality is simply and profoundly about *not doing harm* to, and not causing suf-fering for, yourself or others. That's a large part of what drew me to it. When I was twelve, at summer camp, I read the transcripts of the Nuremberg trials of Nazi war criminals, trying to under-stand why the great-uncle I was named for had been murdered with most of his (and my) family. Even then I was already stunned by, and felt a need to try to understand, why people can show such cruelty (sometimes deliberately, sometimes care-lessly) towards those around them. Years later I came to see that Gotama Buddha had a powerful answer to my "Why?"—a teaching that could not only reveal the roots of human hurt-fulness, but show the way to uproot them.

The Buddha taught that actions which cause harm invari-ably spring from three roots: *greed*, *ill-will*, and *ignorance*. Innocence has nothing to do with any of those. True innocence doesn't have much to do with babies, either. So-called "inno-cent" two-year-olds scream when they don't get what they want, poke dogs in the nose, and snatch toys from each other. Plenty of greed, ill-will, and ignorance there! The fact that many adults don't act much better is the tip-off that deep down they're basically still babies!

In reality, *true* innocence is the highest of human accom-plishments. It's the defining mark of those who have achieved genuine victory in facing life's innumerable challenges. *Not doing harm* requires the utmost in awareness, effort, and courage—that's why, of all known organisms, humans are the only ones capable of fully achieving it. And it's anything but naïve; it calls for *wisdom* (facing the truth) about the potential for harm in the world and in human nature—in *your own* nature! To fully achieve that wisdom would require the *complete* uprooting of the greed, ill-will, and ignorance which—as Gotama, Jesus, and Moses, among other spiritual masters, knew so well—grow as wild and tough as crabgrass in every human mind and brain. If you like challenges, Patrick, you can't find a bigger one than that!

Similar misunderstandings plague the words "virtue" and "virtuous." Do you think they sound uptight, priggish, and prudish? Well, I have a surprise for you. They come from words in both Latin and Sanskrit for "courageous man" or "hero"! Both of these words came down to us through medieval French and English, where they still meant "potency" or "strength." They are derived from the same root as "virile"!

One who is virtuous must be a hero because it takes real strength and courage to achieve mastery over one's self. The Buddha compared the strength needed to that of a chariot driver who has the ability to steer, rather than be pulled along by, a charging team of horses. Only self-mastery, which results from a clear mind, will enable you *not to harm* yourself and others. The alternative is being stampeded and trampled on by the wild horses inside you. Or even worse, allowing them to trample on others.

Don't think for a moment that *not doing harm* is merely passive or negative, like not doing much of anything. The Buddhist texts describe virtue as a tremendously active, energetic state, one that calls for focus, skill, and coordination, as well as strength. It's not enough just to hold back from acting out of greed or anger. You also need heroic self-control to follow through on your best intentions and the positive commitments you've made. *The keeping of promises,* as the great Scottish philosopher David Hume pointed out over 250 years ago, is a fundamental building block of morality. Men and women of character used to say, "My word is my bond"—a vow that they would allow no inner impulse or outer distraction to overpower their resolve. They took pride in that feat of self-mastery, and it made this world a more trustworthy place than it's become today. You could plan your life, and give your heart, in confidence that other people would keep their promises far more often than not.

That's the kind of "innocence" we've lost—or more accurately, thrown away—and must retrieve.

But if the connection between innocence and virtue is clear, where does *ceremony* come in? There's a clue in another poem Yeats wrote around the same time as "The Second Coming." Here is what he said near the conclusion of "A Prayer for My Daughter," written as a blessing for the future of his sleeping baby girl:

And may her bridegroom bring her to a house
Where all's accustomed, ceremonious;
For arrogance and hatred are the wares
Peddled in the thoroughfares.
How but in custom and in ceremony
Are innocence and beauty born?

"Beauty," it seems, is another strong word that has lost its ancient virtue in the modern marketplace. Women like Madonna, Jenny McCarthy, and Pamela Anderson Lee sure seem "beautiful" (silicone and all), but no one would accuse them of being "innocent." What could Yeats have been thinking when he linked innocence and beauty so closely?

Seeing those two words paired, almost like identical twins, should start you thinking about what beauty really is. Could it be that innocence, the absence of the harm that leads to suffering, is the essence of *real* beauty? Well, I say it sure beats the R-rated version that gets shoved in your face on every TV and newsstand. And I say this: Peace is Beauty. Freedom from fear and craving is Beauty. And freedom from "arrogance and hatred" and their "peddling" (basically the business of Hollywood today) would be a good start toward achieving Innocence. Consider this: "sex goddesses" are exactly that— sexy. Real beauty is something else altogether.

Why is it that a lot of kids today seem to understand these kinds of things better than many "adults"?

And why did Yeats hold "custom and ceremony" in such high esteem? *Ceremony,* remember, is the blessing of taking serious things seriously, marking occasions like your coming of age—or a first date—in ways that impress us with their true significance. Such ceremonies are like gateways, insuring that we will never cross one of life's most important boundaries carelessly—promiscuously—without sufficient preparation or awareness of what's at stake. *Custom,* or morality (which is derived from the Latin word for custom), is the everyday practice of the commandments and precepts that restrain our unruly human nature and protect us from its great potential for harm. "Custom and ceremony" also imply plain good manners—the small rituals that counter "arrogance and hatred" and guide us to treat one another with respect.

Yeats deeply believed that custom and ceremony are the powerful guardians of innocence and beauty, and the well-tended garden in which they grow. We've seen what happens to a society that "liberates" itself from them. It becomes a society that has abandoned innocence, and that is a very harmful—and ugly—place to live.

But there's still plenty of room for optimism, Patrick. You and your peers now have the chance of a lifetime—an opportunity that too many of today's adults threw away long ago. You have a *bona fide* chance to be heroes! And if anything remains certain in our uncertain times, it's that heroic deeds are badly needed.

By challenging all that's reckless and ruthless in our culture, you and your friends can not only protect yourselves from it, *you can change it*—and help to protect us all. In truth, every living being (God's Children one and all) yearns to live in a world more pure, safe, sane, and hopeful than the one we live in now. That's why, as we approach a new millennium, the world is anxiously waiting for new heroes to emerge. Every generation is called to its own epic battle. I believe that restoring the purity of our ethosphere is yours.

Here I am, a grown man, telling you, a new adult just turned sixteen, that I'm looking to you and your generation to return our world to a safer and less toxic condition. A Big Request, no doubt about that. But please believe me, I wouldn't ask if I didn't genuinely think you could do it. And I promise you this: I'll provide you with tools I know can do the job, and I'll be with you every step of the way.

Your friend,
Jeff

HOW TO BE A HERO

Dear Patrick,

I know, it sounds like an absurdly huge assignment I've laid on you and your generation— to clean up a moral mess it's taken the better part of a century to make. You could even call it a Herculean task. Have you ever read the story of how Hercules had to clean the Augean stables?

That was the least glamorous of the legendary Greek hero's impossible labors, which he was sentenced to perform as penance for throwing his own children into the fire. True, he was out of his mind when he did it—driven mad by a jealous goddess—but the Greek gods didn't accept the insanity defense, or the abuse excuse. A man, and especially a hero, was account-able for his own actions, not to mention his own children, so Hercules had to pay. But as a consolation, he was promised that if he served his sentence in full, and succeeded at these ten superhuman labors (later upped to twelve), he would become immortal.

Eleven of the labors were your typical dramatic superhero stuff—slaying beasts and monsters, fetching heavily guarded treasure and magical animals from the ends of the earth. But the fifth labor—cleaning all the manure out of the stables of King Augeas, the biggest livestock rancher in Greece, in *one day*—was not exactly the kind of job would-be heroes have in mind when they sign up. Hercules did it by using brains, as well as brawn. First, he offered King Augeas a deal: he'd clean out the stables in a day in exchange for one-tenth of the livestock. Augeas agreed, because he didn't believe Hercules could do it. Hercules brought Augeas's son along to watch what became a major engineering feat—or perhaps the world's biggest ever flush toilet. The hero made an opening at each end of the cattle yard and then diverted the courses of two nearby rivers so that they flowed right through the stables and washed out all the manure.

Hercules' conniving, however, sabotaged his triumph. When Augeas learned that this labor was supposed to be part of Hercules' penance, he broke his promise to fork over the 10 percent. And when Hercules tried to sneak a profit on the side from one of his labors, it didn't get counted as part of his penance either. That's how he wound up doing twelve instead of the original ten! One moral of this story certainly is: Use your head, by all means, but don't get *too* clever. Whenever you try to outsmart the Law of Consequences, you just end up making more trouble for yourself. The other moral is that heroes don't just do high-profile things like slay dragons and rescue maidens. Sometimes some serious house-cleaning is the most heroic thing they can do.

Fortunately, to have a powerfully purifying effect on this world, you don't have to (and in fact, you can't) clean up other people's messes for them. Remember that "law of moral physics" that says what you do to yourself, you also do to others (and vice versa)? The positive corollary of that law is that what you do *for* yourself, you also do for others. In Gotama's words, *"Protecting yourself, you protect others; protecting others, you protect yourself."* Start with yourself, and how you live your own life—always remaining aware that no one else, not even the Buddha himself, can do it for you. "You yourself must do the strenuous work," he said. "Enlightened Ones can only show the way."

It's a fact that the daily choices you, one young man, make right now *(Should I cheat on this test? Should I manipulate that girl?)* have so much power that the ripple effects they cause will eventually touch people you'll never know. It could be a little kid in a small town in Ohio, it could be an infant in an inner-city neighborhood in L.A. It will definitely be the people your mother interacts with every day—if only due to the joy or anxiety your choices cause her. For example, consider how what you do affects the children of the people your mother works with. Those kids' lives are touched by the effects your mother has on their parents, which is affected by her mood, which is affected by you! And so on and on and on. That's just how the world works.

The choices you make, and the actions *(karma)* they lead to, are part of what creates the moral environment we all must live in. This is one of those principles we seem to have no trouble grasping in relation to the ecosphere. You've undoubtedly been drilled in the basic principle of ecology, that every part of the environment is connected to every other part. This means that you can't ever really throw anything *away,* because what you throw in the sea is eventually going to turn up in our drinking water. If you ask environmentally concerned young people, "Why *not* throw that paper cup in the street? Why pick it up if it's already there?" you discover that they have a sense of their own power to make a difference, for harm or for good. They've *seen* the ecosphere get worse and then get better as a result of many such small actions *(karma).* No one doubts that every time you choose *not to pollute* the natural environment, you're making a significant difference in the purity and beauty of our world—and that everything you do *to pollute* has the opposite effect.

This principle of ecology is actually based on one of the deepest of spiritual truths: that each person's actions, for good and for bad, affect us all. Why should this same truth be so hard to grasp when it comes to the inner world? It doesn't make sense to worry about throwing out a Styrofoam hamburger container but not to worry about throwing out a hurtful, thoughtless word or act. Neither is going to go away; both are going to add more toxic waste to the environment. Just as with the ecosphere, you contribute either to our ethosphere's pollution or to its purity by how you live your life.

There are still places we can go in the ecosphere, like that wilderness camp you loved so much up in Canada, where the air is pure and the streams run cold and clear. You've spent time in the wilderness, Patrick, and come out stronger, smarter and calmer. You *know* why it's so important to protect and restore it—and you basically know what that takes. You've clearly seen the harm done by greed and carelessness, the restorative power of awareness and care—and the difference it makes to *you*. But because the healing of our *ethosphere* has barely begun, there aren't many places, especially in a sophisticated big city, where you can readily see moral values in action and experience firsthand just how big a difference they make. Once you get past obvious examples like helping to feed the poor at a shelter (as important as that is), where do you look next? I haven't run across www.moralvalues.com lately on the "information superhighway," have you?

Yet, mysteriously, you are able to imagine and long for things you've never seen. When you were younger, if I had invited you on a quest, and told you we were going to fight our way through many obstacles and dangers to a kingdom that was pure and undegraded, inspiring and invigorating, wouldn't you have wanted to leave right away? You *still* would—except that sixteen-year-olds know that's just a fairy tale. There's no such place in reality, right?

There is, but it's not in the outside world of the five senses. It is *within* you. That's how I know you can do the job I've asked you to do.

There's a deep place in you, and in each one of us, that recognizes and responds to moral values. It's the part of us that makes us uniquely human, different in kind from any other living thing. That is our destination on this journey of life, but it's also our spiritual source. It's through neglect of that inner source, and the difficult, heroic journey it takes to get back to it, that our society has gotten into such a mess. But that place is always there, waiting for us to come home. One of its names is Innocence, and the great spiritual masters of our species have left signposts to help guide us back to it.

He never claimed it was an easy place to get to.

Gotama Buddha was a hero who found his way back to Innocence and blazed a trail for others to follow. He never claimed it was an easy place to get to, but he promised it could be done. He said, "You who have trodden this path will make an end to suffering." He considered this quest the greatest possible challenge and adventure. The journey, the goal, the guide who knows the way, the enemies who will try to stop you—all are within you. (Even the Augean stables are within you, when you take too much pride in your inner "animals" and allow them to multiply—and that's no bull!) Everything good and bad about the cosmos, as well as the path to true mastery, all can be found, as Gotama said, "in this fathom long body." To blaze this cosmic trail within will require the same undaunted courage possessed by all great explorers. For if you dare to undertake this journey, you will be a true pioneer—helping to show others the way.

But whatever you choose to do, remember this: The state of the world, and of its future, begins right here—in the state of your mind.

Your friend,
Jeff

TRAINING YOUR MENTAL FORCE I: THE POWER OF MINDFULNESS

Dear Jeff,

You might have heard from my mom what happened at the rowing championships. I was a little embarrassed. Everyone else's parents were there, and my dad came up, and his friend who was with him was completely plastered. He passed out, and my dad had to drag him to the car! My dad didn't seem perfectly sober, either. It was a big day for me, so that kind of put a little dent in it.

But now I'm at camp. It's hard, but great. Rowing's one of those things where you just have to do it a lot to get better, and I have that opportunity here. Basically, it's row, row, row, and row some more—like the song. I look forward to getting your letters though.

Patrick

MEET YOUR VEHICLE

Dear Patrick,

It's Father's Day as I write to you today, a holiday which must evoke considerable ambivalence for you—and for millions of your peers. How can you not have mixed feelings

91

about someone so vital to your existence, yet so distant from your everyday life? Not to mention so undependable when he *does* show up?

This morning's newspaper features a full-color ad with the headline ABSOLUT DAD. The ad goes on, "Happy Father's Day, you're one in a million"—but there is no human face, no strong arms. Instead, across the page wriggle hundreds of sperm (with heads shaped like Absolut vodka bottles). The ad agency probably thought they were just being clever, but they've unconsciously captured one of the most ravaging trends of our time—the reduction of fatherhood to a biological function. It's no wonder your mother refers to such men as "the Inseminators." And all in the service of marketing an intoxicant! A cruel irony, if you think about it.

Well, Patrick, it just underscores the urgency of this task you and I have taken on.

This is obviously going to be a summer of intensive training for you—first at that camp, which I understand has produced quite a few future Olympians, and then later this summer when you'll work on getting your driver's license. So I'm sure you'll be glad to hear that I'm about to add yet another kind of training! Seriously, the mental training I'm going to introduce you to can be done simultaneously with your physical training (and anything else you happen to be doing), and will actually complement and enhance it, helping you to be a better rower and driver, as well as a better man.

There are actually some useful parallels between becoming a good driver and becoming a good man. Both involve freedom, power, and independence—but also responsibility. You can go wherever you want on your own, but only after you've learned to control your own actions safely and skillfully. It's no coincidence that sixteen is considered about the right age to go through training for both. Modern neuroscience has discovered that it takes about that long for the "insulation" on the wiring in your brain—the myelin coating that protects nerves—to develop completely enough to insure that electrical "messages" will reach their destinations without short-circuiting. That enables you to have an idea and carry it out without a dozen distractions and random impulses interfering. That level of nervous system maturation basically means that nature has prepared you for the challenges to come. But there's still a lot of work left to do to properly "program" your nervous-system wiring.

In the case of driving, of course, our society requires you to take lessons and get your learner's permit. First you must practice regularly under a teacher's supervision. Then you've got to pass a written exam as well as a practical on-the-road driving test. Only after meeting all these standards do you qualify as a legal driver. All this is done to prevent you from hurting yourself and others. When you're going sixty miles an hour in a ton of metal, in close proximity to other whizzing tons of metal, no one doubts for a minute that, as Gotama said, "Protecting yourself, you protect others; protecting others, you protect yourself."

For the journey of life, however, you've been provided with a far more amazing and potent "vehicle": a human body, fully equipped with a genuine brain to steer it and keep it running smoothly. While this magic vehicle is quite capable of running on automatic cruise control—which, unfortunately, is the only way many adults operate theirs—on its own it will never get you to Innocence. Without your awakened and trained intelligence at the helm, it can *only* drive you down the roads of greed, ill-will, and ignorance! That's why traditional societies approach this human "vehicle" with much *more* respect and caution than we lavish on the automobile. They require intensive "driver" training and testing before you're deemed ready to "take the wheel" of your own life.

Many East African tribes, for example, mark the transition from childhood into adulthood with elaborate rites of passage. These initiation ceremonies require a young man to demonstrate poise and self-control in the face of intense physical pain. For instance, elders of the tribe perform ritual circumcisions, and the initiates must endure them without so much as flinching or even blinking an eye—or else bring shame to their families. After this demonstration of self-control for the sake of honor, they are required to perform tasks demonstrating their courage and self-reliance, such as surviving in the bush alone for several weeks or stalking and killing an adult antelope.

The purpose of these complex rites and rituals is to inculcate in the young men of the tribe a sense of fearlessness and composure when confronting danger. These are the qualities that the tribe requires an adult to possess, as they are necessary for him to fulfill his main duties in life: feeding and supporting his family, and defending his tribe. Certainly courage and composure are every bit as crucial for protecting your soul and family from the dangers of today's all too often vulgar and violent society.

These rites of passage demonstrate a profound insight that our society has almost totally forgotten: we human beings don't become adults automatically. The achievement of real adulthood is not determined solely, or even primarily, by biology. The ceremonies of these so-called "primitive" tribes reflect their deep cultural awareness that young adults need, at least to some degree, a formal introduction to their new physical, sexual, and mental powers. For genuine maturity to develop, a person must be taught how to use his or her newfound powers wisely and skillfully. For this nature of ours contains tremendous potential for both good and evil.

In the last few years, Patrick, I suspect you've had thoughts and feelings so intense they seemed like they might become, or actually became, genuinely scary—feelings so powerful and intrusive they seemed inescapable, maybe even uncontrollable. Those feelings mark the end of childhood. They're *your* share of the raw power that creates Olympic records and moon landings, Shakespearean plays and skyscrapers, saxophone solos and the U.S. Constitution—but also of the power that built the concentration camps in Nazi Germany and Bosnia and that tears families apart every day. It is a power that in good people can become creativity and in bad people can turn into violence. To be human and have that much raw power at your disposal is quite a challenge. It brings great opportunities, but they sure as hell come with significant risks. Skillfully driven, your human "vehicle" can take you anyplace you can dream of. Steer it poorly, inattentively, or drunkenly, though, and it can do both you and others tremendous harm.

What I've written to you so far has corresponded to the "drug and alcohol course" and the "traffic rules course" you're required to take as part of your driver training. You're more aware now of the dangers of all kinds of intoxicants, and you're familiar with the principles of the behavioral guidelines laid out in the commandments and precepts. These fundamental "rules of the road of life" are solidly based on the moral Laws of Reality, in the same way that traffic rules aren't merely arbitrary but are based on the underlying physical laws of mass, energy, and inertia. The purpose in both cases is very practical: to prevent harm and injury, enabling you and others to have a safe and enjoyable journey and to "arrive alive" at your goals.

But that's all just book learning till the moment when you get behind the wheel, turn the key, and begin to experience what it actually feels like to drive. Now, obviously, at the end of this summer you'll be seriously driving a car for the first time—but you've been running around in a human body and brain for sixteen years! However, you may not have fully grasped that you *are*, in fact, the "driver;" or fully understood the basic nature of your "vehicle"; or even realized that they're not exactly one and the same—because we're no longer taught to think of ourselves that way.

In order to provide clear instruction, I will have to introduce you to both the "vehicle" and the "driver" within you, and show you how to be aware of the difference between them. And there's also a third aspect of your inner being—we can call it the "navigator"—that will be crucial for keeping you on course, on what Buddhist philosophy calls life's Middle Path, which avoids the destructive extremes of both excessive pleasure and needless pain.

On any long journey it's very important to have a companion with you: a good friend to keep you company, keep you awake, and help you read the road maps. An expert navigator with accurate information about the "lay of the land" is extremely important. After all, without top-notch navigation, even the Starship *Enterprise* ends up Lost in Space! Of course, I'll be with you on the first leg of this journey, but it's a journey that will last your whole life (and I'm sure we both hope you're gonna live longer than me!). So I'm going to introduce you to a friend who will be with you at all times, who you can call on at any time of the day or night for guidance and encouragement. Like everything else on this journey, that friend is within you. But before you meet this inner companion and navigator, it's important to get acquainted with your "wheels."

Because its wiring is quite similar to that of a chimpanzee (our closest nonhuman relative, who shares 98 percent of our genes), your human "vehicle" has goals, desires, and impulses of its own. Hopefully, these are not identical to yours. But keep in mind that this vehicle is wired to do everything in its power to convince you that its goals *are* the sum total of yours, to the exclusion of all others. Your vehicle, in other words, is a very special kind of machine: it's an animal! (In that sense, "driving" it is more like riding a horse—but with millions of "horse"power.)

Like riding a horse—but with millions of "horse"power

Before I go on, Patrick, tell me how you and your friends think about animals—and about nature in general. Do most people you know share the view that nature is pure and good and animals are innocent? In some environmentalist circles, that view has been elevated to the status of a religious belief. Unfortunately, as a guide to human life and a goal for human evolution, it's no substitute for the real thing.

Your friend,
Jeff

Dear Jeff,

Everyone's got a different animal they like. I like dolphins and all water animals, because I like the water a lot. And there are a couple of instances of dolphins saving somebody's life. I have friends who like other animals.

I do know a lot of people who think, "Oh, things are natural, so they're good." A lot of my friends who aren't religious think that way.

I don't take the view that things that are natural are always good, but I do really care about the environment. I love to go on camping trips. I think it's relaxing and peaceful and really beautiful.

Hope that answers your question.

Patrick

VIVE LA DIFFÉRENCE:
ANIMALS VS. HUMANS

Dear Patrick,

Equaling "natural" with "good" is one of our culture's most dangerous errors. It dates back to the philosopher Jean-Jacques Rousseau, whom I consider the evil genius of the modern era. It's not that nature itself is evil, but it is deeply and fundamentally flawed. As the Buddha taught in his First Noble Truth, nature is filled with suffering *(dukkha)*. Anyone who's ever watched the nature shows on the Discovery Channel would know that!

In fact, Gotama taught that to be an animal is to live in what is called a Woeful State—a condition only one step removed from hell. Why are animals in such an unhappy state? Because it is quite difficult for them to act out of any wholesome motive at all. For that reason, those dolphins that save lives, and some of the noble things dogs do, should be viewed as particularly heroic! But it's important to remember that even dolphins aren't always such nice guys. They seem to have a high craving level. Male dolphins have been observed to team up and "gang-rape" a female!

Mostly, animals are just on a constant treadmill of responding to craving, fear, and ignorance. Especially in the wild, they tend to either want something or be afraid of something, to be either resting or restless, almost all of the time. And there are many humans that don't act very differently. That's the *real* danger of our culture's sentimentality about animals and nature: it becomes an excuse to give *our own* animal nature free rein—with disastrous results.

I in no way mean to deny that animals are living beings who deserve kindness and respect. And I certainly don't mean to say that they are insensitive or unfeeling. I am simply pointing out that they're largely driven and automatic—*and so is your animal "vehicle," and mine!* Animals, including the human animal, are preprogrammed to get food when hungry; to fight or run away when faced with a threat; and to find and mate with fertile members of the opposite sex. Social animals like canines and primates, including us humans, are also preprogrammed to seek status and a sense of belonging in the pack, because their (and our) survival depends on living in a group. With the rare exceptions I just noted, animals basically have no goals beyond survival, reproduction, and whatever immediate activities will help them to survive and reproduce. The curiosity, pleasure, playfulness, and affection that wild mammals undoubtedly feel are never ends in themselves but are ruthlessly subordinated to the uses of survival and reproduction.

From where I sit, people are obviously different. But I've had more than a few animated discussions with my fellow scientists and philosophers who think the differences are less monumental than I do. You might say they see the differences between humans and animals as more a matter of quantity than quality. In essence, they think people are just very sophisticated animals. While I agree there is no shortage of people who fit that description (not to mention the ones your average animal wouldn't call sophisticated!), I also believe people have a unique capacity to rise above mere animal status. Perhaps not that many humans fully actualize that capacity, but the fact that *some* do means we *all* have that capacity. The existence of a Moses, Gotama, or Jesus has implications for our entire species. Or as the poet Robert Browning put it: "Ah, but a man's reach should exceed his grasp, or what's a heaven for?"

One big difference between people and animals that everyone agrees on is that we have a part of our brain called the *prefrontal cortex,* which is especially highly developed. "Prefrontal" means we're talking about the front of the front of the brain, principally the part located right behind your forehead. *Cortex* refers to the furrowed outer layer of "gray matter" (gray because it consists of tightly packed nerve cells and their support system) that covers every higher mammal's brain. Its job is to receive, recognize, and coordinate complex input from the senses and to send out orders for appropriate responses. But the prefrontal cortex is something special, the *crème de la crème* of brain tissue. Enabling you to imagine, anticipate, memorize, plan, and conceptualize, it is the most amazing piece of computer processing equipment ever developed. Think of it, Patrick, as a magic carpet: it can whisk you away from the here and now into past, future, or fantasy. Or think of it as a genie in a bottle: almost anything it can imagine, you have the potential to make happen. Remember, I wrote to you recently, "The state of the world begins in the state of your mind?" Because of the tremendous power of the prefrontal cortex, what's *in there* is going to be projected *out here*.

So will it be something beautiful, or something harmful? That depends on who's in control.

You see, the mere possession of a prefrontal cortex isn't (despite what some scientists and philosophers will tell you) the *biggest* difference between humans and animals. Because a lot of the time, animal drives are *running* the prefrontal cortex on a sort of "automatic pilot," using it as nothing more than a very fancy way to get food, sex, belonging, dominance, and security. Many of our most cherished likes and dislikes, fantasies and feelings are actually mental elaborations and justifications of those basic animal drives. For example, much of what is called "love"—especially in American pop culture—is really mere sexual desire. And a lot of what we call "friendship" is really animal pack behavior. (Remember the "cool hierarchy" at school that made Jaime feel ashamed to be a virgin?)

Often, when we say "I want," it's really our animal vehicle talking. Unaware that we are harming ourselves and others, we're content to go where *it* wants to go and to take its strong feelings for our own sense of self and identity. We mistake the automatic pilot for the driver. And when we do that we basically *act* like an animal—and sometimes not like a particularly sophisticated one. But because we are human, we always have the capacity to *realize* we are acting like an animal.

And that, Patrick, is the *really* big difference between a human and an animal—a difference not just of degree but of kind. What I'm about to tell you is the heart of your first, and most important, "driving lesson." Once you fully grasp this, the skills you need to steer toward Innocence will follow. *You are more than the sum total of your body and brain.* In my opinion— and this is a scientist talking—even your fabulous prefrontal cortex is ultimately just another part of the vehicle. *You* are the driver. You can take control.

Today, that is a revolutionary idea. It's ironic, because before the modern age began, people knew much less about their "vehicle," but they had a whole lot more wisdom about the power of a good driver. When modern science came along it gave us tremendous power over the material world, but at what price? We seem to have paid for it with a loss of power over ourselves. And as Jesus said, "For what shall it profit a man, if he shall gain the whole world, and lose his own soul?"

Now we must take that power back. We must take all the scientific knowledge we've gained about our "vehicle" and put it in the hands of a new generation of reawakened drivers. And those clear-minded drivers will carry with them the power to transform both science and society. Will there be obstacles and resistance? There sure will—but the discipline it takes to overcome that resistance constructively will just help strengthen the minds of those dedicated to completing the journey. Of course that's a truth known by the pioneers and explorers of every generation. All in a day's work for seekers of the Promised Land.

Your friend,
Jeff

HERESY TODAY, DOGMA TOMORROW OR THE LIMITS OF SCIENCE

Dear Patrick,

Do you know what a heretic is?

It's important for you to know, because according to what I like to call the "High Church of Modern Brain Worshippers," you're talking to one. Yes indeed, in the most powerful scientific and philosophical circles of our time, what I told you in my last letter—*you are more than the sum total of your body and brain*—amounts to modern-day heresy.

Before the modern age was born (a long and difficult birth that took from about 1450 A.D. to 1700, if not longer), the institutions of organized religion had final authority not only over people's births, marriages, and deaths, but over their minds. All over medieval Europe, the Catholic Church was the guardian of an official body of beliefs called "dogma," rooted in Holy Scripture and in the pope's divine authority to interpret it. People were expected to accept Church dogma as the ultimate truth. If someone openly challenged any part of dogma, even if he had good reason to believe that a part of it might be erroneous, he could be tried for the crime of heresy. The penalties in those days were very harsh. A conviction of heresy brought death, generally by burning at the stake.

Strange as it sounds to us today, in our age of free speech and triumphant science, in 1633 the pioneering physicist and astronomer Galileo Galilei was condemned for "vehement suspicion of heresy" and sentenced to detention for life for daring to insist that the earth goes around the sun, rather than vice versa. Now, the key word here is *insist*. The old idea that the sun went around the earth wasn't exactly a central point of Church dogma—until Galileo launched his all-out attack on it! It was based on common sense and traditional pretelescope astronomy, so, of course, it appeared to be the view in the Bible, too. But the Church's main concern was that people's lives continue to revolve around God, and it was remarkably willing to tolerate the purveyors of new astronomical theories, like Copernicus, who first proposed the theory that the earth orbits the sun, as long as they didn't push into the realm of theology and start calling the Bible a liar. But that is, in essence, what Galileo did. "[H]e was not a tactful person," writes George Sim Johnston. "[H]e loved to score off people and make them look ridiculous. . . . he became obsessed with converting public opinion to the Copernican system. He was an early instance of that very modern type, the cultural politician."

You may be frowning, Patrick, because this isn't quite the Galileo you've heard of—the hero of a dramatic showdown between the courageous new science and the rigid, corrupt old Church. But that tale is a myth, fostered by our own High Church of Science. The real story is far more complex. Of course there were people in the Church, as in any established power structure, who were rigid and corrupt. But there were also minds as broad as that of Cardinal Robert Bellarmino, the Church's Master of Controversial Questions. Sounding not so different from a good scientist, Bellarmino wrote that if only Galileo would "content [himself] with speaking hypothetically and not absolutely" unless and until there was "real proof" that the earth went round the sun, he would "run no risk whatsoever." Now, in 1633 there was nothing even approaching "real proof" that the earth wasn't stationary! Yet Bellarmino went even further in his open-mindedness. "[I]f a real proof be found," he said,

> then it will be necessary, very carefully, to proceed to the explanation of the passages of Scripture which appear to be contrary, and we should rather say that we have misunderstood these than pronounce that to be false which is demonstrated.

But Galileo wasn't at all tolerant or accepting of Bellarmino's very reasonable offer of a compromise position. He was so sure he was right that he kept on pushing the point—all the way to openly insisting that the Church make its theology conform to his almost totally unproven theory! Finally, after many attempts at compromise, the Church felt it had no choice but to condemn him. Even then, it was only for "*suspicion* of heresy," and he got his sentence knocked down to house arrest by publicly renouncing the Copernican theory and agreeing to keep his mouth shut about it for the rest of his life. He died peacefully in his bed in 1642.

Meanwhile, of course, the earth went right on revolving around the sun. And in 1741, after much more scientific research on the question had been conducted, the Catholic Church tacitly recognized that Galileo was correct in that assertion by okaying his complete works. The modern understanding of the solar system was officially recognized as a part of Church teaching in 1822. One moral of the story is this: today's heresy can turn into tomorrow's truth . . . and sometimes even tomorrow's dogma.

There's also a lesson in there, which I think is very important, about "questioning authority" with all due respect and not being obnoxious just because you happen to be right. For one of the secrets of living with grace is to strive for what Eliot called "the wisdom of humility." Now today's dogma, Patrick, at least among "intellectuals," is an updated version of Galileo's heresy: materialistic science. But I remain optimistic that our "High Church of Science" has members in its higher ranks as open-minded as Cardinal Bellarmino!

Patrick, I know you're interested in science as a profession, and I have every intention of encouraging that. There are many fine things to be said about science, and probably the best thing about it is its "Prove it. Show me" attitude. Good science won't regard something as true till there is hard, objective evidence for it, gathered through carefully designed experiments that produce the same results again and again, no matter who does them. It is due to this careful skepticism and insistence on objective proof that we've gained so much knowledge about the physical nature of the universe and so much power over the material world.

But science has limits. Anything that is *non*physical—which means anything outside the realm of the five senses—is not a concern of science and is basically out of its ballpark. That includes most of life's deepest truths. Wise scientists admit this. I personally know many scientists who hold serious religious beliefs, and some who are even active in their local church. And a recent survey in the journal *Nature* revealed that 40 percent of American physicists, biologists, and mathematicians believe in God. All this is at least a tacit acknowledgment that there are extremely important things—like the meaning of life, for instance—which are not explainable in purely scientific terms.

However, it's also true that many of the most influential scientists of today are dogmatic materialists. That is, they're as sure that everything worth knowing can be explained in physical terms as the medieval Church fathers were that the sun circles the earth. What that really means is that they believe everything worth knowing about you, Patrick, can be understood by understanding the physical Patrick—i.e., your body and brain. And while they don't claim to understand you completely yet, they insist that someday they will, if they're just given enough time and money.

Now the last time I checked they didn't burn people at the stake or throw them in the slammer for daring to suggest otherwise, but they hadn't yet started to give out any prizes or promotions for it either. That's why most of the scientists who *aren't* dogmatic materialists often prefer not to talk about it too much, especially to other scientists. For today's heretics, it seems the safest course is still silence!

That's why, when I go public with these ideas I'm writing to you, I'll be taking a significant risk with my scientific reputation. But that risk will be worth taking, because too many of today's most outspoken and publicly active scientists have overstepped their bounds with an arrogance more dangerous than Galileo's. The business of science is to show us how the material world works—and yes, how we can manipulate it to our benefit. It has been so successful that today we're beginning to be able to manipulate the matter *we ourselves* are made of— our own brain chemistry and genetic code. But the people creating and using these extremely powerful new technologies are just as vulnerable as people have always been to being driven by greed, ill-will, and ignorance! Science can't correct that, or insure that these new wonders don't become tomorrow's horrors—only the proven "technologies" of Moses, Jesus, and Buddha can. Above all, Patrick, science cannot tell us why we're here—or how to live.

Your friend,
Jeff

MENTAL FORCE:
YOU ARE NOT YOUR BRAIN

Dear Patrick,

I know, I'm already giving you a mental workout to match the physical ones you're doing every day! And that's nothing— by the end of this letter, you're going to be in the driver's seat, turning the key!

Science, Patrick, would create considerably fewer problems if it stopped at the laboratory door. But the core beliefs of materialistic science have saturated our whole culture. Almost all those who consider themselves part of the "intellectual/power elite" also believe that just about everything worth knowing ultimately exists within the realm of the five senses. (After a martini or two this becomes: "Everything worth having can be bought.") This belief leads those people to pay a whole lot of attention to the five senses, and even to demean those things, like faith and "old-fashioned" morality, that can't be explained in terms of them. Because these "elite" people dominate the mass media which so powerfully influence the collective consciousness of our culture, physical sensation of the material world has become an all-pervasive yet often unacknowledged foundation for the way most of us think about ourselves and our lives. The result: a culture excessively preoccupied with the sensory world and the gratification of the five senses.

The irony is, we actually believe this all has set us free. Free from superstition, inhibition, and guilt; free from the "oppression" of commandments and precepts that put limits on our desires and impulses; free from the drudgery of old-fashioned "driving lessons" to teach us the discipline and self-control necessary for applying those rules skillfully; free, even, from the burden of responsibility for our own actions and the "damage" that failing to live up to that responsibility can cause to "self-esteem."

You see, Patrick, if this is a strictly physical universe, ruled by the mechanical laws of cause and effect, then whatever you do wrong can be blamed on something "out of your control"—either something that was done to you in the past, or some random molecule ricocheting around inside you. This leads to sleazoids like the Menendez brothers actually trying to con us into thinking they were blameless for their parents' murder because they had a flawed childhood. It's like no-fault insurance for your human "vehicle." No matter how much damage you do, it's not your fault, and you won't have to pay. Society will pay. Never mind that in the end "society" is just individuals like you and me—and that the universe will exact its own inevitable price. From the timeless laws of the ethosphere there simply is no escape. Like the great boxer Joe Louis said—you can run, but you can't hide!

Can you see what's happened? Scientific materialism tried to get rid of those stodgy old "driver's" licensing and liability laws (a.k.a."custom and ceremony") by getting rid of the "driver"! Here's the current and damaging dogma on your human nature:

- You *are* your body and brain, and that's all there is to you. Someday we'll be able to explain your thoughts, your feelings, even what you call your "spirit" or "soul," by diagramming your brain's wiring.

- There is no "driver" or "pilot" involved in life's journey, but that's OK—you don't need one. Human nature is a marvelous mechanism that can be trusted to drive itself. Evolution "designed" it that way through a random process guided by the principle of "survival of the fittest."

- Then why, you may wonder, is the road littered with wrecks? Well . . . the bad news is, this mechanism can be defective. If you were miswired by a bad childhood, or errant genes, or faulty brain chemistry, there's nothing you can do about it—you'll just have to wait for science and modern medicine to fix you up. (Those new "miracle" drugs like Prozac should do the trick, at least until we master gene surgery!)

- Meanwhile, if you keep on cracking up, hurting yourself and others, don't let it affect your "self-esteem." It's obvious you can't be blamed. Please don't worry. It's society's responsibility to repair things, so you can exercise your right to feel good about yourself and live an enjoyable life.

If you buy that, the intellectual powers that be will say that you're a free man, but is that really freedom? I don't think so—except perhaps the "freedom" to self-destruct. Following foolish ideas like these is what has led us to the mess we're in. To *my* mind freedom is having a choice *and* taking the responsibility that comes with it. Freedom isn't hurtling along like a passive passenger on a runaway train—it's taking the controls and choosing which tracks you're going to ride on, which destinations you're going to aim for. It's deciding where *you* want your "vehicle" to go, and going there!

Scientific materialism says that isn't possible, because there can be no "driver" distinct from the body and brain. Yet I'm a scientist and I've *seen* people do it—and not just ordinary people, but people whose brains were more out of control than I hope yours or mine ever will be. These were patients of mine at UCLA who have a biologically caused psychiatric illness called obsessive-compulsive disorder (OCD). You've seen my book *Brain Lock,* so you know that biochemical imbalances in the brains of people with OCD can drive them to wash their hands till the skin starts to come off, or check a lock or stove hundreds of times a day. These brain imbalances also cause them to experience terrible fear if they resist doing a compulsion. According to the dogma of scientific materialism, their best bet would be to take a medication like Prozac, maybe for the rest of their lives.

And yet, for a decade I've been helping people to face down that fear—often with little or no need for medication. By doing so they can take back control of their lives from this terrible disorder. And believe me, if *they* can take control of their "vehicle," you can take control of yours! (I'll have more to tell you about precisely how they did it, but here's a hint—it involved them reflecting on and properly understanding their *karma.)*

I've not only seen OCD patients change their own compulsive behavior to healthy behavior; thanks to a high-tech machine called a PET scanner, I've also seen them *decrease the metabolic activity, the energy use, of their own brains.* And given the amount of focused effort it took for them to slow down and redirect the course of their "runaway brain," it seems entirely illogical to me to say that it was merely the brain itself that was doing all the work. A runaway locomotive with no driver can't apply the brakes and head for safety!

I'm convinced that our research team at UCLA has demonstrated that something genuinely invisible and nonmaterial— call it consciousness, spirit, will, or mental force—can leave a visible and deliberate imprint on the material brain. (Have you ever seen that old movie where you see the footprints of the Invisible Man flattening the grass?) Using the PET scanner, we've actually taken pictures of the inner workings of the brain before and after people systematically trained and applied their own mental force—the kind of hard, objective evidence other scientists sit up and take notice of.

Today's heresy . . . tomorrow's truth. Interesting things are happening as we prepare ourselves for the next millennium.

If you came to my lab at UCLA, I could sit you in the PET scanner and show you the "footprints" of your own will affecting the activity of your brain. But there are much simpler, and in fact even more decisive, experiments you can perform, without any high-tech equipment but what's included in your own "vehicle," to prove to yourself that you are the driver. Here's a *really* simple—yet profoundly challenging—way to experience the reality of mental force for yourself:

Next time you have an itch (and now that I mention it, you're probably feeling one somewhere on your body right now), *don't scratch it!* Instead, just mentally observe the itchy sensation.

See how difficult that is? You *can* prevent your hand from going to the itch, but it takes real effort and constant awareness. And it is that deliberate power, holding your arm in place against the command of nature, that I call mental force. But with even a small distraction the mental force quickly dissipates—and you begin to scratch before you even realize it!

"Itch → scratch" is an ancient and automatic brain circuit, one that goes way back in terms of evolutionary development. (It must have had significant survival value, probably because it prompted animals to remove parasites and dirt from their bodies.) The urge to scratch an itch—as you quickly notice when you try to resist it—is quite a potent and persistent force itself! One good reason for resisting it is that it strengthens your mind and enhances your ability to observe and act as the "driver"—not merely as an automaton. (That's one reason why we take note of itches, but try not to scratch them, when we sit in Buddhist meditation. Another is to observe the changing, impermanent nature of bodily sensations—"This, too, shall pass.") By not scratching, you experience your own mastery over your brain, your power to choose which circuit *you* want to activate—in this case you activate the circuit that *prevents* the hand from moving automatically.

Do you still think not scratching an itch is a trivial exercise? Well, it's directly related to the intense athletic training you're doing now—when all your muscles are screaming for mercy, and instead of responding to the automatic brain circuit that goes "Pain—DANGER! —STOP!!" you apply mental force and order your muscles to give 10 percent *more*. I remember that so well from wrestling—working out in a rubber suit in a hundred-degree room! Using your will to defy the pain signal, and put out *more* effort instead of less, is what makes the difference between being good and being great.

And now, Patrick, try *this* one, devised by one of the two or three greatest "driving teachers" who ever walked this earth, Jesus Christ: "Whosoever shall smite thee on thy right cheek, turn to him the other also." That is a very serious (and far more difficult) application of the same basic principle—stopping instinctive automatic responses—one that, in this case, can stop the infectious spread of harm and bring the world a step closer to Innocence! Martial artists, like the swordsmen in the great film *Seven Samurai,* fight evil in a very different way—they use force in self-defense, and to protect the defenseless—yet their underlying mental state is much the same. They too have overcome the automatic reflexes of fear and rage; their skillful actions are so effective precisely because they are directed by cool mental force. Such is the way of all great warriors.

Every great spiritual teacher has a unique way of conveying these truths. Jesus was a divinely empowered, and at times fiery, poet who said, in effect, "This is the Revealed Truth: it is God's Word." Gotama Buddha, another of the all-time great "driving teachers," was more like a cool-headed scientist: he made his discoveries in the inner world of consciousness by using undistorted observation and empirical demonstration, just as today's scientists do in the outer world of matter. And Gotama didn't expect you to take his word for any of this. (That's why he can reach people whom our skeptical, scientific age has made resistant to religion.) Like a scientist, he respected the maxim "Show me. Prove it." Jesus said "I am the way." Gotama said, "Come and see." Jesus revealed the Truth; Gotama taught a method of discovering it for yourself.

Next time I write to you, that's what you'll continue to do. But always keep in mind that, as Gotama said, "the strenuous work must be done by *you.*"

Your friend,
Jeff

Dear Jeff,

You're right, it's really hard not to scratch! It's surprising that it takes so much "mental force" to fight against something so small.

Speaking of pain, I've been really busy with rowing, rowing and rowing. But I'm also in the middle of a really good book, The Amateurs *by David Halberstam. It's about four scullers who are trying to make the national, and only one of them can go to the Olympics. One aspect the book touches is how rowing is still an amateur sport that hasn't been corrupted by commercialism, and it goes into why do people row, when they don't get fame or money. It turns out that they get something more. They are rowing for more personal reasons, to complete something that they were missing as a child, or to get their aggression out, or something. It goes into these four rowers' lives, the history of each one, and why they're rowing, and how they got to where they are. Really, really good, really captures rowing. If you ever get a chance, you should read it.*

One of the big things the book talks about is the amount of pain that the rowers have to go through, like in a seven-minute sprint. It's really challenging, it's one of the hardest sports in the world. And it talks about how when the rowers think about rowing, the first thing that comes into their minds is pain, and how painful it is to race. It's sort of a torture, and the worst part about it is, it's self-inflicted! It talks about how you have to be really mentally different to want to row, not mentally deranged, but mentally different. Kind of like people who climb Mount Everest.

Patrick

MINDFULNESS AND
WISE ATTENTION

Dear Patrick,

The amount of mental force it takes not to scratch an itch is just a very small hint of what every "driver" of a human "vehicle" is up against! Fortunately, the more exercise you give the "driver," the stronger he gets. So we're going to proceed directly to Lesson Two.

Look at your hand. While you're looking at it, make a fist.

Now, would you say, "I'm clenched"? Of course not. It's your hand that's clenched. You're the one who decided to clench it.

Now "look at" your mood—that is, make a mental note of it.

I bet you'll immediately think something like, "I'm happy," or "I'm sad," or "I'm restless" or "bored" or whatever it happens to be right now. But I've got news for you: the very fact that *you can observe your mood and describe it*—just as you could your hand—means that *you are not it.* Remember this, because it's the heart of the matter: *If you can observe it and describe it, it's not you*—not the core you, the real you, the "driver."

Of course, you already intuitively know this about the body you live in. That's why you call it "my body." It's a part of you, sure, but it's not the essence of your sense of self. There's a separation, a little gap, between "I" and "my body." You take for granted your ability to observe and describe your body's sensations. (If there were no gap, you couldn't— just as your eye can't look at itself.) And you take for granted your power to "steer" your body where you want it to go— though it takes a lot of effort and practice to train it to do complex things well, like rowing or swimming. But with enough will, and with the right exercises, you know you can train your body, shape it, change it, so that it responds with ever more speed and precision to your commands. That's exactly what you're spending your summer doing.

It's harder to grasp, but you are not just your feelings or your thoughts, either. Those are actually the workings of your brain. And as such, *even feelings and thoughts* are intrinsically a part of your physical vehicle and of the material world, "the realm of the senses." Gotama actually called the mind our sixth sense! And that means that, through will and practice, you can also train your mental, moral, and emotional self to be more skillful, coordinated, and responsive to command. (It's worth noting that the Pāli word Gotama used to mean "morally wholesome"—*kusala*—also means "skillful"!)

If it's hard for you to imagine thoughts as physical events, almost as *things*, just think of the expression "a train of thought." You know how your mind tends to connect one idea, memory, or fantasy to the next and the next and the next—almost like a railyard worker hooking boxcars together. In 1738 David Hume described three principles that cause ideas to associate or cluster: resemblance (a photograph of a person makes you think of that person), proximity (that in turn reminds you that the very nice girl who sat next to you in sixth grade was his sister), and cause and effect (thinking of the brother tends to remind you of the sister—the same people caused both of their births. Another example of association of ideas by cause and effect is when you jump off a diving board and you immediately think of the water).

Freud showed that likes (if his sister wasn't nice you might not have thought of her) and dislikes (the guy who sat in front of her was a real jerk), desires (she was really pretty, you wish you'd kept in touch) and aversions (that guy probably ended up on drugs, you'd rather not think about him), also have strong effects on the flow of ideas. What seems memorable and what gets ignored is determined by a variety

Acting like a "runaway" train

of very complex factors. Because of all of this, there is a strong tendency for thoughts to "wander off" on their own, sort of like a dog in heat, especially if you're not alert. And if a "train of thought" picks up a little momentum, you know how easily it can start acting like a "runaway" train!

Usually we can't directly watch brain cells at work, but in special circumstances, such as surgery for epileptic seizures, we actually *can* "watch" them through very fine electrodes placed in the brains of seizure patients before and during the operation. Because of research like this, neuroscientists are pretty sure that each time your mind makes one of those lightning-fast connections, at least two and probably many more of those cells, called *neurons,* are making a connection in your brain. In fact, they are constantly making *new* connections, so that some of your thoughts are insights and intuitions you've never had before. No man-made computer can do that—at least not yet. But as amazing as that is, it's still not the most fantastic thing about you.

The most fantastic thing is that *you* can choose to step in, stop a "train of thought," and redirect it—and you can do so with unimaginably rapid speed. You perform this miracle casually all the time.

I'm sure, Patrick, that you sometimes drift off into daydreams when you're studying—especially studying Latin. You wouldn't be human if you didn't. (As Gotama said, "The mind is hard to pin down, flighty, alighting wherever it desires.") But you also know that in an instant you can "wake up," shake yourself, and go back to your books. I know it doesn't sound like much. But that moment when *you notice* your mind wandering—in that split second, Patrick, you recognize and make use of the fact that *you* are not the same as your mind. The Buddha would have called that a moment of *mindfulness*—a moment of genuine "awakening." And in that moment, *you* are free—free to choose and even create the next circuit to fire in your brain, deliberately different from the one your "automatic pilot" would have chosen.

Buddhist mindfulness meditation (which I do for at least an hour every morning) is, to a significant degree, practice in "brain-watching." (I can think of some good movie titles here—*Closely Watched Brains? Brainspotting?*) Meditation is working—and *work* is the right word!—at getting better and sharper at noticing the constant, subtle changes in your own feelings and thoughts. This means developing the skill to clearly observe your own brain in action. Why do we who meditate do this? Well, one good reason is to learn about how our own mind works. It's an incredibly useful source of knowledge. After some practice, you can actually see how cleverly, how subtly, yet how automatically, your mind goes on hooking one thought to another. You can see how a thought, mood or feeling surges, peaks, and subsides. And you can see what's really driving all these "trains." (Remember greed, ill-will, and ignorance? You haven't heard the last of them!)

A very important reason why we meditate, of course, is to get better control of our "runaway brains." One of the things you come to understand from watching your brain is that, left entirely to its own devices, it's not going to take you anyplace very good. Its animal nature, with all the associated biology, tends to take control, and to drag the weak, lazy, or unpre-

It will require a whole lot of taming from you.

pared mind right along with it. (A strong statement, I know. I don't expect you to take it on faith; I'm giving you the tools to find out for yourself.) For your brain to take you someplace peaceful—such as Beauty or Innocence—it will require a whole lot of taming from *you* . . . with a little help from your friend, that one I mentioned you have within you.

Fortunately, taking control begins with the very same act of watching. So the same mental action that shows you *why* taking control is so important actually *puts* you in control.

(For how long depends on how good a driver you are. As you practice and become more skillful, you can stay in control longer.) At the same time as you are learning about how your mind works, you're also exercising and training the mental "muscles" and developing the strength you will need to keep your vision sharp and your gaze steady. Just as you are now training your body in the swift, reliable response to command that you'll need to captain the rowing team, with the right exercises you can train your mind to move your brain toward wisely chosen goals, as smoothly and forcefully as a rowboat (I think you future Olympians call it a shell) moves through water. Do these exercises regularly enough, and your brain will start running more smoothly. Sure, it takes practice, and no question, it takes effort. But the plain fact is, it can be done.

As your mind becomes stronger, and the brain runs smoother, life's rough spots can be handled with much more skill. With practice, you'll see that you can even learn how to change your mood—without any "mood-altering substances." It's all a matter of skillful driving, of paying wise (as opposed to unwise) attention to the road of life. We'll talk more about wise and unwise attention, but you'll remember that wisdom begins in facing the truth. The essence of wise attention is seeing what's really there, as opposed to what you imagine or wish were there. Wise attention is the key to skillful "driving." It allows you to find the true path and avoid the dead ends.

You can do all this, not as simply, but just as surely, as you can close and open your hand. The Buddha taught that wise attention, which the ancient texts define as "going along with the grain of" (as opposed to resisting) the true nature of things, is the power that opens closed minds—not just closed fists! And in that fact lies the beginning of true freedom.

Before you can change or redirect anything your brain is

doing, however, you have to know that *it* isn't identical with *you*. Even when sadness or anger feels like it fills your whole world, there is a part of you that is potentially outside of it and free of it. You only need to awaken that part. This is the part we call *the Impartial Spectator*. Next time I write, I'll show you a very simple way to awaken this source of all empowerment—the "innocent bystander" and wise guide within you.

In the meantime—from the sublime to the ridiculous— tell me what your favorite fast food is! (You'll see why.)

Your friend,
Jeff

Dear Jeff,
Ice cream! ! !
Is the "Impartial Spectator" the same as the "friend within"?

Patrick

MEET YOUR NAVIGATOR

Dear Patrick,

Good insight! The "Impartial Spectator" is the part of your mind that has the ability to become aware of the difference between "me" (the watcher/observer) and "my brain" (the thought or feeling). And when it comes to living a skillful rather than a harmful life, that ability is your best friend.

It's as though you were standing outside yourself and watching your inner experience, sort of like "reading your own mind." As you work on keeping this awareness of the difference between "me" (the watcher/observer) and "my brain" (the thought or feeling) clearly in view, the awareness becomes sharper, clearer, and more intense.

The exercise I'm about to teach you is a very simple, yet powerful way of doing this. This exercise itself is full-fledged meditation—even though you don't have to sit still for it. It contains the essence of Gotama's teaching on meditation, in a form you can carry with you wherever you go. It utilizes and strengthens a mental ability possessed by all people. This ability was termed Bare Attention by the great Buddhist scholar/monk Nyanaponika Thera. Born to Jewish parents in Germany in 1901, he emigrated to Sri Lanka and became a monk in his thirties. In 1962, in his landmark book *The Heart of Buddhist Meditation,* he described Bare Attention as "the clear and single-minded awareness of what actually happens *to* us and *in* us. . . . It is called 'bare,' because it attends just to the bare facts . . . observed, without reacting to them." He also wrote a wonderful little pamphlet on it called *The Power of Mindfulness.*

This exercise to strengthen Bare Attention involves a technique called "making mental notes," developed earlier this century in Burma by the great meditation master Mahāsi Sayadaw. When using this technique, he said, "the knower can be distinguished from the known . . . without any preconception. One recognizes the phenomena without giving any thought to them. In other words, recognition is spontaneous."

Making mental notes of what you experience is, because of its profound simplicity, very different from just *thinking about* it. The very word "about" indicates the tendency of thinking to go round and round something instead of straight to the point. Bare Attention, or Mindfulness, mentally *confronts* the object (such as a feeling, sensation, or thought) you're experiencing. The ancient Buddhist texts explain that it keeps the mind steady, instead of letting it bob about like a pumpkin in water— it is the *opposite* of superficial attention. So when your Bare Attention confronts the object you're examining, your mind doesn't "float away" and let another "train of thought" carry it in some other direction.

Here is a very brief introduction to technique of "making mental notes," as developed by Mahāsi Sayadaw.

"Look at" (become aware of) your mood again. But this time don't say "I'm happy" or "I'm restless" or whatever it may be. Let's take it a step further: don't even say *"My mood is happy (etc.)."* Just say (to yourself) what is there: "Happy feeling." And as feelings change, notice the change: "Happiness fading. Restlessness arising. Restlessness fading. Sleepiness arising," and so on.

The clearest mental notes are often made by using a one-word label and gently repeating it (to yourself) for emphasis. So, for example, when examining a happy mood you would note, "happy, happy," and observe with a clear mind. If restlessness arises note the change by saying (to yourself) "restless, restless," and so on. It's like having a label-maker, and just sticking a neutral, factual little label on each event in the stream of experiences that constantly flows through your mind and body.

Another example might be, "Stomach is growling. Want some ice cream." As mental notes this could become "growling, growling," "wanting, wanting." *What you're trying to do is clearly observe and note the most prominent experience in the present moment.* The words themselves are not so important. Your mental notes could even have been "hungry, hungry," "stomach, stomach," "ice cream, ice cream." *The stress is on the observing.* For now, don't worry about *doing* anything to that parade of events. Just watch, and practice making mental notes. It does take practice. (You may discover that as you watch your thoughts and feelings, they change in some way. If so, observe the change and make a mental note of it. Your ability to see things change will increase as you continue to practice.) As you go through your day, every time you remember, just check out what's happening with you and make a mental note of it.

You may find it hard to believe that it's really *that* simple—that something so straightforward as just alerting yourself with a simple word or two to whatever you're doing or thinking really makes that big a difference! The reason it does is at least partly because so much of what we do and think is quite automatic and passes by very quickly and almost totally unexamined, unless an effort is made to pay attention to what's going on in the present moment. All mental notes are is a tool to help us pay closer attention to what's actually going on, especially in our minds, from moment to moment—and to note how quickly it changes. It's the paying attention part, not the notes themselves, that really makes a big difference.

So making mental notes may seem like a small change in your thinking, but it's small the way a key is small, yet can open a bank vault full of treasure or command a turbocharged Porsche or a huge Mack truck. By making mental notes, the "driver" gets better and better control of the "vehicle." The very process of observing makes good things happen to your mind. It begins to grow stronger and calmer, and the brain starts to run more smoothly. As your mind gains strength, the power to observe grows into the power of self-control. As you will see, that is true even of such powerful passions as sexual desire and anger. And control over such basic biological drives clearly implies, as we've already shown for the "drives" of OCD, that the brain itself is under better control.

I hope you're beginning to see that you've just been handed the key to the one kind of power that can really change the world: power over yourself. It's a magic key, because making mental notes awakens wise attention, and that not only puts you in command, it also activates and strengthens your companion and navigator—your friend within. And I'm sure you already know that it's a big advantage in life to have a powerful friend.

Your "driving teacher" (and friend),
Jeff

Dear Jeff,

One thing I wonder about "brain-watching" and making mental notes is if it could make you more self-conscious. I haven't got the hang of it yet. It seems kind of awkward.

Is there any way to get people to feel less self-conscious about themselves? My girlfriend is really self-conscious. She was always saying "I'm fat," and I was always telling her, "You're not fat, you're beautiful. Don't be so hard on yourself." When I first got into the relationship I felt like I had to always make her laugh, or make her smile. That put a lot of pressure on me, and it made me self-conscious. I was always aware of her feelings, which was a good thing, but I was always aware of myself also, like I had to push myself and try and be funny. I was more self-conscious then than I am now, but do you have any suggestions that I could tell her?

Thanks!
Patrick

TRUE AND FALSE FRIENDS

Dear Patrick,

Self-consciousness is a painfully awkward and inhibiting feeling—one that's all too familiar to me and anyone else who's ever been sixteen! It's a very good question, whether this method of self-observation I'm teaching you—using Bare Attention to watch your own thoughts, feelings, and sensations by making mental notes of them—could turn into another form of self-consciousness. Obviously, that's something you need like a hole in the head!

The answer is: just keep at it. Making mental notes does feel a little awkward at first, because it's different from anything you've done before. But as you practice and it becomes more natural, you will find that this clear self-awareness—Mindfulness—is completely unlike the self-consciousness that sometimes plagues you and your friend. It is, in fact, the diametrical opposite of it. Indeed, it is the antidote to self-consciousness.

Among all the other good things it is the key to, mindful awareness also empowers you to free yourself from the paralyzing grip of self-consciousness. Anytime you apply wise attention to a situation by making mental notes, your freedom increases because you are in touch with reality. The total, night-and-day difference between "watching yourself" *mindfully* and *self-consciously* really comes down to the difference between listening to true and false friends. And as with everything else you encounter on this journey, you have both types within you. The friends you make on the outside reflect—and then influence—which one you choose to listen to within.

You already know what a true friend is. I've met some of your friends at school, and I am very confident that you have true friends among them. You have no feeling of self-consciousness in front of true friends, because you already know that they accept you completely. They also share your deepest values and goals. There's no need to hide parts of yourself from them or pretend to be something you're not. In their supportive presence you can reveal doubts and vulnerabilities, with no fear that they'll take advantage of you or reject you.

But being with true friends does increase your self-*awareness,* because they are people you care about, so you want to be the kind of person they respect and admire. An almost paradoxical thing about good friends is that at the same time as they *accept* you, they also *expect* the best from you, and want the best for you. It hurts them when you screw up, and it gladdens them when you do well. In that way they are very much like family. And while you have a healthy fear of disappointing them, it is very different from self-consciousness. Your concerns, and even anxieties, about not letting true friends down don't paralyze you. On the contrary, they inspire and energize you to push the edge of the envelope and excel. (It is worth noting that in all of these ways they are very similar, indeed intimately related, to your Impartial Spectator or "friend within.")

The people you feel self-conscious in front of, by contrast, are people whose acceptance you crave and whose rejection you fear. (Because that's what self-consciousness really is, at bottom: a *fear of rejection* grounded in a *craving for acceptance.*) People who strongly elicit that feeling are almost always false friends, because good people don't *want* to make others feel self-conscious. Now, when the feeling of self-consciousness is not so strong, it may be that they're just people you don't know very well yet (the way you didn't know your girlfriend very well at the beginning of your relationship). And sometimes behind their cool façade it's merely that *they're* afraid of being rejected by *you!* Often you can put them at their ease just by being friendly, and they'll quickly return the favor.

But when people consistently act in some way that makes you feel like the real Patrick won't do, it's time to take three steps back and look very closely at what's really going on. If you can feel them judging you, as if on a scale of 1 to 10 (the way girls must feel when they're being rated—generally by morons—on their appearance), and you feel a strong inner pressure to adopt their point of view and judge *yourself* (in a vain attempt to avoid their rejection), it's probably time to boogie. You didn't sign up to audition for a beauty contest, and nobody appointed them the judges. Never underestimate the power of simply walking away—at least temporarily. Or as I sometimes like to say, "Time to give it a rest."

Next time you have this universal experience, observe it and make mental notes! This is where your Impartial Spectator's powerful built-in bull & baloney detector comes in particularly handy.

It's generally not quite clear exactly what you'd need to do to be "in" with false friends. The only thing that's obvious is that it's something bad. Other than that, it's like a little secret game, an in-joke shared among them by looks, signs, and gestures that keep you guessing. That brings a sinking feeling of uncertainty *(how can I win this game when I don't know what the rules are?)*, which is one of the reasons why self-consciousness is so paralyzing. Of course, the other, far more important, reason for the churning stomach and inner tension is that there's a fight going on inside you. Because there's always at least one thing you do know: to get false friends to like you, you will have to act in ways that will make you not like yourself. Or, what amounts to the same thing, in ways that disgust your "friend within." At the very least, to be considered an "insider" will require despicable behavior like putting down "outsiders," even if they're people you actually like and sympathize with. And acting like that on a regular basis will make you feel like throwing up when you look in the mirror. So reflect carefully before volunteering for a life of sustained nausea.

It's when facing choices like these that you really need a powerful *true* friend on your side. Because the craving for acceptance by your peers, and especially by what Jaime called the "cool hierarchy" among them, is a very powerful drive, and it's one that can take you down some bad roads in a big hurry. Next time I write, I'll tell you why.

Your friend,
Jeff

Jeff,
When I was reading your last letter, I circled "ways that disgust your friend within" and wrote next to it: "Being mean to anyone makes me feel like garbage."

Patrick

RESISTING THE CALL OF THE PACK

Dear Patrick,

That is a very wise and wholesome response. And it is probably the one that most young people feel spontaneously, in their heart of hearts. What is it, then, about the craving for the "cool hierarchy's" approval that can be strong enough—in an untrained mind—to override what you know is right?

While it feels like a very human emotion, *the drive for peer acceptance is actually a deeply entrenched part of your animal "vehicle."* It's physically hardwired into your brain, and it's activated by hormones. The struggle for dominance and status (because that's what it really is) plays your emotions like an organ, because levels of mood-regulating brain chemicals fluctuate in response to social "success" or "failure," as interpreted by parts of your brain you share with rats and lizards. Indeed, it's quite likely that one major reason why the brain generates these emotions so powerfully in social situations is to promote survival and security in the hierarchy of the animal pack.

Soon after puberty, young primates start to work out the power structure, the pecking order, in their own generation, and it's generally done by pretty crude criteria: who's biggest, strongest, most effective in exerting aggression, best-connected, most seductive, and who smells best. In monkey, chimpanzee, and gorilla "societies," this process is both influenced and held in check by the authority of adult males and females. In traditional human societies, it's the job of adults to subordinate the crude primate criteria to the evolved standards of the community and to harness young people's competitive drives into the shaping of better citizens. That's one of the uses of *ceremony,* like the tests of courage in initiation rites.

But in a society like ours, where so many adults have abdicated both authority and ceremony, we have a situation that doesn't even exist in nature: groups of young people with no stronger force in their lives than each other. You're lucky, Patrick—you have a strong mother and a strong relationship with her. But I'm quite sure that you know kids (your pot-smoking friend, for example) for whom status in "the animal pack" means *everything*—more than their future, their karma, or their soul. They're the ones who will do anything—buy hundreds of dollars' worth of the "right" CDs and running shoes (large corporations, as well as urban gangs, feed on the need for pack identity and insignia), pierce every body part that sticks out, use and deal drugs, count sexual conquests—to build a reputation for being "cool" or "famous." And by the very nature of things, those kids issue a powerful and confusing call to your "vehicle." A part of you wants to respond, and that's your *false* friend within. (Remember him, because Buddhists give him a name—Māra—and he'll be popping up often along this road.)

Practicing mindfulness, by making mental notes in the present moment, summons and strengthens your *true* friend within to come to the rescue by getting your mind back on track (or on the *path*, as Buddhists call it). This true friend will wake you up from the intoxicating dream of belonging to the pack and remind you where *you* really want to go. Whenever you observe your stream of experience mindfully, from the objective viewpoint of the Impartial Spectator, you're acting exactly the way a true friend does: both *accepting* everything, and *expecting* the best.

"Be kind to yourself," writes the Venerable Henepola Gunaratana, a Buddhist monk and scholar from Sri Lanka who now teaches meditation in West Virginia and is the author of the best introductory book on how to meditate, *Mindfulness in Plain English.* "The process of becoming who you will be begins first with the total acceptance of who you are. . . . Accept your feelings, even the ones you wish you did not have. Accept your experiences, even the ones you hate. Don't condemn yourself for having human flaws and failings. Learn to see all the phenomena in the mind as being perfectly natural and understandable. . . . Don't fight with what you experience, just observe it all mindfully." This compassionate, curious, and even humorous self-acceptance is the exact opposite of self-consciousness (so if you want to help your girlfriend, teach her how to make mental notes!). As you'll see, it is also the best antidote to the feeling of loneliness that arises from the craving for others' acceptance.

But self-acceptance is just the beginning of your Impartial Spectator's true friendship to you. Unerring guidance is also available at a moment's notice. To get it, all you need is mindful awareness. "Mindfulness," the Buddha declared, "is *always* helpful." That's because mindfulness automatically brings wise attention with it. The more clearly you see, the more wisely you choose, and that protects you from trouble, pain, and suffering. Doing *what is right*—that is, what *will not harm* yourself or others (remember, in reality those two cannot be separated)—follows naturally, even effortlessly, from clearly seeing *what is so*. When you see clearly, the basic truth—"Protecting yourself you protect others, protecting others you protect yourself"—is quite obvious. The hard part, the part that takes so much effort and will, especially at first, is keeping your eye on *what is real* when all your animal "vehicle" has eyes for is *what it wants*. But that's the purpose of making mental notes: to get in touch—and *stay* in touch—with reality.

When you can truthfully see *yourself*—what's really going on inside you, right now—the major obstacle to insight is removed. It then becomes a straightforward matter to clearly comprehend what's going on *around* you as well. A helpful way of looking at it is that your own thoughts and (especially) emotions are like sunglasses. If you completely forget you have them on, you might start to assume the world is tinted gray, or greenish brown. But if you remember you're wearing shades, you can look *over* them to see the world's true colors. Similarly, if you make a mental note and observe that right now you're "wearing shades" tinted with anger, or sadness—or craving for acceptance and fear of rejection—you become instantly free to look *over* your emotion instead of *through* it, and to see the world directly, clear and undistorted (even though the emotion is still there).

You must experience this shift in perspective for yourself to know what I'm talking about. Try it the next time you're caught up in a strong emotion: remember to make a mental note, such as *angry, angry.* Then observe how different the world looks!

The moment you *see* your own state, you're no longer blinded by it. And then, you can see *beyond* yourself and beyond the present moment. You become more aware of what's *around* you—the feelings, attitudes, and agendas of other people—and what's *ahead* of you: the future, in which the consequences of your present choices will unfold. Like a good chess player, you become able to think many moves ahead. When you use your Impartial Spectator, you'll find that you can *see* where a given course of action is going to take you, and how you and others will be affected. The destinations of both the true and the false path start to become crystal clear—in advance. That's why the Impartial Spectator is such a good "navigator."

But remember, Patrick—to open that inner eye, you must first take a good hard look at yourself!

Your friend,
Jeff

Dear Jeff,

I'm kind of embarrassed to tell you this, but I'm writing to you from home, not from the competition in Canada, where I thought I'd be now. My mom may have told you that I almost got thrown out of rowing camp for a really ridiculous reason. I didn't, but then they chose the teams for the rest of the summer, and I didn't make the cut. And several kids with slower times than me, did.

Here's what happened.

We had a coxswain in the morning—you probably know the cox sits in the stern and calls the strokes and steers the boat—and she was being really mean to her rowers. She's one of those people who's extremely annoying. All morning, she'd been badgering us. And just at the end of the row, I said, "Oh, must be that time of the month." And I got in a lot of trouble.

She laughed at first. Everyone laughed. It was a little joke. And then she got out and started crying. It was ridiculous. She just totally, completely overreacted, and no one told her she overreacted, and she got me in trouble.

The head coach thought it was really bad. He asked me where I found the humor in the joke. I said it was just a little comment, I thought it was humorous. I had used that joke before in my classroom and the teachers laughed! He didn't think it was humorous. He said, "I'm trying to think of successful scenarios for you to stay, and I can't think of any. I don't know if people will be able to respect you anymore, and row with you." And I'm going, "Are you kidding me? This is way too far. Come on!"

So the end result was, I didn't exactly get thrown out, but then I did, sort of. So now I'm looking for someplace in the city where I can at least work out on machines and stay in shape. I'm kind of in shock. I guess I'll have more time to get my driver's license.

Patrick

ACTIONS HAVE CONSEQUENCES

Dear Patrick,

There's an old cliché that says "Experience is the best teacher." As with most old clichés, there's only one good thing to be said for it—it's often true.

Here I was, telling you about making mental notes and how your Impartial Spectator can protect you from hurting yourself and others, and there you were, reading along, saying "Hmmm!" and nodding your head—and along comes life and hits you with an illustration that makes the point more clearly than anything I could have dreamed up.

What's the big deal? You made a thoughtless remark. While not trivial, it's not exactly a major transgression, either. Prior to our current era of hypersensitivity about "self-esteem," it would have gone largely unnoticed—except by the girl whose feelings you hurt. It certainly wouldn't have almost gotten you thrown out of rowing camp! But nowadays, a mere insensitive remark can be interpreted as the moral equivalent of a vicious attack. Your coach certainly gave you a memorable introduction to "political correctness," and to the extreme, misplaced overprotectiveness that so strangely accompanies our culture's uncaring promiscuity.

I'll say at least one good thing for your coach, though. His overreaction, absurd as it was, threw a spotlight on a small but perfect example of what I've been talking about: *actions have consequences.* Or, as I sometimes like to simplify it, "You pay for your mistakes." ("We pay our debts sometimes," sings the rock group Alice in Chains. But Gotama Buddha said we pay our debts ALWAYS—if not through the purifying efforts of mindfulness, then with pain and suffering.) So there is definitely a sense in which that coach did you a favor. The odds are he doesn't know Sanskrit, but he sure gave you a nice little lesson on what the phrase *karma-vipāka,* "the ripening of actions," means.

Patrick, can you see how, if you'd remembered to use your Impartial Spectator to mindfully observe what you were feeling and doing, you would have avoided this unpleasant scene, and the temporary setback it's dealt to your progress in your sport? Let's look a little deeper into what happened between you and the coxswain, and then take a look at the big difference the small act of making mental notes would have made.

Now understand this clearly: the fact that the coach's overreaction was wrong in no way implies that your remark was right. In my opinion, what the coach should have said to you is short and to the point: *"Young man, gentlemen don't speak like that, especially to ladies, and we only permit gentlemen here."* But let's try subtracting the coach and his reaction from the equation for a moment and see what small but very real harm was done *by that wisecrack itself,* not only to the girl, but to you. Because according to the Laws of Reality, every action cuts both ways. Even if no one else ever heard about your "joke," you could not have hurt her without also hurting yourself. Is that hard to believe? Look deeper.

"Sticks and stones can break my bones, but words will never hurt me." Would little kids chant that if it were really true? This is a simple example of the defense mechanism Freud called *denial.* Words most certainly can hurt, especially when they are untrue, "unceremonious" (disrespectful of serious things), or spoken with ill-will. As we've seen, this is a truth recognized by every great tradition: in the commandments that God gave to Moses, and on the Buddha's Noble Eightfold Path, where "right speech" is one of the ways to Innocence. And the Buddha explained that speech is "right" when it is honest, kind, and helpful. When Gotama speaks, as he so often does, of wholesome or unwholesome "actions of body, speech, and mind," he is saying that words, too, are actions, and are therefore part of your *karma.* (So too, it's worth noting, are the thoughts you have *before* you speak.

Thoughts are often willful actions of your mind, and as such they too are part of the wholesome or unwholesome *karma* you generate.)

Why did the coxswain burst into tears when you said to her (after having unwholesome thoughts contaminated by mild, but real, ill-will), "What is it, that time of the month?" You know why: it embarrassed her by making a public reference to a private function. With a little effort you can imagine how it would feel if someone said something roughly equivalent to you, especially in front of girls. You also insulted her by reducing her to a biological machine whose behavior was driven by her hormones. It may well have been; as we've seen, most people—regardless of sex—*are* operating mechanically much of the time. However, we generally get better results from people by appealing to the part of them that's *not* a machine, rather than humiliating them for the part that is.

Why did the coxswain then feel the need to run and tell the rowing coach what you'd said instead of handling it herself—by slapping you across the face, for instance? Because one lesson too many women seem to have taken from feminism, rather than "empowerment," is that they are helpless victims who need protection. It's one thing for a woman to call the police when she's been genuinely assaulted, but women are at least as potent as men when it comes to speech; they hardly need to call the thought police every time they feel insulted!

But let's go back to the part that was under your control. You knew before it came out of your mouth that the remark was embarrassing and insulting, so why did you say it? You know the answers here, too. First of all, you obviously felt she had it coming. You felt she had spoiled the training session for everyone, and so you felt justified in letting loose some of your annoyance and frustration. Then, too, you were playing for laughs. You'd made a similar remark before, and everyone had laughed. It's a remark that displays a fairly sophisticated familiarity with the ways of women, for a sixteen-year-old male—familiarity which indeed you have, as the son of a single mother who isn't exactly a blushing Victorian about the facts of life. Let's face it, Patrick—you were showing off a little!

But suppose the coach's wrath hadn't descended on you—what harm could that mildly tasteless remark have done to *you?*

By way of an answer, let me ask you another question. Did you have the slightest, momentary feeling, right before you said it—like a warning light going on—that it was a little bit unworthy, that you were about to score off a cheap shot? Think back, and answer this question carefully.

Your friend,
Jeff

Dear Jeff,

I didn't think that remark would get me into trouble, but right before I said it, I thought maybe it would make her feel a little down, like we felt down all day in the boat. It was sort of like an attack at her to make her feel the way we were feeling. I didn't want to really hurt her feelings, it was just like, we've had to deal with you all morning, acting like this—OK, now it's your turn to take a little.

Patrick

THE GUARDIANS OF THE WORLD

Dear Patrick,

Very good! So you *knew*, right before you made that remark, that you were acting out of ill-will—however justified it may have seemed by *her* ill-will. But Gotama Buddha said unequivocally that acting out of ill-will *always* harms *you*—whatever your reasons. It's worth quoting some of the very first words of the *Dhammapada*, the most well-known collection of inspiring statements made by the Buddha:

1. . . . If one speaks or acts with an evil mind, from that suffering follows one, as the wheel follows the foot of the ox.
2. . . . If one speaks or acts with a clear mind, from that happiness follows one like a shadow that never leaves.
3. "He abused me, he beat me, he defeated me, he robbed me": in those who harbor such thoughts, hatred is not appeased.
4. "He abused me, he beat me, he defeated me, he robbed me": in those who do not harbor such thoughts, hatred is quenched.
5. Hatreds never cease through hatred in this world; through loving kindness alone they cease. This is the eternal Law.

So Gotama's advice on acts of revenge—big or small—is that it's not worth the cost *to you*. His insight is much closer to Jesus' "Whosoever shall smite thee on thy right cheek, turn to him the other also," than to its Old Testament precursor, "An eye for an eye, and a tooth for a tooth." If you still have trouble seeing why a mean-spirited wisecrack is, *by its very nature*, harmful to you, these words of the great modern scholar/monk Nyanaponika (the one who was born a German Jew) should help to make it clear: "[B]ad deeds and words, and the thoughts motivating them, may fail to harm the other, *but they will not fail to have a damaging effect on the character of the doer* [my italics]. . . . It will be a wholesome practice to remind oneself often of the fact that one's deeds, words, and thoughts first of all act upon and alter one's own mind. Reflecting thus will give a strong impetus to true self-respect which is preserved by protecting oneself against everything mean and evil."

Here, then, is another extremely simple but powerful technique for protecting yourself and others. Whenever you feel any doubt or hesitation about something you're about to do or say, stop and ask yourself, *"Why am I doing this?"* If the answer contains elements of greed, ill-will, or ignorance, don't do it!

But let's back up, and look at that split second of doubt and hesitation that so often "gives us pause" on the brink of doing something wrong. Gotama said that little warning feeling is very important, and he had a name for the cause of it: *hiri*—the same word that means "appropriate shame" when it comes to the body and sex! We don't really have an equivalent word in English; we generally only talk about the "shame" and "guilt" we feel *after* we've done something unwholesome in body, speech, or mind. But Gotama taught that any time we have even a little bit of kindness or generosity in our hearts, at that moment we also have at least some awareness of how bad we'd feel if we did, said, or even thought something ugly or cruel.

The Pāli language actually uses *two* words to make a wonderfully subtle distinction between two aspects of that awareness: *hiri*, which can also be translated as "disgust at wrongdoing," and arises out of self-respect; and *ottappa*, which means "dread of wrongdoing," and arises out of respect for others. Both imply an awareness of the suffering that will result for you and others if you commit a bad or unwholesome act.

Now it's obvious that normal people would feel *hiri* and *ottappa* at the thought of, say, killing someone. (And yes, many people *do* feel them at the thought of having an abortion.) What's interesting is that if we are genuinely sensitive, in the good sense of the word, they guard us against lesser wrongdoing as well. And in fact, that's exactly what Gotama called *hiri* and *ottappa*—our guardians. "Monks," he addressed his followers, "these two bright states are the guardians of the world. Which two? *Hiri* and *ottappa.*" Without them, he said, no woman would ever be safe, and the world would degenerate into a condition suitable only for "goats, cocks, pigs, dogs, and jackals." (I've walked down the Sunset Strip some nights when it looked like we might already be there!)

The ancient texts had, to say the least, a highly vivid way of clarifying these terms. They explain *hiri* and *ottappa* by asking you to imagine an iron rod, one end of which is cold and smeared with feces, and the other end heated till it's red hot. A wise person wouldn't grasp the filthy end out of disgust, and would not grasp the red-hot end either, due to a healthy fear of being burned. *Hiri* is compared to the first example, *ottappa* to the second. (I think you'd agree that this is a bit stronger than our somewhat faint word, "conscience"!)

If, in the instant before you spoke, there was even the slightest awareness in your mind that by sinking to the level of mentioning the cox's bodily functions, you were going to make an embarrassing mess that soiled *you*—that was *hiri.* You couldn't have foreseen the "politically correct" hysteria you were about to unleash, because such consequences are largely artificial, but if you felt even a split second's anxiety about the real blame you would deserve for hurting her feelings, that was *ottappa.* Gotama taught that *hiri* and *ottappa* always arrive together, like twin lifeguards, and they protect you from wrongdoing by delivering a wake-up call to your Impartial Spectator. Their function is to make you recoil from evil. They give you a chance to grab the wheel and steer in a better direction.

In the Bible, what Gotama calls *hiri* and *ottappa* are portrayed as the voice of God. It is God who gives Cain a moment's pause, a chance to wake up from his anger and act with a clear mind, when the envious Cain is about to slay his brother Abel:

> And the Lord said to Cain, "Why are you angry, and why is your countenance fallen?" [Why are you doing this?]
> "If you do right, shall you not be accepted? And if you do not right, sin crouches at the door. And to you shall be its desire, and yet you may rule over it."

And yet you may rule over it. That is the message of all the great traditions with regard to every one of our baser motives and passions. And the method of "ruling over it" begins with self-observation—with making mental notes. (In our Western tradition, this often involves prayer and self-searching.)

The automatic response to an annoying person is to get annoyed. Without *mindfulness* and *wise attention,* which are the only ways to avoid acting like a machine, annoyance will automatically arise and grow whenever the mind is confronted by an annoying situation. It isn't called "pushing your buttons" for nothing! But what do you suppose would have happened if, instead of reacting to her, you had observed yourself?

What if, instead of saying to yourself, "Boy, is *she* a pain," you had made the mental note, "*Annoyed, annoyed*"?

The answer is this: the annoyance which had, perhaps unavoidably, arisen would have stopped growing then and there. You would have realized that her bad attitude was literally infecting you, and that you were about to spread the infection further. In the words of another great modern meditation teacher, the Burmese monk Sayadaw U Pandita, the Buddhist scriptures illustrate the foolishness of engaging in such quarrels "with the image of a person enraged, taking up a handful of excrement to fling at his or her opponent. This person befouls himself or herself even before the opponent." You're quite right that in this case, the coxswain flung it first—but did you have to *catch* it?! As your mind grows more nimble, it gets easier and easier to duck!

And while "getting even" provides you with a certain animal relief and satisfaction, at the price of increasing the amount of ill-will in the situation, you can never predict (as you found out the hard way) *how much* ill-will the next turn of the screw will generate—or where it's going to land! ("What goes around comes around" . . . and around . . . and around, unless someone puts a stop to it!) That's one reason why the difficult art of self-control is worth mastering: it's so *practical.* It not only leaves you feeling much cleaner, it also tends to keep things cool and calm. And only a fool prefers friction and strife over cool and calm—that's part of the Buddha's definition of a fool!

Now if you had mindfully observed your own annoyance and stepped aside from it instead of acting it out, what kinds of better choices would have opened up to you? You could have said, "You don't seem to be in a great mood today, but please try to keep it out of the boat, okay?" You could have taken the cox aside after training and asked her what was bothering her. You could have gracefully asked the coach to try to counsel her. And if that didn't help, maybe *she* was the one who didn't belong in rowing camp, not you! I can guarantee you this: it would have increased the chances that your coach would see it that way!

If you reflect on it, I think you'll see just how graphically the whole experience illustrates the Buddha's words, *"Protecting yourself, you protect others; protecting others, you protect yourself."* To protect yourself better from now on:

1. Always try to make mental notes, especially before you leap to the attack!

2. Be alert for the "danger signals" of your Guardians, *hiri* and *ottappa*.

3. Whenever you feel that little warning about something you're about to do or say, pause and ask yourself, *"Why am I doing this?"* That question is virtually guaranteed to wake up the "navigator." To answer it, observe mindfully.

Remember what the Buddha said: "Mindfulness is *always* helpful!"

Your friend,
Jeff

"SPIDER SENSE" VS.
THE FORCES OF EVIL

Dear Patrick,

Now that you've met your friend the Impartial Spectator, we're almost ready to take a guided tour of your "engine," your brain, from its deepest and most primitive to its most unique and sophisticated levels. You'll discover that nearly everything you do or experience, from the basics such as breathing, eating, sleeping, waking, and sexuality to your most complex feelings and thoughts—everything, in fact, but the observer who is aware of it all and the will that makes a choice—has a physical basis in your brain.

This knowledge strengthens the Impartial Spectator, because it helps to break the controlling grip of an unwholesome thought or powerful feeling when you can remind yourself, *"It's not me, it's just my brain."* It's this kind of wise attention that can tame an unruly brain. This becomes particularly important on those "bad brain days" when that sucker simply will not stay in place, even for a second or two. These are the days when that phrase you always hear in hair spray ads, "unruly split ends," seems like a good description of how your neural pathways are firing. I think we're living in an age when more people have frizzy brains than frizzy hair!

Once you've mindfully observed how this amazing biological machine called a nervous system operates on automatic pilot, and you begin to realize that, with the help of your awakened "friend within," you have the power to step in, redirect, and even reprogram it—you gain confidence that through your actions, you can reliably add to the Beauty and Innocence of this world, rather than to its ugliness and harm. Make no mistake about it—an unruly brain necessarily leaves behind it a trail of destruction, wreckage, and sorrow. And what inevitably follows from that is, as Gotama described it, "grief, lamentation, pain, mental upset and despair." Or, as he termed these states in his First Noble Truth, *Dukkha*—Suffering.

But wait! It gets worse! Because when a "bad brain day" grows, unchecked by mindfulness, fed by a toxic stream of unwise attention, into a bad brain week, or month, or year— then the ugliness begins to reach increasingly disturbing levels of power, intensity, and unpleasantness. The scummy residue exuding from the cesspool of a bad brain life, and the ugliness it leads to beyond this life, I'll leave for another time (or you can refer to masterpieces like Dante's *Inferno).* But I'll give you a hint—the name Māra isn't derived from the word for Death for nothing!

It was precisely for the purpose of helping you avoid such a disaster that Gotama the Buddha spoke the following words to his disciples:

> *"Abandon evil, O monks! One can abandon evil! If it were not possible to abandon evil, I would not ask you to do so. But as it can be done, therefore I say 'Abandon evil!'*
>
> *"If this abandoning of evil would bring harm and suffering, I would not ask you to abandon it. But as the abandoning of evil brings well-being and happiness, therefore I say 'Abandon evil!'"*

Which brings us back to our Guardians, *hiri* and *ottappa*, those twin words for "recoiling from evil" that are so much stronger and more direct than the English word "conscience." Gotama Buddha held *hiri* and *ottappa* in the highest esteem, for without them, he taught, abandoning evil is impossible. Because to accomplish this ultimate task, the only task that really matters, you will need the power and speed of a genuine *moral reflex* to help you fight against the cunning, craftiness, and many disguises of our "human animal" nature. *Hiri* and *ottappa* can sense, like the "spider-sense" of the famous superhero, when you're about to do or say or even think something harmful—even faster than your unpracticed Impartial Spectator can wake up and see it. They are a superb early-warning

The cesspool of a bad brain life

system. But to function properly, *hiri* and *ottappa* require our respect and wise attention. And instead, much of our culture today does everything it can to disregard, discredit, and deafen us to our inner Guardians.

What are some of the ways our culture tries to drown out the voices of *hiri* and *ottappa*? Well, there are drugs and alcohol. They can't *completely* knock out your Impartial Spectator (otherwise no one would ever stop taking them)—yet another hint that the Impartial Spectator is not merely another part of the brain. But intoxicants certainly do "turn up the volume" of the animal passions, until the "still small voice" of your Guardians is no more than a whisper in a hurricane.

Then there's that most false, pernicious, and foolish of ideas: that actions don't have consequences. *Ottappa* is telling you in no uncertain terms that that's a lie. Yet so much in our culture feeds and encourages that *other* voice within you, the one that says, "Go on—you can get away with it." Beware! That's the voice of Māra, your false friend—your mortal enemy—within.

Another pernicious idea that has come to permeate our culture was stated to me most recently by a scientist friend of mine. We were discussing the basis of ethical principles, the foundations of right and wrong, and my friend said to me, "It's all man-made." Now, this is a man for whom I have the utmost respect, who is also a very good person. And yet, even he has bought into the dangerous nonsense that is the heart of "secular humanism" (if it *has* a heart): that "right" and "wrong" are nothing but human creations.

The existence of *hiri* and *ottappa,* and their profoundly similar function in human minds all over the world, are strong evidence that *that's* a lie. As another friend of mine, social scientist James Q. Wilson, reports in his book *The Moral Sense,* University of Chicago researchers have discovered that "there are some things that young children regard as wrong" in societies as different as middle-class Chicago and village India—such as "breaking a promise, stealing flowers, kicking a harmless animal, and destroying another's property." Just as you have physical senses, like the balance organ in your middle ear, that orient you to the physical laws of momentum and gravity—and are essential for driving a car safely—*hiri* and *ottappa* are your "moral senses," which orient you to the equally absolute and objective moral laws. The unerring information they give you about right and wrong are essential for "driving" your human "vehicle" without harming anybody.

That's why it's so tragic that our culture's "war on *hiri* and *ottappa"* is aimed with particular intensity at teenagers, who are just starting to "drive" on their own.

Speaking of which, Patrick, be sure to let me know when you're going down to Florida, so your two kinds of "driver's ed" can go forward together!

Your friend.
Jeff

COURAGE AND THE
IMPARTIAL SPECTATOR

Dear Patrick,

Thanks for the call, and your Florida address. The fact that, as you say, these letters have been arriving with uncanny timing, "just happening" to address questions and issues in your life that you haven't asked me about yet, is a sign that we're on the right track. I wonder if courage is one of those issues.

"Aw, c'mon, don't be a wimp": my sixteen-year-old friend Sara in St. Louis tells me that's what kids today say when they're pushing you into actions you intuitively recoil from, like getting behind the wheel drunk, or proving yourself sexually, or trying a drug. In my day, they called you a "chicken." But regardless of what the word is, the insult is a challenge very few teenagers can resist—for a reason.

Young adults *need* challenges and testing. One of the things you most need to find out about yourself is whether you have courage. That's because it's a quality absolutely essential to a successful adult life. There may be no more saber-toothed tigers, but you will be called on to protect and defend the people, principles, and property that you care about, from dangers just as serious and a lot more insidious. And that requires guts. So there are very good reasons why young people are extra sensitive to the accusation of cowardice. In a healthy culture—and in the remaining healthy parts of our culture—you have opportunities to prove yourself and build *real* courage through training systems such as martial arts, demanding sports, military basic training, and outdoor challenges.

Unfortunately, in the two segments of our culture that have the biggest impact on young people—entertainment and education—values have been twisted into a grotesque parody. (As you read this, keep in mind that another part of the Buddha's definition of a fool is someone who finds attractive what is unattractive.) Criminals, addicts, and exhibitionists like Madonna, Marilyn Manson, and Dennis Rodman are marketed as "heroes." Risking mindless danger, being rude, and breaking rules are worshipped as the epitome of courage and cool. This glorifying of destructive over-the-line behaviors is one more symptom of our cultural disease. You don't romanticize lawless self-gratification, or make light of the pain it causes, if you or your loved ones have ever been on the receiving end of the mind games of a pathological narcissist.

One of the worst results of this glorification of sick behavior is that *you often get shamed as a "wimp" for heeding the warnings of* hiri *and* ottappa—your Guardians, who empower you to protect both yourself and the world. This is a perversion in the truest sense of the word! Your healthy disgust at and fear of doing something that's cruel, destructive, or just plain stupid is mislabeled as cowardice, usually by false but "glamorous" (real meaning: brimming with false confidence) "friends." To a young person, this is genuinely and deeply confusing (also to an old person with the maturity level of a young person). You can be talked into feeling ashamed of your deep and natural hesitation to "cross the line," just when you're most entitled to feel grateful and proud that your "spiritual instincts" are in good working order! This is where *true* courage is called for—otherwise you can be tricked into fighting against your protectors as if they were your enemies, trying to suppress their voices instead of listening to their wise guidance. And for what? To avoid rejection by a bunch of phonies who spend too much time posing in front of a mirror.

This is how many tragedies happen. For example, several young people have been honest enough to tell me that the first time someone "offered" them marijuana, or "invited" them to get drunk (we should probably use more aggressive verbs than that), they were uneasily curious, reluctant, and scared. They felt a little sick to their stomachs, and their hearts beat faster—physiological signals of fear and dread. They were worried about what was going to happen to them, whether they would lose control of themselves or become distorted beyond their own recognition. (This is *ottappa*.) Often they had found it repulsive to watch other kids who were sloppy drunk or stoned; that didn't look like fun, it looked ugly, stupid, and scary. (This is *hiri*.)

My guess is that those feelings are pretty universal. And of course, they are accurate! Drugs *are* dangerous. The years of your life (or your life itself) that you could lose to addiction, the potential for brain damage, the alterations in your personality, the loss of control of your life—to fear these is quite simply to perceive reality. And yet, millions of kids are taunted into taking those feelings, not as a wise warning, but as a challenge. When *hiri* and *ottappa* say "Don't go there," *that* becomes the "cool" place to go. Otherwise, you're a wimp. It's as if, on the road, when you saw a STOP sign you felt obliged to stomp on the accelerator.

Another, closely related problem kids often have with listening to *hiri* and *ottappa* is that the "two bright states" within your own heart are sometimes telling you the same thing your parents, teachers, and people like me are telling you. "Don't do drugs! Wait for sex! Get your studying done before you go out with your friends!" Even when they're right, they're such a drag! Ever since the '60s, the knee-jerk attitude of American youth culture has been, "If an authority figure says it, reject it," without pausing to evaluate the real source, or the real merit, of what is said. And that's just as stupid and mindless as knee-jerk obedience. Why bother to "Question Authority" if you lack the integrity to appreciate a good answer when you hear one? Asking a question when you have no intention of even listening to the answer is an act of hypocrisy, or worse.

So you might, at times, confuse this important form of self-control with parental and adult control—something you are trying to get away from. You may think that the warnings of *hiri* and *ottappa* are no more than the internalized voices of your parents (after all, that's the crux of what Freud said about how we acquire a "conscience," or "superego"), and that therefore obeying them makes you childish. Your false friends, the allies of Māra, your false friend within, will be only too happy to sneer that yes indeed, if you hesitate before harm-doing you are a baby, a goody-goody, a mama's boy, *and* a teacher's pet!

Well, Patrick, you know by now that anyone who taunts you for choosing not to harm yourself or others is a very false friend, as well as a very big fool. To follow *hiri* and *ottappa* when they lead you away from the animal pack takes *true* courage—but that is the priceless gift of your "friend within."

Your "friend without,"
Jeff

P.S. Give me, if you can—and I'm sure you can—an example of a time when you fooled your mother, but *still* didn't feel good about whatever it was you got away with.

Dear Jeff,

Everyone says when you're a teenager you're trying to get away from parental authority, but I don't really have that problem. Nowadays I can make judgments on my own, so I don't even need my mom—I don't need to go to her or get away from her.

A time when I fooled her? I've bought stuff that she didn't want me to buy. A heart-rate monitor, for my rowing. She didn't want me to waste the money on it, and so I bought it anyway, and I never told her. I told myself it was all right because it was for my training, and it was pretty important. I did sort of need it for what I'll be doing this fall. But I felt a little bad about it.

And when I was a little kid, not doing homework—a lot. I'd say I did my homework and I hadn't done it. And I felt bad about that.

Patrick

WHAT IS TRUE FREEDOM?

Dear Patrick,

What a great answer! It provides us with a powerful demonstration that your Impartial Spectator is an essential part of *you,* and not a mind-control implant from your mother (though there's no question she nourished it). In fact, it is what makes you capable of real independence— from both her *and* your peers. Parents don't install their child's Impartial Spectator, or instill the "spider sense" of *hiri* and *ottappa.* You are born with this natural radar for right and wrong, in seed form. Each of us comes into the world preequipped with the *potential* for mindfulness, wisdom, and Innocence.

It is, of course, true that for this potential to work at its best, it must be cultivated and fortified. *That* is the major task of all parents, and one I think your mother has done remarkably well. However, the fact that the moral sense of most people functions reasonably well, even when their parenting has been far from inspiring, provides significant evidence that the awareness of right and wrong occurs naturally and isn't just a parental implant any more than it's just a cultural implant.

But the sense of right and wrong doesn't kick in *quite* as automatically as our physical senses and animal instincts do. And because it so often has to do battle against them, it needs the backing of wise authority, the support of custom and ceremony, the fighting spirit of true courage—and, most of all, the light of mindfulness to see by.

More than two hundred years ago, Adam Smith, the Scottish Enlightenment philosopher and economist who coined the term "the Impartial Spectator," described how the small flame of our social nature—our desire to be approved of and admired by others—lights the much bigger flame of our spiritual nature, our desire to act admirably whether others are watching or not. "When we first come into the world, from the natural desire to please, we are accustomed to consider what behaviour is likely to be agreeable . . . to our parents, to our masters, to our companions," Smith wrote in 1759 in his book *The Theory of Moral Sentiments*. To figure that out, we have to use our imagination, putting ourselves in their place and judging our own actions through their imagined eyes.

But very soon, the approval of others is not enough. If it were, we'd all conform to H. L. Mencken's sarcastic but quite insightful definition: "Conscience: The inner voice that warns us that someone may be looking." We'd be hypocrites, behaving well only when others were watching, and letting our hidden thoughts run wild—which is exactly how sociopaths, people with poorly developed *hiri* and *ottappa*, live. For such people lack what Congressman J. C. Watts so aptly defined as character when he said, "What is character? Doing right when nobody's looking."

Instead, in those of us fortunate enough to have some character, a wonderful and awe-inspiring metamorphosis takes place. The eyes we imagine watching and judging us actually become our own—but our own in a very special sense. "When I endeavour to examine my own conduct," Smith wrote, ". . . and either to approve or condemn it . . . I divide myself, as it were, into two persons. . . . The first is the spectator," whom Smith describes in other passages as "fair and impartial," a neutral observer, "the man within." "The second is the agent [the one acting and being observed in action], the person whom I properly call myself. . . . The first is the judge, the second the person judged of." In this way, Smith said, "We suppose ourselves the spectators of our own behavior."

When I showed these passages to Sayadaw U Silananda, a senior Burmese Buddhist monk, and my meditation teacher, he said, "Oh! *That is mindfulness.*"

That really is quite remarkable, considering that Adam Smith probably never heard of Buddhism, much less any of the actual teachings of Gotama! And yet, in 1759, Smith could, and did, independently discover and describe the basic practice of mindfulness! It strongly suggests that this practice involves a universal human ability, available for use by anyone willing to make the effort. And out of this very universality comes a natural opportunity for two of the world's great cultures to constructively engage and reinforce each other, with potential benefits for all the peoples of the world. This is one of the major reasons I believe we are living in genuinely monumental times—for the opportunity to advance the cause of mindfulness in the world is one which your generation must work hard to bring to full fruition!

Mindfulness, the inner observer which is always accessible to us, provides the awareness we need to assess our *mental* actions (thoughts and motives), as well as our outward bodily acts. Because of this tremendous breadth of vision and insight, it actually holds us to a higher and more rigorous standard than other people do. Look at your example: even as a little kid you couldn't "get away with" not doing your homework and lying about it—in the gaze of your own budding Impartial Spectator, you felt badly. And, to the extent that your dad's values sometimes haven't been so great (as when he recently told you to break the rules of your school this fall by getting a car and hiding it off-campus), there is a queasy doubt mixed into your pleasure at his advice or approval.

So you can readily see that your Impartial Spectator is stronger and purer than parents and other merely human authority figures. In fact, it's directly attuned to (in Adam Smith's words) "those principles and rules which Nature has established for the direction of our judgments," by which Smith clearly meant God and His Laws—Laws whose moral content matches so closely the Noble Truths of Gotama. And while Smith knew that looking at ourselves through the Impartial Spectator's eyes requires "a considerable, and even a painful exertion," he also knew that the Impartial Spectator's "early warning system," which Gotama called *hiri* and *ottappa*, can always awaken us to the Moral Law within us:

> It is he who, whenever we are about to act so as to affect the happiness of others, calls to us, with a voice capable of astonishing the most presumptuous of our passions. . . . [T]he natural misrepresentations of self-love can be corrected only by the eye of this impartial spectator. It is he who shows us the propriety of generosity . . . and the deformity of doing the smallest injury to another. . . . It is not the love of our neighbor, it is not the love of mankind, which upon many occasions prompts us to the practice of th[e] divine virtues. It is a stronger love, a more powerful affection . . . the love of what is honourable and noble, of the grandeur, and dignity, and superiority of our own characters.

Their passions forge their fetters.

It is this very love that lays the foundation for *truly* free action. What is our current culture's definition of *freedom?* Isn't it to be free to do and get what you want? Buddhists say that, on the contrary, *true* freedom is freedom *from* what you want— freedom from the fierce mechanisms of basic animal brain function, all of which are driven by grinding sensations of craving and aversion. "Men of intemperate minds cannot be free," observed a wise man of our own Western tradition, the British statesman and philosopher Edmund Burke. "Their passions forge their fetters." To free onself from the endless treadmill of greed ("I *want* it"), ill-will ("Get it *away* from me"), and ignorance ("Don't *bother me* with the truth") requires some insight into the nature of these roots of unwholesome action—which is what we're going to look at next. But that insight will tend to arise spontaneously in a mind imbued with a love of the truth and an appreciation for the honor, nobility, and dignity necessary for the attainment of freedom.

Your friend,
Jeff

TRAINING YOUR MENTAL FORCE II: THE OWNER'S MANUAL FOR YOUR BRAIN

Dear Jeff,

Greetings from Florida in August. My driving course starts tomorrow!

You say, "true freedom is freedom from what you want." But I was thinking about that, and I thought that "I want it" isn't always such a bad or greedy way to think. Don't you always want to improve? If you're setting a goal, and you want to achieve that goal, isn't that good?

Patrick

YOUR "OLD BRAIN": THE DRIVESHAFT

Dear Patrick,

That is a very insightful and sophisticated question. On that very point, the Buddha made a sharp distinction between the material and spiritual worlds. Different, even opposite, Laws govern the realm of the senses and the realm of spiritual striving and self-transcendence.

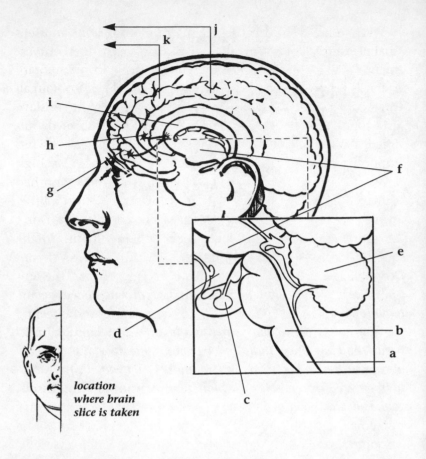

Figure 1. *The location of some key structures of the brain. The solid box shows magnified view of structures contained within the dotted lines.*

a. *SPINAL CORD: sends signals to body*
b. *BRAIN STEM: basic life support control center*
c. *PITUITARY GLAND: hormonal control center*
d. *HYPOTHALAMUS: master switch for survival drives*
e. *CEREBELLUM: coordinates movement*
f. *THALAMUS: switchboard for sensory traffic control*
g. *ORBITAL CORTEX: alerts us when "something's wrong"*
h. *CINGULATE GYRUS: can cause heart-pounding, gut-churning fear*
i. *CAUDATE NUCLEUS: gearbox—part of basal ganglia*
j. *FRONTAL CORTEX: action control and fine tuner*
k. *PREFRONTAL CORTEX: thinking, planning, imagining*

When it comes to desires for material possessions and sensual pleasures, Gotama taught vigilance, restraint, and contentment with what you've got. (His Greek contemporary Heraclitus, too, counseled: "It is better for men not to obtain all that they wish.") These are the kinds of desires that can enslave and torment you, that by their very nature can never be fulfilled. But when it comes to the striving for self-mastery and Innocence, he said, don't be contented even with a very high level of development! He was saying this to monks who had achieved quite a lot, and were letting down their effort a little. Strive ever onward, Gotama said. Never be complacent. Don't be satisfied with anything less than Enlightenment. So the question to ask yourself is, when a voice within you says "I *want* it," who is speaking—the "autopilot" or the "driver," the animal brain or the Impartial Spectator? A similar process occurs when, for example, someone offers you drugs, and the feeling "Get it *away* from me" arises—that's *hiri* and *ottappa*, not ill-will. Learning more about your brain's strengths and weaknesses will help you to tell the difference.

So, by now you've had your first official driving lesson! This is one of those firsts in your life that you'll always remember. Across the street from where I grew up was a shopping center with a big parking lot, and when I was just a beginner I used to go over there early on Sunday mornings and drive around the empty parking lot by myself, practicing. To this day, whenever I see a big, empty parking lot, I remember being sixteen, concentrating on getting the hang of making turns correctly.

Because an automobile is an inanimate machine with no "drives" of its own, you can safely assume that you have the basic abilities required to be a good driver. A reasonably well-running car is going to go where you steer it, at the speed you tell it to go—it has no particular preferences about where it wants to go, or when. It does pretty much what you want it to, usually without arguing. And so aside from practice, all it really takes to control a car is normal vision (or a pair of glasses), decent reflexes, and some common sense about safety and self-preservation. As wonderful as those things are, they're so familiar and work so automatically that you don't have to give them too much thought.

Learning to be a skillful driver of your human nature is a very different story. The basic abilities required of *this* driver—the clear and far-seeing vision of mindfulness, the moral reflexes of *hiri* and *ottappa*—aren't so obvious or automatic. Now that I've pointed them out to you, I'm sure you can recognize times when you've used these spiritual senses to guide you. But unlike your physical senses, they won't function consistently or reliably in the absence of conscious, wise attention. You don't have to work at focusing your eyes; you do have to work at focusing the various aspects of yourself that we might call your "I's." That's why I've taken care to introduce you, in some detail, to the basic skills needed by a top-notch driver—so you'll be really ready when we turn our attention to your own "magic vehicle." It takes a fair amount of basic training just to understand what a driver of the human vehicle is really up against!

Because, as we've noted, your body is not just some powerful but obedient hunk of metal. It's a living creature, built from the genetic code of an animal! And its engine, your brain, has a "driveshaft" at its center which focuses the force of millions of years of struggle for survival. That driveshaft, the *thalamus* and *hypothalamus*, connects with a "gearbox" called the *basal ganglia*, which functions a lot like the automatic transmission of a car. Working closely together, the driveshaft and the gearbox constantly send and receive messages to and from the frontal and prefrontal cortex—areas where you do your thinking, planning, and imagining. This incredibly complex interactive communications system transmits detailed information about what your inner feelings are, and what you should do about them.

Scientists generally agree that the innermost core of our brain, the thalamus, hypothalamus, and basal ganglia, is part of what is often called the "old brain"—structures which we in essence share with reptiles, birds, and the simplest mammals, like opossums and tree shrews. To judge both by anatomy and by a great deal of human motivation and behavior, we have pretty much the same hypothalamus and other "old brain" structures as your basic lizard, crawling around on its belly and hiding under rocks.

The "old brain" is directly involved in generating and coordinating your sensations (painful, pleasurable, and neutral), appetites (including sexual desire), and primitive emotions (like fear and rage)—all responses related to your basic survival as a living organism. However, the intensity and crudeness of these emotional responses is modulated (sort of like the volume, bass, and treble controls on a fine stereo) by the structures of what is called the *limbic system,* a brain region unique to mammals, the animal class to which we humans belong *(see p. 164)*.

This class of animals is characterized by the fact that mammalian mothers nurse and care for their young. Because this requires close social interaction between the mother and her offspring, the great neurobiologist Paul McLean has said that *"the history of the evolution of mammals is the history of the evolution of the family."* It remains to be seen whether we modern humans will prove to be a credit or a disgrace to our animal class. Unless we can reverse many of today's trends, we have reason to fear what's to come. For absent fathers, serial divorces, and overworked or workaholic parents rob young humans of the nurturing and security they need for their brains and their character to develop properly.

Needless to say, the communications system linking our various brain regions involves a web of interconnections so vast it makes the Internet look pathetic! There are those who think someday computers will be able to match the incredible complexity of the human brain. Who knows, they may

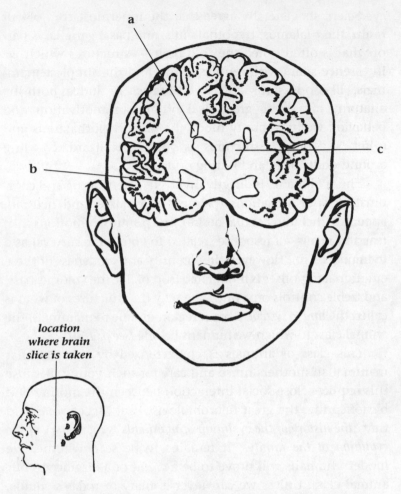

Figure 2. *The location of three key gray matter structures of the brain.*

a. *CAUDATE NUCLEUS: the gearbox/automatic transmission for the front of the brain; part of the basal ganglia habit system*

b. *AMYGDALA: the LIMBIC SYSTEM's central headquarters for emotional regulation and processing*

c. *THALAMUS: the switchboard for control and modulation of sensory signals*

even be right. But after speaking to experts in that field of research, I can guarantee you this: it's an achievement that's not on any horizon anyone alive now can see.

Now, apart from us humans, all other animals have no choice but to interpret the messages from the driveshaft of the old brain as orders which they must obey. Whatever "thinking and planning" they do is exclusively in the service of more efficiently following orders from the thalamus and hypothalamus. If you've ever had a dog or a cat, you know that these animals do appear to anticipate and perhaps even picture what they want—the leash, an open door, a bowl of food. But their prefrontal cortex is so rudimentary that it pretty much restricts them to responding to what's going on at the present moment. We humans, on the other hand, can nurse a grudge or a craving for decades. You don't exactly picture a dog patiently waiting for the moment when he finally runs across that guy who stepped on his tail ten years ago!

The horror of being human is precisely this: that our highly developed prefrontal cortex offers the lower brain centers a virtually unlimited menu of ways to elaborate and indulge their primal passions. The wonder of being human is that we, and we alone, can refuse to be driven by these very powerful but primitive messages from our animal brain driveshaft. At least to some degree we can, in effect, disengage the driveshaft and redirect its power in ways that other animals are incapable of. Because of this, we have a genuine choice. *We can take control of our fabulous brain away from the animal within.* Indeed, as our research at UCLA on OCD (obsessive-compulsive disorder) patients has shown, by changing the ways we humans decide to respond to those "old brain" messages, we can actually change how the wiring of our basal ganglia works! And then our human brain can be a powerful engine for good.

As we go through this blueprint of your engine in a little more detail, Patrick, and talk about the subjective experiences and feelings you have that correspond to electrical activity in some of its structures, I'd like you to remember, and even repeat to yourself, these two phrases: *If I can observe it and describe it, it isn't me*—not the core you, the real you, the driver. And: *What I can observe and describe, I can control.* That capacity for conscious control penetrates remarkably deep into the brain. There is very little, if anything, in a human being that must be totally automatic (although I'd be the first to admit that for some of the most basic of those mechanisms to *stop* being automatic, you'd have to get pretty close to the level of a Jesus or a Gotama).

At the top of the spinal cord, where it enters the skull, is the oldest "brain" of all, called the *brain stem (see diagram on p. 160).* Something quite like it already exists in insects and other animals of the arthropod class—the ones with compound eyes and antennae. This part of your brain is largely, though not totally, out of reach of the driver. While you don't will your heart to beat, and you can't will it to stop beating, you *can* deliberately speed it up or slow it down. Overall, however, the functions of the brain stem are very much of the automatic, or reflex, type. You might say the key to this part of your engine was turned not long after your father's sperm fused with your mother's egg!

For example, you can't decide to stop breathing for long. Your brain stem keeps these basic life-support systems going. You also can't stop the pupils of your eyes from contracting when exposed to a bright light. This reflex reaction is one of the first things emergency medical technicians check at the scene of an accident, because its absence shows that the brain stem is not working properly—and that means that basic life-support systems like breathing, blood pressure, and heartbeat may be in imminent danger of failure.

Just about everything else that is necessary for your survival as an individual organism and for the survival of our species—the maintenance of normal rhythms of waking and sleeping, body temperature, drinking and eating, and the appropriate behavioral expression of fear, aggression, and sex—all of these are regulated in some part of the hypothalamus, with close cooperation from the thalamus, basal ganglia, and limbic system. These brain structures work to focus your attention on those sensory stimuli that are relevant to the survival and reproduction of you as a living animal.

Now, Patrick, please note this carefully: stimuli relevant to survival are of two fundamental kinds—those that promise the fulfillment of basic needs (which you experience as pleasant and attractive), and threats of danger (which you experience as unpleasant, frightening, infuriating, disgusting, etc.). Your "old brain" works to motivate and coordinate your response to these stimuli by arousing emotions and linking them quickly to actions (e.g., danger → rage or fear → fight or run).

In many ways, the hypothalamus could be called the master switch of survival. Among other things, it's the hypothalamus that triggers puberty, signaling the *pituitary gland* (which is connected directly to it) to release the hormones that "switch on" the testes or ovaries and start them producing the sex hormones that have so dramatically changed your body and feelings over the last few years. And the role of the hypothalamus in sexuality doesn't stop there—for sexually mature animals, including humans, that sustain damage to certain parts of the hypothalamus lose all interest in sex. Working closely with the thalamus (sensory regulation), the limbic system (emotional regulation), and the basal ganglia (automatic transmission)—which allows you to automatically shift from one behavioral gear to another and to develop and perform habitual behavior patterns—the hypothalamus supplies the driving force behind what I have called your animal vehicle's "automatic pilot."

But you, as the driver, have the potential ability to disengage that autopilot and hand-fly your vehicle to a remarkable degree. Next time I write, we'll see how deeply conscious control can penetrate even into the dark realm of the "old brain."

Your friend,
Jeff

Dear Jeff,

I used to think learning how to drive a car would be difficult. Compared to the stuff you're telling me, it's nothing!

You wouldn't believe how hot it is down here. I look forward to getting back to New England after Labor Day.

Patrick

THE COSMIC BATTLE FOR
YOUR BRAINPOWER

Dear Patrick,

You've just provided an excellent example of a seemingly automatic function of the hypothalamus.

It's to this crucial part of your brain's "driveshaft" that you owe your body's ability to maintain a constant internal temperature within a degree or so of 98.6 degrees Fahrenheit, whether the air temperature around you is 40 or 90. When you walk out of your dad's air-conditioned condo on your way to your driving lesson, and you quickly begin to get overheated in the muggy furnace of Florida in August, the front of your hypothalamus detects the rise in blood temperature and sends out signals to start you sweating, as well as to relax and expand the blood vessels in your skin so some of your blood's heat can escape through the skin surface. When you then turn up the car's A/C full blast, and after a few minutes you start to get chilled, evidence from animal studies indicates it's the back part of the hypothalamus that responds, ordering blood vessels to contract and—should your blood temperature continue to drop—signaling your muscles to start up heat-generating movements like shivering.

All of this happens without and, you might think, beyond conscious control. So firmly ensconced is the hypothalamus in the driver's seat of our culture—especially since the discrediting of its main counterbalance, religion, among our "intellectual elites"—that we assume much of what it does is totally involuntary (like the regulation of body temperature), and the rest is inevitable (like the male's pursuit of sex, or the female's longing for children). Well, there's a lot more to the human drama than just that! Unlike any other animal, we have the capacity to live truly unique lives, endowed with tremendous subtlety and richness. But

The cosmic battle for your brainpower

to accomplish this worthy goal we must gain access to a power that's unique in all of nature—the power of the Spirit. By applying this power—for example, in the form of an awakened Impartial Spectator—we can exert willful control even over so-called "involuntary" brain centers.

Take temperature regulation, for instance. Australian aborigines used to sleep on the ground, unclothed, even on cold nights. They knew how to suppress the shivering reflex and rest in an energy-conserving state of lowered body temperature till the morning sun warmed them. Some Tibetan Buddhist monks, experienced meditators, can raise the skin temperature of their hands and feet fifteen degrees, or lower their heart and breathing rates to levels that would be dangerous to you or me.

How do people achieve such control over the so-called "involuntary"? I've never personally tried to do any of those things, and Gotama himself said feats such as those are not important for spiritual development. But they are, at the very least, an impressive demonstration of the power of the Impartial Spectator—for I can tell you with confidence that doing such things involves a process of *inner observation*. Remember—if you can observe it, it isn't you, and what you can observe, you can control.

Proof of that comes from the modern practice of biofeedback. A biofeedback machine converts electrical activity in some part of the body or brain (picked up by electrodes) into a signal, say an audible tone, which changes pitch as the electrical activity changes. The tone directs a patient's attention to the subtle inner sensations associated with the change. Once these sensations are recognized and observed, they can be voluntarily controlled. (If you can observe it, you can control it.) By this method, ordinary people, who aren't experienced meditators at all, can learn to deliberately relax the capillaries in their own fingers and toes to gain relief from a painful constriction of these tiny blood vessels in response to cold, called Reynaud's syndrome. They can also learn, among other things, to raise or lower their own blood pressure, and to reduce the hyperactivity of the gut called irritable-bowel syndrome—all in the province of the "automatic" parts of the hypothalamus and brain stem.

But as remarkable as all that is, Patrick, and as much disciplined concentration as it takes—that's the *easy* stuff! Controlling the shivering caused by *fear* takes far more mental discipline than controlling the shivering caused by cold. For as we saw way back when I told you "Look at your hand," it's much easier to step back and observe your body—and therefore, to control it—than to get that same crucial little distance from your emotions and your thoughts. That's why I taught you how to make mental notes! As a human being, your emotions and thoughts form the core of your internal sense of "I." It's quite a revelation (and not a very pleasant one) to discover the extent to which that "I" ordinarily does the bidding of its "master"—the lizard brain!

For the hypothalamus to make your body sweat or shiver in response to heat or cold is a direct and neutral process. But to control your complex behavior—even just to make you go get a cold drink or put on a sweater—the hypothalamus has to involve much *more* of your brain. It has to enlist your basal ganglia and limbic system—dressing up the naked survival drive in a package of habits and feelings that naturally feels like "me" or "mine." ("It's hot! I want a Coke!" or "It's cold! I should put on my sweater!") And then, with lightning rapidity, comes that familiar running commentary of thoughts, opinions, and reflections—indicating that your prefrontal cortex can't help but stick its two cents in: "I like Coke much better than Pepsi," or "I really look great in this sweater!"

Your prefrontal cortex, Patrick, that part of your brain behind your forehead that makes you uniquely human, is where the information from your inner and outer worlds meets. This is the place where your plans are made and the consequences of your actions are thought through. It is here that the weighing of alternatives occurs—a process essential to making informed decisions.

But it's also in the prefrontal cortex, in your thinking mind, where that most subtle and dangerous of all deceptions—self-deception—takes place. For this is where the drives of our "old brain," the one we share with animals, can slyly disguise themselves in that costume of purity and uniqueness we call the Self—*My* goals, *My* wishes, *My* desires. But this, sad to say, is nothing but a charade and a delusion. For from your "animal brain" nothing truly pure or unique can ever come. *Mistaking animal drives for a unique Self* is by far the most common reason for distorted thinking and faulty reasoning about what the *real* consequences of acting like an animal will be. This is the mistake that underlies the vast majority of human tragedies. Tragedies of any other sort are generally considered Acts of God.

So that's the downside—the big mistake to avoid. Animal drives and animal survival are very real and very powerful forces, but pure and unique they are not.

Now here's the upside: it's also right there, in the prefrontal cortex, that your *spirit* has its maximum power to intervene. That is the battleground where the Big War is perpetually fought. This is the energy field that your spirit and your inner animal—empowered by either God or the Devil—are fighting to control and possess.

In Buddhist cultures this battle is personified in the struggle between Gotama and Māra, whose name literally means "Killer," and who the Buddha addressed as "Evil One," "Dark One," and "Enemy of Freedom." He is master of the sensory world and the implacable foe of Enlightenment and liberation. Just as he did everything in his power to hinder Gotama's ascent to Buddhahood, he will wield his weapons, drawn from his arsenal in the world of sensual cravings, attempting to destroy any being who dares to strive for Enlightenment. Like his close ally/alter ego Satan, the world of the inner animal is his most favored habitat—the dark jungle in which he thrives.

Whatever purity and uniqueness the human soul can aspire to will be found by joining the cosmic conflict against these vicious enemies of Truth on the Godly side of the battle. That requires *using the power of your Impartial Spectator to gain control over the animal drives of your hypothalamus.* And failing to heed the Impartial Spectator's call only assures you of being on the wrong side of the struggle—for in this, the most important of all battles, neutrality is not an option.

But you can't take control if you don't know you're out of control! So I'm going to ask you to work with me in a little exercise, one which is basic but has the potential to bring you a taste of Enlightenment. And it's an exercise which, as you continue to practice it, will further strengthen the most important power you possess.

Here's the exercise:

Patrick, try to sit still in a chair, in a quiet room, for twenty minutes, and just watch yourself breathe. (This is Buddhist mindfulness meditation, which I practice for at least an hour every morning.) Pick a time and a place when you can be reasonably sure no one will interrupt you. Close the door to minimize outer distractions. Sit comfortably in a chair, or cross-legged on the floor, with your hands resting in your lap. You can close your eyes, or you can keep them open but unfocused (but closing them is probably easier).

Place your attention on the inner rim of your nostrils, where you can feel the subtle movement of air as you breathe in and out. Now, watch your breathing go in, go out, go in, go out. Make a mental note for each in-breath and out-breath, e.g., "Breathing in," "Breathing out," or "In," "Out." Try to be aware of the entire in-breath, from the time it starts to the time it stops. This is the time to make the mental note "Breathing in," if that's the mental note you choose to make. (As always with mental notes, don't worry too much about the words you use. It's the process of observing that counts.) Then try to be aware of the entire out-breath, from the time it starts to the time it stops. This is the time to make the mental note "Breathing out."

If you suddenly notice that your mind has wandered away from your breathing, just make a mental note of that (e.g., "wandering, wandering"). Then gently bring your attention back to an in-breath or out-breath, and continue observing and making mental notes, as I've just described.

If it sounds simple, that's because it is. But if you think it's going to be easy, my friend, you're in for a surprise.

Let me know what happens when you try this!

Your friend,
Jeff

Dear Jeff,

I didn't try that till I got back to school, which made it harder to find a time when no one would bother me. But I did.

What happened is that I didn't make it to twenty minutes! I couldn't really do it for that long. Within a couple of minutes my mind started taking off. It's surprisingly hard, and kind of frustrating. After about ten minutes I started thinking, "I really should be doing my homework now!"

Talk to you soon,
Patrick

THE ENEMY WITHIN

Dear Patrick,

I'm glad to know that you arrived back at school safely. It's good, too, to hear the results of your meditation exercise.

You are amazed and chagrined at how hard—indeed, for a novice, nearly impossible—it turns out to be to sit quietly and just watch yourself breathe for a "mere" twenty minutes. I know! It's not long—ten seconds? thirty seconds? a minute?—before your mind leaves your in-and-out breath and dashes off down some trail of thought like a hound on the scent of a rabbit. You bring it back, only to watch it take off again . . . and again . . . and again! The novelty of the exercise quickly wears off, and you feel restless and frustrated, annoyed by the monotony of watching your breathing, yet also fascinated by the unexpected difficulty of it. I *know* you must have been getting pretty desperate if you started thinking you should be doing your homework! (Maybe Buddhist mindfulness meditation ought to be introduced into all high schools—to generate *that* thought, if for no other reason!)

Patrick, you can rest assured that this is all entirely normal. Losing track of your breathing doesn't mean you've stopped meditating. Losing track is part of the whole process! *I* still lose track all the time. As long as you're still sitting there, mindfully observing whatever happens, you're still doing it.

I can't improve on what the Venerable Henepola Gunaratana has to say to beginning meditators in *Mindfulness in Plain English:*

> Somewhere in this process, you will come face to face with the sudden and shocking realization that you are completely crazy. Your mind is a shrieking, gibbering mad-

house on wheels barreling pell-mell down the hill, utterly out of control and hopeless. No problem. You are not crazier than you were yesterday. It has always been this way, and you just never noticed. You are also no crazier than everybody else around you. The only real difference is that you have confronted the situation; they have not. So they still feel relatively comfortable. That does not mean that they are better off. Ignorance may be bliss, but it does not lead to Liberation [what we are calling Innocence]. So don't let this realization unsettle you. It is a milestone actually, a sign of real progress. The very fact that you have looked the problem straight in the eye means that you are on your way up and out of it.

That's not to say that that "way" is a short or easy one. Buddhist meditation—sitting still, mindfully watching your own body and mind—is actually the hardest job in the world! And in some countries, like Burma and Sri Lanka, it is the most highly respected. There are people called *Bhikkhus* and *Bhikkhunis* who leave regular life and devote their entire lives to it, and just to see one of them when you walk out your door is considered a blessing. We translate their name as "monks" and "nuns," but in reality they are the highest form of martial artists—heroes and warriors in training, constantly preparing to defend the world from Māra's onslaught. They've dedicated themselves full-time to strengthening mindfulness and taming the mind, because they know the untamed mind is where all the trouble and suffering in the world begins.

But the Buddha clearly stated that this battle isn't just for the monasteries. It must also be carried into the thick of ordinary life by people like you and me. Monasteries are rather like research laboratories, and it's out here in the world that the "medicine" of mindfulness is so acutely needed. The cure lies in clearly seeing the disease in all its manifestations, right down to the most devious and subtle.

There are two very important things you can see even from your brief ten or fifteen minutes of trying to meditate. The first is how driven your mind is, and the second is the nature of what drives it. Actually, there's a third: you now have another "hot line" to your Impartial Spectator. *You can contact your inner friend instantaneously at any time just by noticing your breathing.* Indeed, mindful awareness of in and out breathing is the first meditation described in Gotama Buddha's *Discourse on the Foundations of Mindfulness*—the core text for all Buddhist meditators.

But you've also now met your *enemy* within up close and personal—the one who pretends to be your best friend and, like all false friends, tells you what your animal brain wants to hear. Your animal brain doesn't want the taming discipline of meditation. It tells you, "Aw, that's too hard and boring. My way is better. I make life fun and exciting and fulfilling. Come, run away with me." Whenever you find yourself tempted by this seductive quality of ordinary, untamed thought, know that you are hearing the voice of Māra, the enemy who tested Gotama's strength and courage as he meditated under the Bo tree (as Satan tried to tempt Jesus in the wilderness) and who constantly tries to distract and tempt people away from mindfulness. Māra is the personification and the master manipulator of the animal drives in the human mind.

The Buddha compared the mind—yours, mine, everybody's—to a wild elephant, and meditation to taming this elephant by tying it with a rope (mindful attention) to a plain wooden post (your breathing). At first, the elephant keeps breaking the rope and running away. Similarly, no matter how hard you try, you can't stop the mind by brute force or coercion—as you noticed, you *can't* keep your attention on your breathing by simply ordering it to stay there. The natural tendency of the untamed mind is to wander, to ceaselessly change its object of attention. All you can do is catch it, bring it back, and patiently tie it up again . . . and again . . . and again.

Fortunately, Patrick, mindful attention is a special kind of "rope": the more you use it, the stronger it gets. And as the mind, like the tame elephant, starts to calm down, it becomes a dependable friend and ally—working with you, rather than constantly fighting against you like some unruly foe.

But *why* does this "elephant" keep running off? (It's no accident, of course, that your mind is depicted as an animal that's very dangerous in its wild state.) What is it looking for? For the answer, try and reconstruct two or three of the trains of thought you got lost in during those fifteen minutes. Can you remember any of them? If not, the next time you catch yourself daydreaming, just stop and notice the content of your thoughts. We've already talked about *how* such trains of thought are hooked together: by the principles of similarity, proximity, and cause and effect. But now we're ready to take a closer look at *why*—at the engines driving those trains.

Your friend,
Jeff

Dear Jeff,

I kept thinking about my girlfriend. Over the summer we wrote to each other and talked on the phone, but ever since we got back to school she's been avoiding me. She won't give me a hug, go outside and go for a walk or anything. I've tried to talk to her alone and she tries to ignore me. It's been making me feel like total garbage. While I was sitting there my mind kept going back to that, remembering how good it was last year, wondering what's going on.

I also daydreamed about places I'd like to be and things I'd like to be doing, like whitewater kayaking. I pictured myself run-

ning a river. (I daydream about that kind of stuff a lot, anyway.) I worried about getting the grade back on a test I don't think I did too well on.

Those are just a few of the things I can remember.

Patrick

THE THREE ROOTS OF EVIL:
GREED, ILL-WILL, AND IGNORANCE

Dear Patrick,

Whenever you observe with that kind of honesty, you'll notice that your runaway fantasies and thoughts are of two main kinds.

One kind concerns objects associated with *pleasant* feelings—like your thoughts about your girlfriend's attractive qualities and the good times you had with her last year, or about kayaking on a wild river. The natural, and extremely rapid, reaction of your mind to any pleasant feeling or desirable object is attachment and craving: holding on, wanting more, imagining or plotting how to get it. The theme of this kind of thought is, "I *want* it." From the point of view of our desire-driven popular

Three Roots of Evil that grow in every untamed human mind

and consumer culture, hey—that's what life is all about! But the Buddha didn't mince words: he called this *greed (lobha* in Pāli), and said that it is the first of the Three Roots of Evil that grow in every untamed human mind. When considered as a Root of Evil, *lobha* includes all forms of lust, craving and desire—even very mild forms. (Mild forms, of course, are much less harmful than intense forms.)

Now, greed may seem like a harsh word to use for something as natural as the desire for a romance to continue. But Gotama called it a Root of Evil because it causes suffering—you want things to be the way they were last year, and the reality is they're not. And even if they were, *lobha* would tend to cause clinging to things as they are and blind you to the inevitability of change. Because of things like that, *lobha* is an impediment to seeing clearly and can drive you to act in ways that will harm yourself and others.

The second kind of thought you will notice concerns objects associated with *unpleasant* feelings like fear or anger—for instance, your hurt and resentment at your girlfriend's behavior, or your worry about getting back that test grade, or any other problem, insult, threat, or frustration. Your mind's natural response to unpleasant objects is to immediately start imagining how to either destroy them (fight) or escape them (flight). For example, you fantasize about how you could talk to your girlfriend, even argue with her, to make her hurtful behavior go away. Indeed, the theme of this kind of thought is, "Get it *away* from me." Gotama called this the Second Root of Evil—*aversion* or *ill-will (dosa* in Pāli)—which includes every kind of negative emotion, from boredom to annoyance (like your irritation at the crabby coxswain last summer) to fear, hatred, and rage.

There's actually a third kind of feeling, which is *neutral*—neither pleasant nor unpleasant. But you won't find yourself having a lot of thoughts about neutral feelings, and those you do have will tend to be superficial and fleeting. That's

Every kind of negative emotion

because your mind reacts to neutral feelings with low-level awareness or total unawareness—if it notices them at all, it goes "ho hum" and tunes them out. A good example is how you feel when you hear the sound of "white noise" at medium volume. It's generally neither pleasant nor unpleasant; that's why your mind tends to ignore it. The mind's tendency to fixate only on what it desires and what it hates, and to overlook everything else, is one aspect of what the Buddha called *ignorance (moha)*. The theme of *moha* is "Don't *bother me* with the truth," and it is the Third Root of Evil.

In fact, the Buddha taught that every unwholesome state of mind has at least some *moha* blended into it—you wouldn't harbor thoughts contaminated with greed or ill-will if you were truly wise! But *moha* can also exist in the absence of these other two roots of suffering and mental torment. A typical example of ignorance in its pure form would be the distracted restlessness of an aimless, wandering mind.

The most common and potentially lethal form of *moha* is denying or ignoring the inescapable truth that your willful actions are going to ripen into consequences. Relieving beings of the suffering caused by this type of ignorance was viewed by the Buddha as one of his most urgent missions.

Maybe, Patrick, you can now begin to match some of these common ways your mind behaves with what you've already learned about the brain!

Yup—you're looking at the telltale pawprints of the Lizard Brain on your very own prefrontal cortex! Remember—the "old brain" is interested only in what will either advance (pleasant) or threaten (unpleasant) the physical survival of your genetic code—that is, the kinds of things involved in perpetuating the species. Anything neutral, it scans and dismisses.

We scientists actually have a pretty good idea how this works in the brain. The information from all your sense organs except smell must pass through the thalamus before reaching your frontal and prefrontal cortex. The thalamus acts like an extremely complex traffic-control system that— *in the absence of mindful awareness*—rapidly directs sensory information to a wide variety of destinations, and does so in an extremely efficient and highly automated fashion. For example, in close "consultation" with the limbic system, the thalamus can screen incoming sensory data for the type and amount of emotional charge it carries, and then rapidly activate other brain areas in order to initiate a response and/or process the information further.

What this all adds up to is that if you're not alert and mindful, your prefrontal cortex may never even get full, true, and accurate news of the world. It—and you—will tend to get only a tabloid version of reality from the propagandists and censors of the animal brain. (This is what Heraclitus meant when he said, "The eyes and ears are bad witnesses for men if they have barbarian souls.") This would provide a highly distorted and sensationalistic picture of the world, yourself, and other people, designed to get you to do what your animal brain wants you to do and go where it wants you to go (which often is straight into trouble!). As a result, many important activities would be performed with little or no thought about possible long-term consequences—they'd basically be animal responses, pure and simple. In other words, don't ever depend on your thalamus to send your prefrontal cortex the message, "What if she gets pregnant?" If your thalamus (and hypothalamus!) gets that message, it'll only be because *you* ordered your prefrontal cortex to send it downstream in the direction of the gland department.

Now, there's no denying it's natural to travel through the world guided solely by feelings of pleasure and pain, motivated and driven entirely by the forces of desire and aversion. But the Buddha's great insight is that *to live like this is to live a lie.* For it represents a total surrender to the deceptions of the animal brain (and its "Big Boss Man" Māra) about what the true nature of reality is, what it all really means for you, and what condition you'll end up in if you keep reacting like an animal.

Remember, I told you that one of our culture's most dangerous errors is equating natural with good, when in reality, the Buddha taught in his First Noble Truth, nature is filled with suffering. The animal tendencies of craving, aversion, and blindness to the Truth beyond the five physical senses are natural, for sure—but they are called the "Roots of Evil" because they perceive fellow sentient, suffering beings as nothing but objects of, or obstacles to, your desires. It's easy to "run over" another person when you don't even see them, but that's what happens all the time when the animal brain is in the driver's seat. Do you think the people who have hurt you in your life really *saw* you? Do you think your girlfriend is really seeing you right now? If she did, would she be able to hurt you like this? Have you *really seen* the people *you've* hurt?

Yet nothing about a human being has to be totally automatic. Through the application of mindful awareness, you can actually gain increased access to the traffic-control system of the thalamus, opening your mind to an ever-widening panorama of the Truth—including even subtler aspects of it, such as the real feelings of another person, or the long-term consequences of an action. These sorts of considerations don't concern your animal brain at all—but they are absolutely essential to your quest for Innocence.

Keep on trying to meditate, Patrick. And whenever you remember during the day, use mental notes to observe your thoughts and feelings. I promise you that whatever happens with your girlfriend, these tools will help you to keep your balance and handle it more wisely. There's a saying that "Mindfulness takes care of the people who practice it." Practice it, and you will find that out.

Your friend,
Jeff

Dear Jeff,

After a week of avoiding me, and a lot of pressure from my friends, my (ex) girlfriend finally told me she wants to break up. It really hurt my feelings that she couldn't just tell me the first night. On top of that, she's been making fun of me for being so involved in rowing—and she was the reason I got into it in the first place! That was a really low blow for me and she understood that and did it anyway. I never did anything mean to her; I tried so hard—I've never been so nice to anyone in my life! I've sort of figured out that she has little regard for people's feelings. It's a big surprise—I used to think of her a lot differently last year.

Is that what you mean when you talk about how your brain censors things, and gives you a distorted picture, a sensationalistic picture of the world?

We were reading Chaucer in English class, and I don't know if you ever read the Miller's Tale, but it sort of ran parallel to that idea. It's about craving immediate pleasure, the idea of trying to satisfy yourself immediately. There are two characters in the story, one that has that point of view and the other who isn't like that. He has a desire but he doesn't go about just trying to satisfy it immediately.

"Do you think the people who have hurt you in life really saw you?" I thought that was good. It's something I wonder about a lot: why so many people don't seem to care that their actions are hurting other people. And you're saying that they don't even realize what they're doing. It gets me down sometimes. Even some of my close friends, who I think are good people, sometimes I don't really want to be around them because of the way they act. I mean, I've definitely hurt people's feelings, too, but it made me feel really badly. I'm a little more aware of it than my friends, I think. And I feel almost like that's really—lonely.

Are there ways to get your friends to be more aware?

Actually, I've been doing that (meditation) a lot. (I still haven't gotten up to twenty minutes.) It relaxes me, and makes me feel less lonely.

Patrick

THE SUBLIME MODES OF LIVING

Dear Patrick,

You talk about awareness and kindness being lonely. It IS lonely! But the Buddhist perspective is that a meditator cultivates solitude, because so much of the time spent with other people is wasted time!

Don't get me wrong—it's good to have friends. And it's good, though challenging, to have a girlfriend, and painful to lose her. When you've decided you're really going to try, when you do everything you possibly can and you're *still* left alone—which Gotama strongly advised as being *much* better than the company of *bad* friends—those are the moments when you really begin to understand the Buddha's First Noble Truth: Suffering. (Of which he gave "separation from those one holds dear" as a cardinal example!)

I started doing meditation largely as a result of the pain of rejections I'd gone through. I had made very heartfelt attempts to develop relationships, one major attempt in college and one in the first year of medical school, that didn't work, largely because I didn't know how to play the game and didn't particularly want to learn. Like you, I was seeking a level of sincere communication that's genuinely rare. I have never given up. And I will say the same thing to you: don't settle for less. Go forward, be sincere, clear your mind and your brain, be free. As T. S. Eliot said, in a line from his greatest poem, "Four Quartets," that I repeat to myself all the time: "So Krishna, as when he admonished Arjuna on the field of battle. Not fare well, but fare forward, voyagers." (In the sacred Hindu epic *Bhagavad-Gita,* Krishna is a god, Arjuna a great warrior.)

How can you help others to be more aware? You have to do that with a lot of awareness and care yourself, because if you're too assertive, people in the grip of their animal brains are going to resent it. Speak the truth, quietly and firmly, and some people will respond. And the people who do are going to be your real friends, though there may not be many. And the people who don't—like your ex-girlfriend, perhaps—you're just going to let go of. And meditation will tide you over the lonely times. The Buddha himself will be your companion on this road.

The reason why meditation makes you feel less lonely is because it has a cleansing effect on your craving. It's uprooting mental impurities. Greed, ill-will, and ignorance, and the suffering they cause, cannot coexist with mindfulness, any more than darkness can coexist in the same space with light. So in any moment when you succeed in observing yourself mindfully, *in that moment* you are freed from loneliness because you are free of craving—even though, a moment later, you can get lost in thinking and craving again! But that

Greed, ill-will and ignorance cannot coexist with mindfulness.

Peace is *always* available within you. And in the moments when you attain it, you'll begin to realize how much of the world's Beauty we normally miss—subtle things that enter our senses but never make it into our conscious awareness because the animal brain filters them out.

Take your breathing, for instance. It isn't particularly pleasant, and it certainly isn't unpleasant. So your animal brain judges it irrelevant. Talk about ignorance—it only happens to be the mystery that sustains your life and connects you to every other living thing! But your animal brain doesn't want to watch something so repetitive and unexciting. It would much rather entertain itself by screening its own private X-rated sex scenes, action sequences, and disaster extravaganzas. It is so addicted to sensation, both pleasant and unpleasant, that it dreams them up even when they're not present. But if you *make mental notes of those enticements* instead of getting hooked by them, that is, if you remain mindful, use wise attention, and come back to your breathing, you will make some remarkable discoveries.

"Breathing, which seems so mundane and uninteresting at first glance, is actually an enormously complex and fascinating procedure," Ven. Gunaratana writes in *Mindfulness in Plain English.* "It is full of delicate variations, if you look . . . and a constant cycle of repeated patterns. It is like a symphony. Don't observe just the bare outline of the breath. . . . Every breath has a beginning, middle and end. Every inhalation goes through a process of birth, growth, and death and every exhalation does the same. The depth and speed of your breathing changes according to your emotional state, the thought that flows through your mind, and the sounds you hear. . . . If the breath seems an exceedingly dull thing to observe over and over, you may rest assured of one thing: you have ceased to observe the process with true mindfulness. Mindfulness is never boring. Look again. . . . Mindfulness looks at everything with the eyes of a child, with a sense of wonder." And wonder, Patrick, is a facet of the human mind that brings us closer to the Divine.

Animals take the flawed, but real, miracle of this world for granted. Because no animal can do this: deliberately redirect the traffic flow of sense information surging through its thalamus, and choose to focus in on *more* of what it's seeing, hearing, tasting, etc. The directing and focusing of an animal's attention is done largely by the automated traffic-control mechanisms of the thalamus. That's why nonhuman animals are aware of little more than where their next meal or mate is coming from. It takes a human to willfully override those mechanisms and actively decide what to pay attention to.

And the human mind is capable of a lot more than that! For example, humans can experience a deep sense of awe and reverence when faced with the marvels that reveal themselves to exquisitely focused wise attention. Curiosity is about the best animals can do. Further, and perhaps most important, a human, but no animal, can ask the critical and life-altering question, "Is my attention going *toward* or *away from* the Truth?" That's the *really* big question—the one that takes the differences between the human mind and the animal mind to the *spiritual* level. For in striving for the Truth, human beings have the capability to transcend not only their animal natures but the very bounds of humanity itself.

We humans have within us the capacity to attain what the Buddha called the "Sublime Modes of Living": loving-kindness (wishing others to be safe and happy), compassion (the sincere wish for the relief of others' suffering), sympathetic joy (rejoicing in another's happiness), and equanimity (mental balance regarding all things, both agreeable and disagreeable). These supremely wholesome states require a human mind (at least!) to attain because a significant degree of mindful awareness is necessary for all of them. These "Sublime Modes" are a natural flowering that comes from cultivating the Three Roots of Good—generosity, goodwill or benevolence, and wisdom. We must develop and strengthen these Three Good Roots, from which all wholesome actions spring, to rid ourselves of their opposites, greed, ill-will, and ignorance, the Three Roots of Evil from which all unwholesome actions spring.

So different, so opposed, are these two ways of using your mind and relating to the world that one branch of our own Western tradition—mystical Judaism—explicitly says they are at war.

Did it ever occur to you that you might actually have *two* souls?

Your friend,
Jeff

Dear Jeff,
No, to be honest, it didn't. I'm not even sure what that question means.

Patrick

THE ANIMAL SOUL VS.
THE DIVINE SOUL

Dear Patrick,

Well, I'll tell you about at least one thing it means. In an eighteenth-century book of instruction in prayer and morality, *The Tanya*, Rabbi Schneur Zalman teaches us that "there are two souls, waging war one against the other in [every ordinary] person's mind, each one wishing and desiring to rule over him and pervade his mind exclusively." Rabbi Zalman calls these two opponents fighting within each of us the "animal soul" and the "divine soul." He describes them as follows: "All thoughts of Torah [Holy Scripture] and fear of Heaven come from the divine soul, while all [thoughts of] mundane matters come from the animal soul."

What a wonderfully clear and graphic description of the struggle for possession of your prefrontal cortex that goes on between the old brain and your sovereign spirit: two souls (the animal soul and the divine soul), waging war against each other in the mind of every ordinary (that is, non-saintly) person. As Rabbi Yosef Wineberg notes, in his commentary on the passage quoted above, "The mind is thus not only the battleground, but also the prize, the object of the battle between the two souls." It doesn't get much clearer than that!

Rabbi Zalman obviously also knew exactly why you had so much trouble watching your breath! In *The Tanya* he writes, "It is known that the way of combatants, as of wrestlers, is that when one is gaining the upper hand the other likewise strives to prevail with all the resources of his strength. Therefore, when the divine soul exerts itself and summons its strength for prayer [and meditation], the animal soul also gathers strength at that time to confuse her by means of a foreign thought of its own." Many people become discouraged, Rabbi Zalman observes, because they mistakenly believe that having such foreign thoughts means they're not praying or meditating properly. That would be true *if* it was the same soul that did both our praying or meditating and our fantasizing. "The real truth, however," the rabbi says, "is that there are two souls waging war against each other," each of them constantly working to gain control over a person's mind.

So your acting-up, runaway mind doesn't in any way mean you're a failure at meditation (unless you give in and let it run away with you). On the contrary, according to the Rabbi—it means you've succeeded in alarming Māra, who is threatened by your striving for mindfulness because he's afraid of losing control of you. (The fact that Rabbi Zalman never heard the name Māra obviously doesn't mean he didn't know about his bag of tricks!) *"Get him,"* Māra whispers to your animal soul, which immediately follows orders from its "Big Boss Man" and unleashes a torrent of appetites, fantasies, distractions, temptations, and obsessions that are designed to totally capture you. But you should only take this as a challenge, *The Tanya* says, "to draw fresh strength, and intensify [your] effort with all [your] power, to concentrate . . . with increased joy and gladness."

If it's such a struggle to remain mindful when you're just sitting quietly by yourself in meditation or prayer, no wonder it's so much more challenging out in the world, where a constant barrage of temptations and threats keeps coming at you! (You could think of meditation as part of your daily workout, building strength for the world-class race of life.) And just to make things *really* challenging, it's been designed so you've got to deal with the greed, ill-will, and ignorance of other people, as well as your own! Having a little trouble keeping your aim steady with a cloud of enemy fire whizzing by your ears? Well, welcome to Reality! But even in the midst of the most intense situation or emotion, remember that you can always contact your Impartial Spectator in an instant, just by remembering your breathing or by making a mental note. (Deeply religious people do essentially the same thing—call on the power and clarity of the Spirit—when they say, "Lord, help me," or "Thy will be done.")

First of all, observe your own thoughts and feelings. If they take the form of "I *want* it," "Get it *away* from me," or "I don't want to know about it" ("Don't *bother me* with the truth"), you can be sure they are coming from your animal brain and soul (compliments of Team Māra!). That means that, by definition, they are blinding you to what's really out there, trying to lure you down the wrong road and into vulnerability, insecurity, and harm. But you can choose not to look at the world through that distorting fog. Once you recognize that it's there, you become able, with the laser beam of mindfulness, to look right through it, seeing your own goals and plotting your own truly human course to them.

The crossroads of the True and False paths exists in only one place—your mind. Every time you encounter something that evokes a pleasant, unpleasant, or neutral feeling, you have an instantaneous choice of how to respond. You can react automatically, like an animal: pleasure triggers craving (a form of suffering in itself), and craving drives you toward heedless taking; unpleasure triggers anger or fear, and their misery drives you to blindly strike out or wimp out; neutrality triggers the mindless channel-surfing response, and a potentially awe-inspiring piece of reality slips by unnoticed. But you can also refuse to let yourself be jerked around by the animal brain like a puppet on a string. Instead, you can stand tall and observe it with your Impartial Spectator's penetrating clarity and all the freedom and control that gives you.

Next time I write, we'll take a practice spin. Now, I'm sure your driving instructor didn't make you take your first test drive on Interstate 95. On the same principle, I'm going to steer clear for the moment of complex maneuvers and start with a deliberately simple, straightforward demonstration of how you can "take the wheel" away from your animal brain. The maneuver I have in mind is *so* simple, it's one I'm sure you've done already. And yet it's directly relevant to the kind of "delay of gratification" you were sharp enough to spot in Chaucer's "Miller's Tale"—and that, in turn, will prove critical for achieving your highest professional and personal goals.

You know how it is when you're studying for an exam, or writing a paper, or working out, and you're really in a groove—and suddenly your stomach growls. . . .

Your friend,
Jeff

THE GROWL OF THE BEAST

Dear Patrick,

A growling stomach in the middle of an intense study or workout session hardly poses a major moral dilemma. Yet it's a familiar situation, and one that offers a clear, simple example of how your vehicle works on automatic pilot, how it works when the decision-making power of your conscious will takes control of the wheel—and how surprisingly different the consequences can be . . . especially when we're talking about not just a single incident but a habitual way of responding to promptings from the animal brain.

You've probably always assumed that when your stomach got empty, it simply growled to be filled. By now, however, you won't be too surprised to learn that, since hunger is a basic survival need, your stomach is actually following orders from . . . yes, your hypothalamus. In this case, animal studies indicate, an area along the side of the hypothalamus detects low levels of sugar (glucose) and fatty acids in your blood, and then sends a message to your stomach to contract—an event you experience as hunger pangs.

Here's an overview of the basic wiring plan, showing how intimately all the brain structures I've been telling you about cooperate and communicate to bring about your basic "let's eat" behavioral response. (The deep complexities of a family meal or a dinner date we'll save for after you're in college!)

Your *hypothalamus* starts things off by making you feel a craving for food.

Your *limbic system* quickly supplies all the emotional associations of eating. As mammals, who are always nursed at the start of life, our brains are wired to associate eating not only with physical comfort and pleasure but also with emotional security and companionship.

Your *prefrontal cortex* then obligingly cooks up a menu plan, which may come complete with full-color fantasy illustrations you can almost smell and taste.

Assuming this ancient sequence of brain mechanisms, developed and time-tested over several thousand millennia, succeeds in persuading you to "Eat Now," your *frontal cortex* will then direct your *basal ganglia* (the automatic transmission) to "Take me to the refrigerator!"

Parts of the brain concerned with actually moving your muscles then spring into action.

The *thalamus* is the traffic cop that keeps this incredibly complex multilayered message flow running smoothly. (Countless other message flows are being processed at the same time!) And since the thalamus also stays in constant contact with the prefrontal cortex, and can jump-start it at a moment's notice, the thinking and planning centers can revise this entire game plan within milliseconds if called upon (or directed!) to. In response to a sudden change of context—for instance, a new priority (the phone rings) or a flash of insight (Hey! I just figured out how to solve that problem!)—your vehicle is capable of turning on a dime.

Now, the natural thing to do when you're hungry—what life-forms have done for millions of years—is to follow the flow of nerve impulses from the old brain, get up, and go get food. And there are plenty of times when that's fine—though I must say that people from more traditional cultures, even Europe, think our American habit of random snacking is savage, more like the daylong browsing and munching of gorillas than like proper human dining, which is by its very nature social and ritual, and filled with the profound complexities found in all human interactions.

We humans are faced with a dilemma. We cannot do without our core animal heritage—eating to stay alive, sex to make babies. Yet we spontaneously feel *hiri*, a kind of aesthetic disgust and embarrassment, at the primitive rawness of our animal appetites (just think of the grotesque obesity of the late comedian Chris Farley, and imagine what it must have been like to watch him eat when he was on a binge), and *ottappa,* or dread, at the intensity of the cravings which drive these activities, rendering them constantly susceptible to spinning out of control—especially when things go wrong, which they always do. (Poor Chris Farley, again, being only an extreme example!)

The truly civilized solution, which humans through the millennia have applied to this eternal problem, calls for *the intense application of custom and ceremony* at precisely those points where the hypothalamus is most powerful. Hence, all the traditional ritual around puberty, dating, and weddings—and hence the insistence in most human cultures on sitting down together with extended family and friends and saying grace before having several courses of beautifully cooked and served food, eaten in accordance with the table manners observed in that locale. (Obeying the simple command "Mind your manners" may be the most practical example of elementary mindfulness there is!)

It's all a far cry from a drive-thru double cheeseburger with fries! And it's worth noting that countries where people sit down to meals together generally have less trouble with obesity, eating disorders, and heart disease. They also have stronger bonds between parents and adolescent children. A lot more goes on at mealtime than just fueling up.

Still, there's basically nothing wrong with getting something to eat when you're hungry—*unless,* that is, you are in the middle of doing something too important to interrupt. If you take a break in the middle of writing an important paper or working out, you may lose your groove. You've probably had that common experience—when even a modest degree of hunger grabbed your attention, and thoughts about food started to create a distraction, leading you to push aside what you were working on, even *before* you got up and went for a quick sandwich. When you came back an hour later—or several hours, if, as often happens, you got further distracted by turning on the TV—you were no longer hot. Your train of thought, or your motivation to work out, was lost. If you managed to get back to work at all, it was a struggle.

We could say, in this case, that your animal soul had won a small victory over your divine soul. And, of course, there were consequences.

The obvious price of giving in to the immediate urgings of your animal soul was that you lost a chance to further improve the quality of your schoolwork or your athletic performance. (Economists call this the opportunity cost: whatever you do is done at the price of using that time to do something else.)

Where people sit down to meals together

JEFFREY M. SCHWARTZ

The less obvious, but more insidious price, Patrick, was that you made it just a little more likely that you'll take the same path of least resistance next time. So in essence, you not only blew an opportunity to grow just a little bit stronger, you also became (mentally, at least) just a little bit weaker, the moment you allowed yourself to keep walking, automatically, to the refrigerator. . . .

Your friend,
Jeff

Dear Jeff,

That happens to me a lot when I'm swimming. My stomach growls, and then I'll start thinking about how hungry I am, 'cause there's nothing else to think about. I can get carried away by that, and I guess it could affect my performance. But I don't actually let it interrupt me very often. My stomach has growled when I'm studying, but I hardly ever stop and get up. I'm conscious that it's there, but I try to keep my focus.

Sometimes at night I can't study, so I'll just go to bed. Because I think about my bed too much. And if I'm tired I don't study as efficiently, so it kind of takes me twice as long to study the same thing. So just going to sleep and then waking back up is better.

Patrick

PROGRAMMING YOUR BRAIN'S HABIT SYSTEM

Dear Patrick,

You've raised a very interesting issue—how to tell when your animal brain is tempting you to goof off, and when it's alerting you to a legitimate bodily need. The Buddha had a very sensible attitude toward the needs of the body, which he called "the Middle Path." He taught that while the body shouldn't be overindulged, neither should it be overly deprived, because that kind of unnecessary suffering doesn't help you attain Mindfulness. Getting enough, but not too much, of needs like food and sleep is most helpful.

Now, getting sleepy during meditation (which I'll bet has already happened to you) *can* be one of Māra's favorite tricks to stop you from becoming mindful—but sometimes it just means you really need sleep! How do you tell the difference? Well, Sayadaw U Pandita, in an excellent book on meditation, *In This Very Life*, recommends "Eight Ways to Stay Awake," some of which are strengthening your resolve, making more detailed mental notes, remembering or reciting inspiring passages of the Buddha's teaching, pulling on your ears, washing your face, and gazing at a bright light. "If none of these techniques work," he says, "[f]inally, a graceful surrender would be to go to bed." That's why I have made it a habit to do my meditation when you do your best studying—in the morning!

I am very glad you make it a practice to keep your focus when you're studying, and not let a growling stomach interrupt you. Have you noticed that that response (or nonresponse) to hunger has become fairly effortless, in fact almost automatic? That's because your brain's *habit system* basically works like a behavioral Xerox machine: it copies whatever behavior you put into it. So life is much easier when you put good ones in! The basic principle is very simple: the more you've done a behavior in the past, the more likely you are to do it in the future—especially when you're not thinking much about it. (Here's the *really* simple formula: For anything you happen to do, the more you do it, the more you do it! Consider this a corollary of the Law of Karma, i.e., what you do has results.)

You know from your athletic training that the more often you repeat an action the easier it gets, till you can perform it automatically, with almost no conscious thought at all. At that point you own that move, because it's programmed into your basal ganglia, your brain's automatic transmission. Well, it works exactly the same way with all other kinds of actions *(karma)* as it does with physical actions. And that means that the basal ganglia can be your best friend or your worst enemy, depending entirely on what *you* program into it. *Each time you unthinkingly do what your animal vehicle tells you to, you wire basic animal drives directly into the automatic transmission.* This tends to lock in the autopilot and bypass the driver—which makes it much harder (though never impossible) for the driver to take control.

On the other hand, when your stomach growls, and you notice it but keep on working, in effect you do spontaneously what making mental notes teaches you to do consciously and precisely. Instead of thinking "I'm so hungry, I want something to eat," you note your hunger as something separate from you. ("If I can observe it, I can control it.") Then you make an inner decision: *I'm on a roll. I don't want to lose my rhythm. I can get something to eat later.* This kind of inner decision is called a *mental resolve.* Gotama, when describing the process of making such a resolve during meditation practice, frequently used these words: "The meditator rouses his will, makes an effort, stirs up his energy, exerts [literally, "stretches forth"] his mind and strives."

You generally do have to strive, at least at first, to ignore your hunger. It takes effort. But then, deprived of the fuel of your *unwise* attention—the fantasizing and ruminating that just gets the animal brain revved up (and that you've noticed can weaken you while you're swimming)—the hunger usually dwindles in strength and fades into the background. And, of course, the more effort you put into mindfully focusing your *wise* attention on the task at hand, the faster and more completely the hunger fades.

Even if the hungry feeling is still there, lingering, it loses its power to bother you. For stretches of time, you remain untouched and unfazed by it. You finish your assignment or your workout, and *then* you go to eat. In this way, not only do you get done what you need to get done—but the sandwich tastes even better! Things always do when they're not tainted by the "bad taste in your mouth" left by good work undone— when they can be experienced with the satisfaction that a clear mind brings. And a clear mind is what your Guardians *hiri* and *ottappa* (those powerful enemies of "bad taste") always give you, when you're wise enough to heed them!

This whole process is really quite remarkable. No animal can do it, that's for sure. Because in every other animal, the link between "hungry feeling" and "get food" is almost totally automatic. So, for that matter, is the link between "sexual urge" and "have sex," or "get mad" and "fight." Animals can't turn the other cheek, as Jesus advised, or restrain their sex drive out of consideration for a partner's feelings. (Animals' drives are regulated mainly by automatic hormonal cycles and by competing drives, as when fear of a stronger opponent overcomes aggression, or immediate danger temporarily suppresses hunger or the mating urge.)

In the animal brain, to sum up, the basic wiring works roughly like this:

hypothalamus (survival drives) ↔ limbic system (emotions) ↔ basal ganglia (gearbox) ↔ thalamus (traffic control/switchboard) ↔ cortex (action control & fine tune) ↔ behavioral responses

It's a system with proven ability to perform quick, highly efficient, and essentially automatic actions—all in the service of keeping the messages encoded in a bunch of DNA moving on down the generational assembly line. These very same links are wired into *your* brain, too—but with one huge difference. You have the unique ability (though most of us don't use it nearly enough) to *observe* the arising feeling ("hungry, hungry"), *notice* how it's immediately followed by the impulse to action ("walk, walk;" "eat, eat"), and then *interrupt* that automatic brain circuitry, and, by deliberately choosing a different action *(karma)*, activate—and even create—*entirely new* brain circuits.

Some of these newly activated circuits may even carry messages not ordained by the merely physical laws of nature, but rather handed down through thousands of years of human civilization. Some may even reflect the kinds of messages which can only be received directly from a spiritual source. By refining your receptivity to messages of that sort, through sustained observation and reflection during meditation or prayer, you can even develop the power to significantly transcend mere animal drives and goals. Monks and nuns, for instance, commit themselves to forgo the transmission of the message in their DNA, in the service of pursuing and communicating an even more important, noncarnal, message. And the names "Christ" and "Buddha" signify human beings who were *totally* free of any remnant of their animal natures—so free that they had *become* the message.

Look around you at the world we live in today. Every good and life-enhancing human achievement you see (and every one you yourself, Patrick, will contribute) springs directly from our unique ability to replace activities generated by old animal brain circuits with new behaviors which are developed with the help of advanced brain circuitry—circuitry created and installed as part of the evolution of human culture. And human culture only evolves towards wisdom and Truth when it is aided and abetted by the messages of great spiritual leaders. In stark contrast are clever but horrific "achievements" like Hitler's Final Solution—complex plans for mechanized genocidal massacre, engineered as a result of the old brain seizing control of the prefrontal cortex's stupendous thinking, planning, and imagining capabilities.

It's of absolutely *paramount importance* for you to realize this: the moment you *choose* a different course of action, *at that very moment,* you not only change your *karma*, you also change your *brain!* And of course the moment you *do* the action, you greatly accentuate both of those changes, and magnify the results they will bring—in part because the actions you choose continuously reshape and reprogram your brain's habit system.

In short, Patrick, always remember this simple formula: *Whatever* action you do, the more you do it, the more you do it! Put that together with the fact that **ACTIONS HAVE CONSEQUENCES**, and you'll really understand the meaning of two old sayings: "Habit is character" and "Character is fate"! Or, as Heraclitus put it around 500 B.C., "Character for man is destiny."

Your friend,
Jeff

Jeff—
How do you know that "interrupting an automatic action" and "choosing a different action" actually changes the brain?

Patrick

USING YOUR MIND TO
CHANGE YOUR BRAIN

Dear Patrick,

The scientific evidence for it comes from our PET scans of OCD patients' brains before and after they practice a form of self-treatment which is based on the use of the Impartial Spectator.

People with obsessive-compulsive disorder have a brain problem: they're getting a false alarm signal from their limbic system, which gets stuck and keeps telling them over and over again that something terrible will happen if they don't wash their hands, check the door lock, or whatever their particular compulsion happens to be. This is true even though they just *did* the compulsive behavior fifty times, and know that there is no real need to do it again.

The PET scans of OCD patients show abnormally high, and very highly synchronized, energy use in three key parts of the brain: the *orbital cortex*, which alerts us when something's wrong in our environment; the *cingulate gyrus*, which makes our hearts pound and our stomachs churn when we're scared; and the *caudate nucleus*, the part of the basal ganglia gearbox that regulates these two structures. (See diagram on p. 160.) In essence, the signals from these brain structures are "locked in gear," which is why I use the term "Brain Lock" to describe the process. Brain Lock causes the minds of OCD patients to be bombarded with very intense, persistent, and bothersome survival-related animal danger signals. The reason why OCD patients will then often do repetitive compulsive behaviors, which they know are nonsensical, is just to try to make the extremely uncomfortable feelings of dread go away.

But they don't: in fact, when you yield to them those feelings just get stronger! It turns out that for OCD patients to change the brain signal and alleviate the dreadful feelings,

How Māra treats his prisoners once he's ensnared them

they must learn to *ignore* the uncomfortable feeling and *not* give in to it. By not giving in, and doing healthy behaviors instead, they actually *change* the Brain Lock signal, and begin to get relief.

There's a big message for *everyone* in this process of OCD self-treatment. Because what's true of the Brain Lock signals in the brain of a person with OCD is also true of the normal and natural animal brain signals we've just been talking about. Whether it's hunger, anger, or sex, *the more you unthinkingly obey it, the stronger the signal and the stronger its control over you becomes.* You've probably noticed it yourself: the angrier you get, the angrier you get. Or even, the more aroused you get, the more aroused you get. And when it comes to overeating, it couldn't be more obvious—the more you pig out, the more you pig out. But the more you mindfully observe, the more you have a choice.

Of course, the big difference between normal signals and Brain Lock signals is that, unlike with OCD symptoms, there will be times when you decide it is appropriate to eat, engage in emotionally meaningful sexual activity, or even get angry. (Sometimes, the expression of controlled and focused anger can actually wake someone up and stop them from doing something harmful. Jesus, for example, used anger appropriately when he drove the money-changers out of the temple.) The whole point is that *you decide,* based on a clear and true view of the situation, what the appropriate behavior is, and when it's time to stop and/or control it. What you should *never* do is follow the path that's sure to lead to suffering for yourself and others—the path of blindly obeying your animal brain, and to hell with the truth and the consequences. Unless you're one of that not-too-select group of fools who insist on finding out firsthand how Māra treats his prisoners once he's ensnared them. (Here's a hint: he's definitely not into rehabilitation or early parole. And being "in for life" is just the warm-up.)

When OCD patients learn how to make mental notes, to observe and label their OCD thoughts and feelings correctly as obsessions and compulsions, and to recognize them as false signals from a malfunctioning brain, they gain the power to willfully change *how they respond* to those signals—which actually changes *how the brain works.* And while normal greed, lust, and aggression aren't malfunctions—they're here precisely because they function so well to keep animals alive—you *can* label and recognize them as *primitive* signals from your *animal* brain. This will help prevent you from responding to them like a puppet and increase your ability to control *your own* responses to your animal brain signals. Over time, Patrick, this strengthens your mental power—a.k.a. your divine soul—by increasing the control your civilized brain has over your animal brain and the animal soul associated with it.

Here's a crucial point to remember: when OCD patients

make mental notes of OCD thoughts and feelings, *it doesn't make those thoughts and feelings go away.* Likewise, be prepared for the fact that making mental notes of your greed, lust, and aggression won't make *them* go away, either. But although their powerful emotions and compulsive urges were still there, the OCD patients began to become *separate* from them. They could now say to themselves, "It's not me, it's just my brain—and I *know better* than to pay attention. What's more, I *certainly* don't have to obey—I'm going to refocus my attention on a healthy, constructive behavior. That's the path to self-empowerment."

This is the essence of wise attention, and it set those patients free. They could now (with effort!) bypass that pathological Brain Lock link between the limbic system (emotion) and the basal ganglia (action). Instead, they could use their conscious will to direct the basal ganglia gearbox to activate a different motor circuit and *do something else*—something enjoyable and at least somewhat worthwhile, such as gardening, rollerblading, listening to music, or even playing a computer game. They worked at doing these activities for at least fifteen minutes at a time, using mindful awareness to avoid being tricked into acting on OCD urges. And when they did this, they discovered that *their OCD urges lost some of their power*—just as you observed that your hunger loses some of its power when you resolutely ignore it and go on working. The same is true of any other powerful old brain impulse that assails you: observing it mindfully robs it of some (and, with enough practice, the Buddha said, ultimately all) of its power.

After ten weeks of practicing this new sequence—mindful observation, increased understanding, redirected action—two-thirds of the patients in our study had taken considerable control of their behavior back from OCD, and were feeling a lot less dominated and terrorized by the disorder. When we looked at their brains with the PET scanner, we discovered that the abnormally high energy use had decreased, and that the three key structures were no longer locked together—i.e., Brain Lock was relieved. These people had used their *mind* to change their *brains*. How? *By changing the relationship between their feelings and their behavior.* By using their willpower to override their automatic response to uncomfortable feelings, they changed their lives from slavery and suffering to freedom and self-respect. And the crucial step, the one I believe actually created new brain circuits, was *putting their will into action*—a.k.a. creating new karma. It was by *doing something different* than their primitive dread was ordering them to do—an act of healthy defiance, noble effort, and real courage—that they made their brains, and their lives, better.

Always remember, "Your karma is what you *do*"—or even more precisely, it's what you *willfully* do, what you do *on purpose*. In other words, by your willful actions, *you create* your own fate. If you remember just that one definition, you'll always be aware of the paramount importance of what you purposely do—both for your own future and for the future of others.

Your friend,
Jeff

Dear Jeff,

Maybe I need to use my mind to change my brain—I started going out with my old girlfriend again. I had gotten another girlfriend in the city. We just went out twice over the holidays. Then I get back to school and R. says, "I still really like you." I explained to the girl in the city—I was totally honest—but she still was really mad. She said "I hope she hurts you again."

She might get her wish. It was really good for the first two days but now I'm getting mixed messages again. It's making me feel really unsure.

Patrick

IT'S NOT HOW YOU <u>FEEL</u>,
IT'S WHAT YOU <u>DO</u> THAT COUNTS

Dear Patrick,

Well, you're heading into another major road test of everything we're working on. When you're assailed by intense feelings of desire and elation, or hurt and rage, it's really hard to remember to be the driver. The temptation is very powerful just to give in and be a passenger on life's most delirious roller-coaster ride. But that is the shortest road to harm and regret. Making mental notes is more important now than ever! *Observe* your feelings, and they won't have such absolute power to intoxicate you, torment you, and drive you. Buffeted by high winds of joy or pain, you'll still be able to direct your actions with a clear mind. (The Buddha said: "Whose mind is not shaken when touched by the vicissitudes of the world . . . This is life's highest blessing.")

We live in a culture that, for over thirty years now—due to the rampant cult of the Self—has *worshipped feelings*. In much of the so-called "human potential" movement, how you feel was supposed to be the key to who you really are and what you should do. From a Buddhist point of view, this is a stupendous philosophical error, which can only lead to practical and moral disaster. In reality, to let your feelings drive your actions is to hand control of the wheel over to your animal autopilot—about as dependable as the drunk driver Princess Diana handed her life over to. This is, as Gotama taught on many occasions, a surefire way to endless suffering!

If that sounds puzzling to you—it's certainly different from what you've been hearing from the mainstream of popular culture—go back to the simple example of hunger. If you let that feeling push you to break off work before you're finished and go for the immediate pleasure and relief of a snack, you end up feeling worse about yourself; maybe, if you let yourself get really distracted, it even causes you some trouble. Now, think about how many relationships, driven at the beginning by passionate attraction, end in battles, betrayal, an ugly breakup or divorce.

We've built our entire concept of love and marriage on feelings, and when feelings change, as they always do ("This, too, shall pass"—the basic nature of reality, the Buddha taught, is that *everything* in this world changes), disappointed lovers often blame each other for their pain and turn into haters. In truth, their pain was inevitable—a direct consequence of the pursuit of pleasure with *utter disregard* for the true nature of reality. "Don't *bother me* with the truth"—how many times has every adulterer said that, by actions if not directly in words? In the pursuit of gratifying their immediate "needs," adulterers (like all unmindful and self-centered lovers) deny the reality of how undependable and ephemeral their own feelings are—and even more, the reality that they will have to deal with the grotesque consequences of their actions.

The sex scandals that have engulfed the U.S. presidency this year are a prime example of "grotesque consequences." All the tawdry quibbling over the details of exactly what happened and the precise motives of the women involved can't disguise a pattern of behavior so lust-driven and ungoverned that it keeps breaking through the most strenuous efforts to keep it under wraps. There's no question that the man we call President has privately hurt and publicly humiliated the wife and young daughter he professes to love. He has also recklessly risked crippling his presidency, and so jeopardizing our nation. To all this, in the moment of passion Bill Clinton consistently seems to respond, "Don't *bother me* with the truth."

This man has tried to deceive himself and us that as long as his poll numbers are high, he has actually succeeded in defying the Law of Consequences. But that is a Law that no one, I mean no one, escapes. Just remember the wise words of Joe Louis—"He can run, but he can't hide!" At the very least, Bill Clinton has irreversibly damaged his place in history, soiled and diminished the image of greatness he so longs for. It remains to be seen whether his presidency can survive two more years and, perhaps, still more sordid revelations. One way or another, his presidency will end, but the harm he has done to his family will continue to haunt him. The heedless pursuit of pleasure causes pain to others, but also, with total certainty, to oneself. One of the most basic teachings of Buddhist philosophy is that there *is* no such thing as "getting away with it."

To be the driver is to understand this simple truth, which unfortunately is the exact opposite of what popular culture says: in reality, your *actions* drive your *feelings*. Note this very carefully, Patrick, and observe the truth of it in your daily life: *It's not how you feel, it's what you do that counts.* In fact, the only *reliable* way to *feel* good is to *do* good, *regardless* of how you feel at the moment! No doubt that isn't the easy way to live—"Know this, good man," the Buddha said, "evil things are difficult to control." But it *is* the effective way, as you know (to return to our beginning-driver's example) from all the times you *didn't* quit working or working out to pursue the pleasure of the impulsive snack.

When you've done what's right, everything in life tastes better! *This is the Law of Karma in action.* A basic teaching of Buddhist philosophy is that all pleasant sensations arise as the ripening of prior good actions. But look at any pleasure through the eye of your animal brain (that is, with unwise attention), and what happens? *The greed for more* immediately arises, urging you to think and act in ways that will inevitably make you feel bad! Look at that same pleasure through the wise and mindful eye of your Impartial Spectator, and you will not be deflected from doing what is good and right. This is exactly the way, Gotama taught, to nourish your Enlightenment Factors: mindfulness, investigation of Truth, energy, joy, tranquillity, concentration, and equanimity—the only genuine path to *"the good life."*

The Law of Karma, as explained by the Buddha, says that *action,* and *only* action (including mental action), has the power to change the quality of your life. Twenty-five hundred years later, our brain-imaging study at UCLA, using the most advanced technology, has shown the scientific reason why this is so: because your actions change the inner workings of your brain. Here's the simple formula:

> What you do affects how your brain works.
>
> How your brain works affects how you feel.
>
> Therefore, what you do affects how you feel.

How, then, can you keep from being driven by strong feelings into unwise, unwholesome actions that will mess up your life and your brain? It's simple, though far from easy. ("Know this, good man—evil things are difficult to control.")

Your animal brain has tremendous momentum behind it—the accumulated energy of countless generations. And it also has a multitude of ways to tempt and trick you, as you'll quickly learn by applying wise attention to all the distracting billboards and deceptive road signs out on the highway of life—such as the supermodel swimsuit posters your roommate has plastered your room with, and the X-rated Websites some of your classmates like to surf. Fortunately, thanks to the basal ganglia, your brain's habit system, resisting the pressures of the animal brain gets easier the more you do it. (Please note that it also gets harder the less you do it.) And here's the bottom line: with practice, you can actually wire your automatic transmission to take orders from your inner spirit instead of your inner lizard.

So get into the habit of *making mental notes* whenever a strong feeling arises, whether it's "hungry, hungry," "angry,

A multitude of ways to tempt and trick you

angry," "hurting, hurting," or even "lusting, lusting." In fact, even "don't know" or "can't tell" when you're *not sure* how you feel are legitimate mental notes! At that point you might simply note whatever posture your body is in: "sitting, sitting," "standing, standing," "walking, walking." The critical point is always the same: *Activate your Impartial Spectator.*

This mental action is very much like disengaging the gears of a car, putting it into neutral, and looking around. The driveshaft of your animal brain will continue to race and roar, making a helluva lot of noise, but as long as it's not attached to the wheels of action, it won't be pulling and pushing you around. So you can take a good look at the truth of the situation, use your wisdom to select a better gear, apply your will to engage that gear—and drive!

Your friend,
Jeff

THE ROAD WARRIOR'S GUIDEBOOK

MENTORS AND ROLE MODELS

Dear Patrick,

Have you heard about the movement to change the requirements for getting your driver's license? I just read about this recently. New drivers who are sixteen have a much higher rate of serious accidents than eighteen-year-olds. The main reason, it turns out, is inexperience. It takes a year or two out on the road, dealing with other drivers in real-life situations, before you really have the knack of handling a car and know the dangers to look out for.

The solution that has been proposed is to grant first-time drivers their licenses in stages. After you completed your basic driving lessons, but before you could get your full-fledged license, there would be a requirement to spend a certain number of hours driving with an experienced adult driver beside you, to advise and guide you and point out potential problems on the road.

It used to be the same way with the skills of living—and in good families, schools, communities, churches, and temples, it still is. During the transition to being on your own, your freedom is increased in stages, and guidance is always available. Of course, adults are far from perfect—all the more

so when they've lost touch with the wisdom of past generations, as so many have today—so they're bound to do this
job imperfectly. Some will be too heavy-handed and will
make a point of flaunting their power over you. Others,
eager to please and unsure of what they themselves believe,
will be so timid they won't be firm enough. Even so, it's still
better on the whole than letting you go out there alone to
learn by trial and painful, costly error.

Kids who have too much freedom—a polite way of saying
too little support and guidance—because their parents are preoccupied with work or with their own problems and desires are
correct to feel abandoned. The kids of today deserve a lot more
than just lip service and so-called "quality time." You need
what everyone needs—hands-on experience with guidance! It's
the adults' job to stand by you while you gain confidence in
your solo skills. To do my job right, I need to do a lot more than
just show you how your vehicle works, toss you the keys, and
say "So long, kid, have a nice trip. Drop me a line." It's essential
that I travel part of the way by your side.

At this point, you no longer need an instructor so much
as a companion and mentor. You already know the basics of
safely and skillfully traversing the rugged terrain leading to
Innocence. You've acquainted yourself with the essentials of
the inner warning and guidance systems you've been
equipped with. Keeping you in touch with the skills you
already have, and inspiring you so that you always keep
improving them—these are my main assignments. My core
responsibilities are to be aware of what you're doing and to
remind you at strategic moments, "Wake up! Look out!
Activate your Impartial Spectator!" I can also point out some
of the dangers along your way, dangers you may not recognize as such—since they're often disguised as roadside attrac-
tions!—but that I've already encountered, done battle with,
sometimes even vanquished . . . only to have them come
back at me again!

You see, Patrick, though I've been "on the road" much longer than you have, the journey remains quite a challenge. If you think bandits, roadblocks, ambushes, even sorcerers and monsters are things of the semimythical past, now safely confined to videogames, think again! This journey to Innocence is no game. It's still as perilous and adventurous as it ever was, because it's still the same inner journey it's always been. Indeed, in some ways it's *more* dangerous and difficult today, for quiet access to your own inner space is now under constant assault by modern electronic weaponry—barrages of false messages, booby traps, and emotional landmines lurking in every TV, computer, and loudspeaker, all instantaneously activated by the flick of a switch.

One of the most important things adults can do is to let you know candidly that we're still fighting the exact same battles you're just starting to get embroiled in. They don't quit. They are timeless and eternal. The same lusts, the same frustrations, the same lures to ignorance—Patrick, *I'm* still struggling with them on a daily basis! The only difference is that experience, study, and meditation have given me some familiarity with the sneaky ways and subtle tricks of Māra, the enemy, as well as some basic skills in freeing myself when I do fall into one of his traps—and a deeply instilled confidence that my "friend within" is more than his match.

To inspire young people, older adults don't have to be, or pretend to be, perfect. But we *do* have to make a sincere effort to protect what is good and to struggle against evil—in ourselves first and foremost, and then in the world. It's not enough just to mouth the right words. Talk is cheap. And since evil things are difficult to control, one generally must move more than one's jaw to make things truly better. (There's a saying a friend of mine is fond of: "When all is said and done, a lot more is said than done.") The acid test is the way we conduct our own lives and govern our own impulses. At the very least, we adults are supposed to fight *that* battle in a way you can look up to and learn from. And that, Patrick, is a responsibility I'm afraid we fall down on all too often.

Here's where your generation may be able to show mine a thing or two. For remember, wisdom doesn't come automatically with age and it isn't beyond the reach of youth. The fact that I can point out dangers to you doesn't mean you can't also alert me to something *I've* missed, due to a personal blind spot or a lapse of attention.

The fifth of our Ten Commandments is "Honor thy father and thy mother," and Gotama Buddha called "Giving support to parents" one of the highest blessings of life. There are no exceptions. It doesn't say "Honor and support your parents *if* they prove worthy of it; otherwise, sneer at them and treat them like clueless oafs." No—you, Patrick, are called upon to honor and support your father even when he lets you down. And no parent is ever so high and mighty as to not be in need of that kind of support. For instance, Chelsea Clinton has been called upon to honor and support *her* father throughout his largely self-inflicted crisis, even though it must cause her great embarrassment and pain. Now if that doesn't seem necessary, or even fair, it will probably become much clearer when you understand that Gotama wasn't talking mainly about material or even emotional support. He considered *spiritual* support—helping your parents enhance their own level of moral awareness—to be the highest and in fact the only genuine form of support. You could say that "Honor thy father and thy mother" means "Awaken your parents' honor."

Maybe it is Chelsea alone who has the power to awaken her father to the *hiri,* or appropriate shame, and *ottappa,* or dread of consequences, that he so plainly has a tendency to ignore. For this man who was elected twice to govern the United States sometimes seems to lack the will or the skill to govern himself. And perhaps the worst consequence of the unworthy behavior of the First Role Model is that it will contribute to a deepening of your contemporaries' painful cynicism.

That's not to be puritanical or unforgiving. Anyone can (and just about everyone does) lose an occasional battle to the potent temptations of the animal brain that Gotama called the Ten Armies of Māra and our own religious tradition calls the Seven Deadly Sins. But this seems to be something more than a lost battle—more like an abject surrender to the Enemy within! It's often said that a nation gets the leaders it deserves—but maybe leader isn't the right word. Bill Clinton, a man without a father, may actually be the living embodiment of the sorry condition of America's soul. It ought to be part of the oath of public office that "I will remain alert to the fact that the state of the world begins in the state of my mind." If the country's leading citizen can't be bothered to inspire us with that basic form of heroism called virtue, who will?

You will, Patrick—you, and Chelsea, and the leaders of your generation. You are the young warriors who will take up the battle too many of *my* generation ran from—the one within, the battle against the animal soul. So prepare yourself to meet Māra's Armies, up close and personal!

Your friend,
Jeff

Dear Jeff,

Well, it happened again. She was nice for two days, treated me really badly for one week, and then she turned around and said, "I never actually liked you. I just felt jealous because you had a new girlfriend. I never really felt the flame come back." I was crushed. The first night I couldn't even go back to my room. I just stayed in the boathouse.

The only good thing about it was that I found out who my close friends are. A couple of them were really good, and they got me through it. I'm OK now, but it's a small world here. We still have to see each other every day, and I'm not speaking to her at all.

When the scandals first broke everybody was talking about the President. That girl he messed around with isn't that much older than us. There's a lot of cynicism, a lot of jokes, but also a kind of feeling of disgust and sadness.

Patrick

THE STRIKING FORCE OF DARKNESS

Dear Patrick,

When I said you were about to meet Māra's Armies up close and personal, I didn't know it was going to be *that* personal!

It doesn't get any easier the second time around, does it? You're experiencing a classic form of *dukkha,* which everyone goes through at some time in life—and many of us go through repeatedly, now that we're "free" to jump into love without the guidance and protection of family and community, custom and ceremony.

As bad as it feels, though, for training your mental force, this is some of the best practice you can get. (And you thought *rowing* took pain tolerance!) The behavior of your ex-friend, as well as the hurt, bewilderment, frustration, and anger you're feeling, give us a superb opportunity to observe Māra's Armies in action and strategize how to effectively defend yourself, and ultimately defeat them.

To suggest the true menace of these battalions, I'll tell you a story. It comes from an extremely thought-provoking show I once saw on TV—as I recall it was an episode of the old, black-and-white *Twilight Zone.*

A man was involved in a car accident, but afterwards he was able to drive away. Soon he saw a plain but somehow sinister hitchhiker—a small, drab man in nondescript clothes—standing by the roadside with his thumb out. The driver didn't stop—but twenty or fifty miles down the road, there was the same hitchhiker again!

The man began to be frightened. He drove faster. He changed his route. He dodged down twisting dirt side roads. But no matter where he went, again and again the drab little hitchhiker was waiting for him. I don't remember what finally stopped him—maybe he just ran out of gas—but as the hitchhiker walked over and climbed into his car, the man finally understood why there was no escaping him. The hitchhiker was Death. The man had been killed in that car accident.

The hitchhikers who will keep trying to waylay you on the road to Innocence don't look anything like Death. On the contrary—they appear as all the enticements and excitements that we think of as the essence of Life. And yet, they are all just different disguises put on by a very devious and clever being whose name means "Killer." (That name can be quite literally true: surrender to the Armies of Māra can be fatal—as the death of Chris Farley, following in the footsteps of his idol John Belushi and many other "high livers," shows!) Māra is every bit as inescapable as the little hitchhiker in the story. You're going to meet him on this road again and again and again. He's everywhere. And because he is such a master of disguise, it's helpful to get a briefing from that great warrior and wayfarer, Gotama Buddha, who faced him on numerous occasions both before and after his own journey to Pure Unadulterated Innocence (a.k.a. Enlightenment), and along the way, learned how to see right through him.

The Buddhist tradition describes Māra's notorious exploits at great length. Māra's most common tactic of attack is to disguise himself by taking on a different form, a trick he's the total master of. For example, he is reported to have transformed himself into an elephant, a cobra, a bull, a simple farmer, or a Hindu priest, all in order to sneak up on the Buddha and his disciples and attempt to ensnare their minds. What invariably happens is that the Buddha looks right at him and says, "Oh, *you* again, evil one!" At that point Māra exclaims, "He knows me! The Blessed One knows me!" and scurries off in temporary defeat—only to try again . . . and again . . . and again. (He's still trying right now to defeat all attempts at mindfulness.)

The first, and most famous, of several decisive battles between these two adversaries took place on the eve of

Gotama's enlightenment. In a scene that bears some striking similarities to the Devil's temptation of Jesus as he fasted in the wilderness, Māra made an all-out last-ditch effort to stop Gotama from becoming the Buddha, the Awakened One, who would achieve complete freedom from Māra's sensual prison for all time. On the occasion of his final struggle to attain Buddhahood, Gotama declared that he would not be fooled or defeated by any of Māra's most common, lethal forces of destruction—his "Ten Armies." Let's quote Gotama's names for these Armies directly:

> Your first army is **Sensual Desire**.
> Your second is called **Boredom and Dissatisfaction**, then
> **Hunger and Thirst** compose the third,
> And **Craving** is fourth . . .
> The fifth is **Sloth and Torpor**,
> While **Cowardice and Fearfulness** is sixth,
> **Excessive Doubt and Uncertainty** the seventh,
> **Hypocrisy and Stubbornness** the eighth.
> **Ill-won Gain, Honor, Renown, and Fame** is ninth,
> **Praising Yourself and Denigrating Others**, the tenth. . . .

It's worth pausing here to notice that Māra's Armies are at least close cousins of, and in some cases identical with, our own tradition's "Seven Deadly Sins": *Pride, Envy, Wrath, Sloth, Avarice, Gluttony,* and *Lust.* Lust is essentially the same as Māra's First Army, Sensual Desire; Gluttony is the Third Army, Hunger and Thirst, reinforced by an alliance with the Fourth Army, Craving; Avarice, the greed for wealth, is a form of Craving, and so is Envy, which is a violation of God's Ninth and Tenth Commandments, "Thou shalt not covet . . . any thing that is thy neighbor's"; Sloth (and Torpor) has a place on both lists; and Māra's Tenth Army, Praising Yourself and Putting Down Others, is the sin of Pride.

It's perhaps an interesting cultural difference that Gotama doesn't include anger (Wrath), while the Seven

Māra's forces of destruction — his Ten Armies

Deadly Sins omit fear. But don't forget that fear and anger are just two aspects of the same Root of Evil—*dosa,* or ill-will. Both have a closely related physiology, involving the limbic system and hypothalamus, as well as adrenaline, the "fight or flight" hormone. My meditation instructor, the Venerable U Silananda, teaches that fear is a form of passive ill-will. A good way to explain both the difference and the kinship between fear and anger is that Wrath says, "Get it *away* from me!", while Fearfulness says, "Get *me* away from *it!*"

Well-trained warriors, from the Japanese Samurai to the Navy SEALs, have always known that Wrath can flip into Fear in a split second, and that when fighting to defend the Good against Evil, the only way to prevail without being contaminated is to keep a clear mind, focused steadfastly on your goal. "Valor without wisdom is insufficient," said Frederick the Great, "and the adversary with a cool head . . . will finally be victorious over the rash individual."

There are other fascinating similarities between Māra's Ten Armies and the Seven Deadly Sins. Both were discovered and described by people who had withdrawn from the tumult of worldly life to engage in full-time meditation, contemplation, or prayer. In a sermon titled "The Seven Deadly Sins," the Reverend G. Bradford Hall of St. Margaret's Episcopal Church in Palm Desert, California, said, "Though each sin has many roots in Scripture . . . the seven deadly sins—or cardinal vices, as they were once called—originated within the desert monastic movement of the early Christian church around the 5th century A.D. In the lonely and cloistered world of monks, nuns and hermits, these seven were the temptations that erupted most in their private holy lives." It's because these Enemies were observed—by Gotama, too—in such carefully controlled conditions, as far as possible excluding external stimulants and contaminants, that we can be quite confident they spring from the very nature of the human mind.

And spring they certainly do! In the Bible, too, sin is not portrayed just as a bad action *(karma)* we commit, but as a malevolent force that attacks *us,* first—from within. If Gotama, who was born into a warrior caste, describes each of Māra's assaults as an army, the Bible, reflecting its desert wilderness origins, depicts sin as a predatory beast. You may recall God warning Cain, right before he killed his brother, that "if you do not right, sin crouches at the door. And to you shall be its desire. . . ." In each case, the "cardinal"[1] sin is not an action, like murder or adultery, but *the state of mind that precedes and conduces to it.* "Along with their own gravity, the seven deadly sins are distinguished by their power to generate other sins," Reverend Hall writes in his sermon. "They are in essence 'evil states of mind' that tempt us into a variety of evil acts." Gotama's psychology is, in some ways,

[1]"Of foremost importance; paramount"—the American Heritage Dictionary.

Boredom and Dissatisfaction is an evil state of mind.

even more subtle; he's aware, for instance, that "Boredom and Dissatisfaction"—the fidgety ignorance of an animal brain that's getting antsy for some crude sensation—is itself an "evil state of mind" that will quickly invite another Army to jump on us. But the Buddha's concluding statement about Māra's entire assault force is essentially identical to God's admonition to Cain about sin: *"and yet you may rule over it."*

> *"These are your armies,* Namuci *["Enemy of Freedom"],*
> *the striking force of darkness.*
> *One who is not a hero cannot conquer them,*
> *But victorious, one gains complete happiness."*

And then Gotama says something extremely assertive to Māra, something which I have repeated to myself on many occasions: "Better for me to die in battle, than to live defeated. . . . I go forward to fight, so that Māra may not drive me from my proper place."

Namuci is another name for Māra, which could also be translated as "enslaver." Māra and his Armies will try to confuse you, Patrick, by claiming that they are the ones who are offering you ecstasy and freedom. But it's the "freedom" of your animal brain doing what *it* wants—pursuing the blind and bottomless cravings of nature—and as we've seen, that really means nothing but slavery and suffering for *you*. Māra will lure you, lull you, frighten you, whatever it takes to get you off the one road *he* doesn't control—the road to Innocence. But of course that's the road that requires you to stay awake, alert, and as vigilant as a warrior on patrol.

Pick up that evil hitchhiker in any one of his guises, Patrick, and he'll invite all his allies to pile in, like a nightmare version of the Keystone Kops. They'll distract you till you've lost your bearings, mislead you with directions rooted in greed, ill-will, and ignorance, and run you right into a smash-up. And right now, with all your emotions in turmoil, you're particularly vulnerable to their combined assaults. I'm going to show you Māra's Armies at work in your own mind and heart—but first, we'll take a quick look at two recent, highly publicized casualties of their unholy alliances.

Your friend and foxhole buddy,
Jeff

DEADLY TEAMWORK:
TWO CASE STUDIES

Dear Patrick,

The most insidious thing about Māra's Armies is the way they work together and strengthen each other. If you let just one of them get to you, and weaken you, the others will tend to rush in through the breach in your defenses and try to finish you off. This can easily be seen in two of the celebrated instances we've already talked about.

For example, it's a fair guess that Māra's primary attack on comic Chris Farley—who started life as a chubby kid—was by way of his Third Army: Hunger and Thirst. But that threw open the door to the Fourth Army, Craving, which quickly magnified Chris's pleasure in food and drink into Gluttony, resulting in Chris bloating himself up to as much as four hundred pounds. Worse, Chris developed a Hunger and Thirst for drugs and alcohol, which are like throwing gasoline on the fire of Craving. Put into the animal brain, intoxicants tend to trigger an insatiable craving for ever more intense highs of all kinds, while simultaneously damaging the capacity for mindfulness and good judgment. And of course with regular use, full-blown addiction sets in, leading to terrible Boredom and Dissatisfaction the moment the effects of the intoxicants start wearing off.

That made it easy for the Second, Third, and Fourth Armies to team up with the First (Lust) and overrun Chris's sexual life as well. He would hire prostitutes or strippers (to whom he could be kind and affectionate—he wasn't a mean or Wrathful guy, unless you took his drugs away) to share his marathon binges of cocaine, heroin, alcohol, sex, and food. He was found dead the morning after one of those—a total victory for the Killer and his Armies. No doubt they simply high-fived and moved on . . . just another night on the graveyard shift for them!

Bloating himself up to as much as 400 pounds

Then, of course, there's Bill Clinton, whose presidency has been seriously jeopardized by his surrender to Māra's most powerful alliance: Armies One (Sensual Desire, or Lust) and Four (Craving). That, in turn, has compelled him to chronically risk alienating the American people with a never-ending campaign of spin, evasion, and denial (Army Eight: Hypocrisy and Stubbornness), in order to try to hold on to both his approval rating in the polls and the favorable judgment of history (Army Nine: Ill-won Gain, Honor, Renown, and Fame).

Many sophisticated observers think that this constant need for approval contributes to Army Seven, Doubt and Uncertainty, undermining Clinton's ability to govern. His constant anxious attention to what the polls say only intensifies the attacks of Craving for approval—Army Four. And so, trapped in the prison of his own high-powered appetites, cursed by what increasingly seems like a perpetual urge to push things to the edge, Bill Clinton seems to suffer both from what his aides describe as a terrible temper (the deadly sin of Wrath) and from significant fear—for example, he is reported to have experienced "tremendous terror" of being found out (Māra's Army Six, Cowardice and Fearfulness), going back at least to when he first considered running for president.

Just think how much trouble a modicum of self-command would have saved him (and us)!

I tell you these things so that you can learn in a deep way that even the most powerful and successful people among us suffer on account of their personal weaknesses. But, Patrick, I'm not here to talk about Bill Clinton or Chris Farley. I'm here to talk about you, and what *you're* going through.

Your friend
Jeff

ANOTHER KIND OF KĀMA SUTRA

Dear Patrick,

As you now know, the pain of love begins with the bliss of love, an all-out attack by the slings and arrows of Māra's first—and most seductive—Army: Sensual Desire. But the other nine Armies are lurking nearby, ready to rush in. In fact, if you look back, a couple of them were probably working you over even before your relationship began, softening you up so Army One's arrows would pierce really deep: Army Two, for instance, Boredom and Dissatisfaction ("Man, I gotta get some more *excitement* in my life!"), and Army Four, Craving ("I *need* a girlfriend. . . .")

The name of Māra's First Army translates as "Sensual Desire," or "longing for sense pleasures," but the original word in both Sanskrit and Pāli is *kāma*—yes, as in the Kāma

Māra's first—and most seductive—Army

Sutra, the famous Indian manual of sexual positions and techniques. Among the translations of *kāma* in the Sanskrit-English Dictionary are "wish, desire, longing; love, affection, object of desire or love; pleasure; sexual love or sensuality; Love or Desire personified; semen." Much can be learned by comparing this word to the Greek word *eros*, the source of our word "erotic" and the name of the god of desire and infatuation. *Kāma*, too, in the Hindu pantheon, was portrayed as a god who shot arrows—tipped with flowers—by which people could get "smitten."

As Freud knew, *eros* encompasses more than just genital sex. Any pleasant sight, touch, taste, smell, or even sound (as any rock 'n' roll fan knows) can arouse sensual longings. The Buddha astutely pointed out that we can even feel a kind of lust for attractive *ideas*, since the mind, in Buddhist psychology, is also one of our senses! But the groin is sort of Eros's home plate, the place most pleasant sensations eventually come around to.

This is especially true at your age, when nature floods both sexes with an overabundance of *Kāma* to make it likely that you will reproduce while you're young and vigorous. (Nature has no idea that most of us now live well into our seventies, or that most of our offspring survive past childhood, or that our kids will be far better off if we have them after we've achieved emotional maturity, the capacity to form genuinely stable relationships, and at least some of our economic and professional goals. From the point of view of the primeval old brain sexual impulse, we—especially we males—might as well be fish, of whose millions of offspring only a handful may survive. That civilization has evolved faster than the brain is true beyond question.)

Because we're human—social primates with a prefrontal cortex brimming with imagination and self-consciousness—many other factors enter into our interest in the opposite sex: loneliness, the need to be reassured that we're lovable, the desire for companionship and closeness, and the desire to gain status in our peer group by landing a desirable "catch," to name just a few. But there's no denying that the powerful undercurrent that gives all these other needs their intensity, drawing the sexes irresistibly together, is *Kāma*.

But if, as the Buddha said, all pleasant sensations are the coming to fruition of prior good actions, why is *Kāma* a treacherous army of Māra, and not the best of friends it pretends to be?

Well, Gotama taught that *Kāma*'s power to hinder the quest for Innocence and Enlightenment is magnified to explosive destructiveness the moment it's mixed with unwise attention. For at that instant arises the First Army's close ally: Army Four, Craving. In his very first sermon Gotama pinpointed Craving as the source of all suffering. Check it out and you'll see it plain as day—especially now, looking back on a relationship that's over. It's the Craving, the intense thirst for *more*, that largely accounts for how quickly and deeply desire can entangle you in the Three Roots of Evil—greed, ill-will, and ignorance—and trap you into feeling and causing pain.

Take greed, just for starters.

When you're attracted to someone, don't you feel as if you just can't get enough of her? You crave more and more of the good feelings between you, with no end or shadow—even though it's been proven beyond a doubt that reality doesn't work that way. You begin to feel more and more possessive of her, believing she is the necessary source of your happiness and pleasure. You want her to be "yours"—even though the war that put an end to one person owning another was concluded in 1865! This, of course, is *lobha*, with the usual generous helping of *moha*—ignorance—thrown in.

Frustrate greed, however, and immediately *dosa*, ill-will, raises its ugly head. For instance, whenever you and your girlfriend are apart, Māra's Second Army—Boredom and Dissatisfaction—quickly attacks. You resent having to take a break from those intensely pleasurable feelings and turn your attention to something less enticing—an upcoming Latin exam, for instance. When you're involved with someone everything else pales, or as Sinéad O'Connor sang, "Nothing compares to you."

Now, Patrick, you come to a very interesting fork in the road. On the one hand, Māra's Fifth Army lies in wait: Sloth and Torpor, a.k.a. laziness or inertia. This is one of the most potent Deadly Sins in the animal brain, and the sworn enemy of every *positive* human achievement—from straight A's all the way to Enlightenment. It is Sloth and Torpor, probably even more than the Sixth Army, Cowardice and Fearfulness, that prevents many basically good people from doing more to combat evil. (It's a real tip-off how rarely Sloth and Torpor interfere with the *negative* achievements of

Sabotage by sleepiness, procrastination and lethargy

JEFFREY M. SCHWARTZ

their fellow Armies. There's usually plenty of animal energy available for seduction, acquisition, gluttony, fight, flight, and the like. It's the *spiritual* energy required by the aspirations of the divine soul that Army Five likes to sabotage with sleepiness, procrastination, lethargy, and so on.) In your situation, you can recognize ambushes of the Fifth Army–First Army alliance by the powerful temptation to lie around fantasizing and ruminating about your girlfriend, listening to CDs, and getting absolutely nothing useful done.

On the other hand, though, if you've chosen with some wisdom, and your friend is someone you admire (which certainly seemed to be the case with yours), you naturally want to impress her. And as you know very well—because you've told me it was the original reason why you first took up rowing and worked so hard at it—you can actually use that as a motivation to excel, channeling the energy of *kāma* into the pursuit of your other goals. Freud called that *sublimation,* and it's a big part of what makes the world go round. Even if it doesn't win you the girl, it can leave you with something that turns out to be more valuable and lasting than the relationship. (As you also know, since athletic excellence has become such an important part of your life!)

This only works, however, when girls are hard to impress—when they value themselves highly enough, and are wise enough, to demand real quality from you. The world isn't going around as well as it should now because girls aren't being taught, as they used to be, about their immense natural value and power, and how to use it carefully to create beauty and good in the world. Instead, girls are under tremendous pressure to trade their "favors" (which they once bestowed with canny selectivity and regal reserve) far too easily for mere acceptance or status.

In this climate of general devaluation, Patrick, you probably know guys who've tried to take shortcuts: why go to all the trouble of *really* excelling when exaggerating or lying about your exploits—athletic, sexual, or otherwise—will do the trick? Is there someone among your friends or acquaintances who does that? Let me know.

Your friend,
Jeff

Canny selectivity and regal reserve

JEFFREY M. SCHWARTZ

Dear Jeff,

A perfect example is this friend of mine—the same one I told you is a womanizer. He always tries to make everything he does sound like it's better than it actually was. This summer he went to this less competitive thing that wasn't as good for his rowing, when it would've been better if he'd stayed and tried to make cuts, make the development team. But he was afraid of getting axed. So he went, and then when he came back to school he was exaggerating how he raced with the junior national Mexican team, and the Canadian junior development team. . . . He actually is really good at making it sound better than it was. Sometimes he fools me!

He does that a lot. It makes him feel like he achieved more than he achieved. And he definitely does it to impress girls. He's a really insecure kid. But I don't understand people who want to win, but don't want to work for it. Even some of the good friends I have seem to get jealous when I succeed and I don't understand why, because they could do the same thing.

Patrick

SLOTH AND ENVY MEET
LUST AND PRIDE

Dear Patrick,

Now you're observing an alliance between the Deadly Sins of Sloth and Envy, or between Māra's lazy Fifth Army and his Ninth—Ill-won Gain, Honor, Renown, and Fame. (The Tenth Army, Praising Yourself and Putting Down Others, often joins in, too.) This unholy alliance is actively nurtured by the way our culture venerates the concept of egalitarianism—the notion that everyone is as good as everyone else, and deserves the same rewards and self-esteem.

Whenever your friends' envy causes you pain, your only genuine protection will come from wisdom: seeing it for what it really is. Envy is an animal-brain response—craving

Envy is an animal-brain response.

JEFFREY M. SCHWARTZ

what others have without being willing to make the effort required to get it. And, of course, this state of mind often leads to thoughts contaminated with ill-will, followed by harmful actions that violate the commandments and precepts: lying, stealing, even killing (remember the story of Cain and Abel!). It's helpful to look for the roots of such unwholesome behavior in others, because then you clearly see that it's their issue, not yours. It even makes you feel a certain compassion for those who capitulate to the Fifth and Ninth Armies. Not only are they getting no real benefit, they're harming themselves, neglecting to program in the good work habits that would serve them for the rest of their lives.

One caution: outside the abstract realm of political rights such as the vote, it is *not* true that all men are created equal. People are born with differing mental and physical abilities. As your coach has told me, you plainly have athletic talent (among others), as well as discipline and determination. Even if your friends trained as hard as you do, they couldn't necessarily row as successfully. (I certainly remember much better wrestlers than me who didn't train nearly as hard.) But they could do *something* as successfully! Virtually no one, Patrick, is born without *any* talent. And true security, the antidote to Envy—and the only *true* self-esteem—lies in finding out what *your* gifts are and working hard to develop them.

But even then, when you've truly excelled by your own honest efforts, Māra has yet *another* vicious Army lying in wait for you: the Tenth—Praising Yourself and Putting Down Others. Pride, traditionally the first of the Seven Deadly Sins and the root of all the others—because in essence, it means loving yourself more than God (the sin we psychiatrists call narcissism)—is also Māra's final Army. For the last and dirtiest trick of the animal soul is to grab the credit and revel in the rewards for the divine soul's essentially selfless achievements. "Pride," the modern English theologian Dorothy Sayers has said, "is preeminently the sin of the noble mind"—and its downfall, as we see whenever scandal engulfs a prominent minister or spiritual master. The moral of *that* story is that if you let even well-deserved admiration go to your head, it can reignite all the cravings of the animal brain and send you back to Square One. No matter how far you come in life, Patrick, remember—it's dangerous to contemplate how far ahead of others you may have the good fortune to be. Always keep your eye on how far *you* still have to go.

When it comes to impressing the opposite sex, wise males are protected from the temptation to falsely embellish their own exploits and excessively disparage others' by their guardians *hiri* ("Only a sleazebucket would act like that!") and *ottappa* ("What if she finds out I lied?"). But those who fall prey to it have been bushwhacked by Māra's Ninth and Tenth Armies. And any girl who falls for your friend's type of phony bragging has, in effect, been raped by the mercenaries of the Ninth Army, Ill-won Gain, Honor, Renown, and Fame. Like all shortcuts to the animal-brain goals of sensual and ego gratification, this is a way, as Jesus put it, of "gaining the whole world, but losing your own soul." (In the original Greek it actually reads gaining the "cosmos" and losing your "psyche"!)

Certainly the craving for acceptance and status plays a large part in high-school sex. But let's not underestimate the greed built into *kāma* itself. It's the nature of sexual desire, as of all craving, to intensify as it grows, always pushing for the next step; it becomes more and more difficult (and takes more and more mindfulness!) to stop short of intercourse. If you consider it mindfully, you know that *not* stopping is sure to raise the emotional stakes and risks of the relationship, and greatly increase the likelihood of someone (including a newly conceived human) getting *really* hurt. But in the heat of passion, you'd rather not think about it ("Don't *bother me* with the truth!").

The survival drives arising like heat waves from the hypothalamus are incredibly compelling. As one of them, the sexual drive can also be considered a part of the Third Army, "Hunger and Thirst," which the great Burmese monk and meditation teacher Sayadaw U Pandita says "relates to the entire range of [bodily] needs and requirements." Just listen to the words of so many love songs—"I thirst for you, baby" (the Pāli word Gotama used for "craving" literally means "thirst"), "I hunger for your touch"!

When assailed by any natural physical appetite, including sexual feelings, remember the Buddha's Middle Path. He taught that the body should not be punished, starved, or deprived. He'd tried those ascetic practices in the course of his quest for Innocence, and he found that they didn't give him what he really needed: the Power of Mindfulness, which, as he later taught, is the only force in the universe capable of defeating Māra. But neither should the body be indulged and catered to, because the more you pamper and submit to its desires, the more they grow into insatiable cravings. (A potato chip—or an orgasm—tends to make you want another one.) And that way lies being nothing more than an animal.

Most important is to realize that, contrary to a culture steeped in the realm of the senses, your body is not the sum total or even the most important part of you. (And, contrary to the false media standards of attractiveness that lead to the tortures of dieting, anorexia, and bulimia, a girl's body is not the most important part of *her*). Your body, however buff, will eventually disappoint, betray, and ultimately abandon you. But cultivating those aspects of the mind that can transcend the world, and experience directly what Buddhists call Enlightenment (*Nirvāna* in Sanskrit) and the Bible calls the Word (*Logos* in Greek), will not. Those aspects of you are forever young, so the sooner you discover them, the better. They're the only place where complete happiness and true security can be found.

A Japanese karate teacher I heard of put it well when he chided a student who was crying over a jammed thumb, "Which is more important—your finger or your spirit?!" Substitute any part of your body for that finger, and you'll get the message. When the Third Army strikes in the form of sex, just as with hunger, don't pamper or flatter it with the overimportance it clamors for. Don't feed it your full and fascinated—unwise—attention. Just observe it, make a mental note, and use your will to do what you know is right.

So far, Patrick, we've talked mainly about how Māra's Armies stimulate the evil root of Greed when a relationship is going well. But you've heard the phrase, "the honeymoon is over." Inevitably, things go wrong, because that *is* how reality works. (When you see it in its true evanescent and impermanent nature, you understand that reality, frankly, doesn't work all that well!) Sometimes the first flaw is as subtle as a little chill between you and your sweetheart, a misunderstanding, a trivial argument. Didn't you have moments like that with your girlfriend—even last year, when things were going great?

This is an even greater test of your mindfulness, because it's pretty easy to be serene and kind and generous (or at least to *think* you are) when things are going your way. But when they stop going your way, you quite naturally start feeling disappointment, frustration, anxiety, anger, and pain—and that's the signal for Māra's nastier Armies to jump all over you. The Armies of lust and craving, insidious as they are, at least stroked and flattered you. *These* guys poke, slice, dice, freeze, and fry you!

We'd better hope for a cease-fire until the next time I write!

Your friend,
Jeff

Dear Jeff,

Yes, there were moments, even last year. She's not a very emotional person, so she never wanted to hug me or give me a kiss in front of anybody else. In private, okay, but at boarding school there's almost no private time, so it was pretty much like all the time. She didn't even like me to put my arm around her or anything. She shied away. So that was sort of upsetting.

Patrick

LOVE'S RUGGED ROAD

Dear Patrick,

"The course of true love never did run smooth," Shakespeare sagely observed in *A Midsummer Night's Dream*. From a Buddhist perspective, it's not difficult to understand why.

Love is the site of a major clash between craving and reality. When we're in love, we want the impossible, and we want it now: permanent happiness, perfect understanding, excitement with security, great beauty with great kindness, gratification (sexual and otherwise) without consequences. We might deny that we're that greedy, but then why—when reality fails to measure up—do we feel such painful dread and fury?

When you're in love, as you noticed, you're alert to the slightest cooling of the relationship's temperature. Suddenly your heart freezes. What's *this?* Those warm, fuzzy feelings were supposed to keep coming! Does this mean you're not lovable? Or that she can't be trusted? In a flash, you're wide open to the onslaughts of Army Six: Fearfulness. "I wonder if she's even thinking about me right now? Worse yet—what if she's thinking about someone else??"

The fear of losing love, especially to a rival, is one of the most powerful and primitive fears we humans face. Many a hardened combat veteran, absolutely stoic in the face of death, has trembled and cried like a baby when the "Dear John" letter he so dreaded actually came. At its worst moments, this form of *dosa* can make you (or anyone) lose all composure and totally forget to check in with that steadfast source of wisdom—your inner friend. (I can readily imagine you sitting in that boathouse all night—it's an inner space I'm all too familiar with!) Without that ever-dependable source of cool and calm, you inevitably tumble back toward the emotions you had as a small child—when your survival really *did* depend on being loved and cared for. In how many love songs do you hear grown men and women singing, "I can't live without you?" That's obviously not true, but the feeling that it is—a craven surrender to Armies Four (Craving) and Six (Fearfulness)—can drive people to act in very destructive ways. And then they *really* have something to fear!

It's bad enough that, in the aftermath of a less than satisfactory meeting, you spend so much time and energy analyzing her every gesture and tone of voice. The *moha*—ignorance—about the true feelings and motives of a girl you like is frequently as thick as pea-soup fog, and it's under cover of that fog that Māra's Army Seven, Excessive Doubt and Uncertainty, likes to attack. This is the Army that makes you constantly question the evidence of your best efforts at mindful observa-

Back and forth you go with that gnawing anxiety

tion. It is the sin of mistrusting your Friend Within. (Could it be because your animal brain doesn't like what he's telling you?) Back and forth you go between your true perceptions, your burning cravings, and your worst fears. "I wonder, what did she mean when she said *that?* Was it just my imagination that she was flirting with my friend, or did I really see it?" And, with that gnawing anxiety, here comes Army Three, Hunger and Thirst, again. Next thing you know you're sitting there with a bag of M&M's and a soda, turbocharging your racing mind with sugar and caffeine.

You'd think that a really good relationship would put much of this fear and uncertainty to rest, and that if such feelings kept nagging you, it would be a warning signal to reevaluate the situation. Is this *really* someone you can respect, trust and rely on? Is the affection she shows you sincere? Is the communication between you as good as it seems? . . . as good as it could be? But no—that doesn't compute within the dark inner recesses of the animal brain.

Instead, what often happens is that one type of excitation feeds another, setting off an explosive chain reaction: the adrenaline of fear *(dosa)* pours psychic gasoline on the testosterone-fueled fire of lust *(lobha)*. In a famous experiment, it was found that if a man saw a woman right after he crossed a shaky suspension bridge, he rated her as much more attractive than if he just met her on the sidewalk! And it does sometimes seem that the more insecure a girl makes you feel, the more desirable she becomes. It probably hasn't escaped your notice that guys who know exactly how to make *girls* feel insecure often have those very same girls falling all over them! (I'll have more to say about the price you pay if you go for the cheap success of *that* strategy.) There's no question that, unchecked by the sword of mindfulness, Māra's Armies will form devastating alliances, driving us ever deeper into that tangled thicket fed by the Three Roots of Evil.

The dark inner recesses of the animal brain

Finally, when your worst fears are realized—and it's amazing how often they are, on *kāma's* battlefield—there's the sharp pain and anger you're feeling now. You went back to your friend with complete sincerity and the best of intentions, only to be stunned by the sudden cruelty with which she cut you off—*again!*

You know, Patrick, it sounds to me like she may well have fallen prey to a particularly vicious attack of Māra's

That tangled thicket fed by the Three Roots of Evil

Eighth Army: Hypocrisy and Stubbornness. This Army's specialty is seen in those acting self-righteous and blameless when they *know* they're doing harm. (Gotama taught that we *can* practice mindfulness by observing the behavior of others—as long as we keep in mind that we ourselves are far from immune to any weaknesses or flaws we may discover. Otherwise we can readily fall prey to Māra's Army Ten, Praising Yourself and Putting Down Others. Just to show you how rooted in the animal brain these Armies are, a primate researcher who has taught American Sign Language to chimpanzees, Roger Fouts, recently wrote that when he broke up a quarrel between two of his chimps, each would try to pin the blame on the other by signing, "Me good! Me good!") It's especially painful to deal with a person bogged down in the Eighth Army's slimy morass—they often get so entangled in their own agenda that they're unable to engage in sincere, open, and compassionate communication. The frustration of trying to reach them can make almost anyone's animal soul snarl, "Boy, would I like to make *you* feel a little of this pain!"

Ill-will? Patrick, I have seen too many people go down this road (and maybe even looked down it once or twice myself . . .), and let me tell you, *this* is *dosa*. The hostile response-to-rejection strain of it *(dosa* responding to *dosa)* is about as virulent as it gets. Apparently, that was the Root of Evil that drove a twelve-year-old in Arkansas, snubbed by a girl, to recruit his even younger friend for a deadly school-yard shooting spree, murdering four girls and a teacher. From age nine to ninety, this form of *dosa*—when allowed to fester in the absence of wise attention—is the main cause of violent crimes of passion. And even those of us who are sure we could never commit anything remotely approaching such a crime must admit that, in all honesty, we've had moments when we shared some of the feelings of those who do.

The hothouse of passionate desire provides fertile soil indeed for the cultivation of greed and ill-will, especially in rejected lovers—this is a fact every human past the threshold of puberty is familiar with. But these first two Roots of Evil require the third for sustenance. "Love is blind," "a fool for love"— these are common expressions for the deep and willful ignorance, or *moha,* in which Māra's First Army immerses us.

You tell me there was no warning of your friend's brutal breakup with you. It seemed to come out of the blue. *This* wasn't the person you knew! Or . . . wait a minute. *Did* you really know her? Or did you just take a few ingredients of her— her tall, cool blond poise, her intelligence, her good breeding— and spin a fantasy around them? Because that's what infatuation usually is. Certainly two key ingredients you put into your fantasy—kindness and honesty—seem to be less than abundant in reality. But let's not be tempted by the Tenth Army into too much *dosa.* Let's just say breaking up is hard to do, and she could have handled it better. She's an inexperienced driver, too.

What do you think? Did she change? Or did your perceptions change? (Since everything changes, the answer is probably "both." . . .)

Your friend,
Jeff

Jeff,
    Now that I look back, I can sort of see—not as dramatically, not as clearly—but I can see little things from last year that sort of matched what she's doing this year. So maybe I just wasn't looking.

    Patrick

PROTECTING YOURSELF—
AND OTHERS—IN LOVE

Dear Patrick,

Aha! Maybe, in other words, the illusion was so sweet that you were saying . . . "Don't *bother me* with the truth!"

We all do it. This is a universal experience; it shows you Māra's incredible power to delude people ("impair their sight," or even "blind them," is how Māra literally put it), and lead them someplace completely different from where they really wanted to go. Now you can have more wise compassion for your mother's romantic mistakes. Undoubtedly, with both your father and your half-sister's father, sincerely hoodwinked by *kāma,* she felt, "He's so gorgeous, so exciting, so protective and attentive and strong—he's the one!" When the truth proved otherwise, it generated a tremendous amount of ill-will and misery for everyone. It's still going on. That is *karma-vipāka*—the ripening of unwholesome actions rooted in ignorance and greed. Which is not to bad-mouth your mother (that would be succumbing to Māra's Tenth Army!). She's hardly alone or unique.

How can you avoid making the same irrevocable mistakes—in particular, that most fateful or karmic of all actions, conceiving a child with an ill-chosen partner? Remember that, despite what "pro-choice" activists want you to believe, *nothing* is more irrevocable than conceiving a child. As a new life begins, *your* life is changed forever, *whatever* choice you make. Because nothing, absolutely *nothing,* can undo or de-karma-ize that coming together of sperm, egg, and spirit once it occurs. That is a totally irreversible event. All an abortion can do is destroy the arisen life, an act of killing for which suffering cannot be avoided. And the other possible choices—a miserable marriage, an adoption, or an effectively fatherless child—entail suffering, too, as you know all too well.

So now is the time to think about how you and your generation can make wiser choices and create more wholesome, lasting relationships, *despite* the universal treachery of the First Army and the howling of our *kāma*-besotted culture. In this, as in all things, the path to Innocence lies with the mindfulness of your Impartial Spectator. ("The one way," as Gotama taught, "for the purification of Beings.")

It's worth remembering that, like the OCD thoughts and feelings of our patients at UCLA, desire and fantasy and jealousy can't be wished or forced away. You've got to get pretty close to Enlightenment before they'll really stop enticing and tormenting you. They are natural, wired into the animal brain. But this unholy trio *can* be *seen through,* labeled and observed with the help of your friend within, so that they don't warp your perceptions and drive your choices. Which is exactly what they do when you view them with unwise attention—the fuel that immediately makes them grow and tighten their grip. Wise attention, on the other hand, weakens their grip, so that you can break free and see them for what they really are—dreams and cravings aroused in the animal soul by *kāma*. In this way, desire, fantasy, and jealousy can become signals to step on the brakes and take a good look, rather than let the autopilot propel you recklessly ahead.

When your animal brain is telling you to speed up, in other words, that's the time to slow down. I know how hard this is to do—after all, it *is* unnatural, like all the best gifts of civilization. Custom and ceremony, and the healthy shame and fear of both divorce and unmarried pregnancy (two of the greatest services of *hiri* and *ottappa),* used to provide the brakes. Now, if your generation wants to break the chain of suffering that has been so irresponsibly laid on you and wisely restore some of the rules and rituals that protect Innocence and Beauty—such as introducing yourself to the parents of a girl you really like—you're going to have to start by voluntarily applying the inner brake of mindfulness. "True love waits" doesn't mean arbitrarily waiting to have sex until the tenth date or the third month or the engagement or the wedding. It means waiting for the right person—someone you trust and respect, as well as desire—and waiting for the right moment to consummate the love that has grown between you.

The next time you find yourself starting to like a girl, don't just look at *her*—observe yourself, too. Mentally note the different components of your attraction to her—your responses to her looks, her voice, her mind, her personality, her popularity, her background. Notice how impatient your mind is to concoct those ingredients into the conclusion, "This is it! She's the one!" Be aware that that long-wished-for girl-of-my-dreams image can partially or totally obscure the real person. (In reality, the girl of your dreams exists in only one place—your dreams!)

Instead of trying to overlook the little things that don't quite fit the image, make mental notes of them, even if this cools your passion somewhat. Try to take your time getting to know each other as friends before you invest your most vulnerable feelings. (I will freely admit that it's easier to give this advice than to follow it. As I said, I'm still fighting the same battles. We all are.) While this is less euphoric and intoxicating than falling head over heels in love, remember your lessons on drunk driving! The only way to get through *kāma's* minefield without serious injury is to keep your most sober part at the wheel as much as you can.

Most important, whatever the physical chemistry between you, make it one of your chief criteria for a girlfriend that she be a true friend. Often the deepest truths are the most simple, and this is a good one: True love waits for a true friend. Remember, we defined a true friend as someone you don't have to feel self-conscious in front of, because you can be yourself and know she accepts you for who you are.

Making physical touching an expression of loving kindness

She is someone with whom you share basic values and goals. She is someone you trust: you can reveal your doubts and vulnerabilities, knowing that she won't take advantage of you or betray you. (As you learned the hard way, that often takes time to be sure of—though sometimes your instincts can be on target.) And she is someone you respect, who expects the best from you.

Is that a tall order? Are people like that really rare—or do many people long to be like that, but fear it's not cool or macho? That's Māra's con. In reality, what could be *more* cool? The ancient Buddhist texts say it in almost exactly these words: true virtue—heroic command of your animal self—will make you cool, calm, collected, and utterly confident in front of others! And if it's guts you aspire to, just reflect on one of my favorite sayings, "He who fears God fears nothing else."

How do you find a true friend? That's simple (though not easy): by being one. By being trustworthy, open, and honest. (I told you this was a tough assignment—definitely not for sissies!) By not letting your own craving allow Māra to blind you to the reality of the other person's feelings. By making *kāma* serve your humanity, making physical touching an expression of commitment and loving kindness. And by fighting off the cowardly attacks of Māra's Sixth Army—the Fear of Intimacy—even when it masquerades as your tough and swaggering protector.

At any moment when you're intimate, you can get hurt, because your guard is down and you're open. Intimacy carries an intrinsic vulnerability with it. And so it takes mental strength to risk being intimate. To make real emotional and spiritual contact with someone takes a lot of courage. But if you do meditation regularly, you'll have that courage.

Your friend,
Jeff

Jeff—

I tried all that. It didn't work!

I tried really hard. I treated her so well. I was totally honest about my feelings. And then she comes back and treats me like total garbage. I was like, "What the—Whoa!!" It sort of makes you question . . . should I be nice to the next person I go out with?

Patrick

A RETURN TO INNOCENCE   259

FREEDOM'S PRICE

Dear Patrick,

I know. Kindness doesn't always work in a world dominated by greed, ill-will, and ignorance. That's why the question you raise—"Should I be nice to the next person I go out with?"—is one that requires the deepest kind of honesty and soul-searching to answer. Indeed, it's one of the profoundest questions that arise when trying to decide how to deal with one of the great challenges we all face—finding a mate.

There's a line from an old French movie called *The Rules of the Game* that puts the profundity of your question into context. It's my favorite line in the history of cinema. Roughly translated it says this: "The thing that makes life so cruel is that everyone has such good reasons."

I guarantee you this: if you were ever able to find out why, from her own perspective, based on her own deep hopes, fears, and beliefs, your ex-girlfriend acted the way she did—you would have to acknowledge that from *her* perspective they were "good" reasons, meaning powerful in the context of her life experience. That doesn't mean the way she acted (her karma) wasn't cruel *(dosa)* and unwise *(moha)*—but it does mean her reasons for acting that way were very real and compelling to *her.* That's why the line is my favorite line from the movies—because it's SO TRUE! But when you've seen the truth of it, one big question remains—What are *you* going to *do* about it??

Well, one thing that's obviously occurred to you is that you could start being cruel and manipulative yourself—and not just to her, but to all women you're physically attracted to. After all, being physically attracted makes you vulnerable—you could get rejected! You could get hurt! (That's Māra's Sixth Army, Cowardice and Fearfulness, talking.)

And then things just go on from there: Why not fight

fire with fire? It's easy enough to justify. And what's more, a lot of the time it'll help you get what most men are supposed to want.

Well, Patrick, consider this: *That* very thought and feeling IS Māra's First Army attacking you, whispering, "*Psst*—try *this. Dosa* will get you more *kāma* with less pain." That's one of the worst traps Māra and his allies can set for you, and I'm happy that you saw it in time—you didn't fall right in. You just made a note of the very strong temptation to do so. Just the fact that you stopped to ask, "Should I be nice to the next person I go out with?" shows that you have already begun to acquire the skill of applying mindfulness and wise attention in challenging situations. The answer to your question will depend on how skillfully you apply them to another question: "What's my goal?"

If it is to make real, moving, and possibly even lasting, emotional contact with another human being, and to contribute to the beauty and purity of our ethosphere, then the answer is yes. By all means, you should be nice to the next person you go out with. If it doesn't work—that is, doesn't get you the girl—it's no reflection on you. It simply means that girl isn't ready for a real relationship, undoubtedly for her own reasons—reasons you'll probably never know. Being ready for a real relationship is no small thing. The kindness and emotional honesty that are required present a challenge that only true heroines and heroes have the courage for. This is what truly separates the women from the girls and the men from the boys. A girl brave-hearted enough to respond may take a long time to find—time during which you may be lonely. Meanwhile, in the process of searching, and meeting a variety of people, you'll be working on your own ability to bring out the best in the ones you meet. How? Through mindfulness and the Four Sublime Modes of Living: Kindness, Compassion, Joy in others' well-being, and Equanimity.

But if what you're going after is sensual and ego gratification—the goals of the animal brain—then the answer, Māra's answer, is no. Don't be nice. Māra will tell you—and he's right—that acting in a cold, unemotional, and calculating manner is a more effective way to get girls—that is, to get access to their bodies and power over their feelings.

What Māra will never tell you is the price—because when the bill comes due, *he's* in control.

If you've ever watched animals mating, Patrick—another way the Discovery Channel has edified us all—you know that there's a very primitive, but natural, erotic charge involved with cruelty. If you harness your human ingenuity to the biological drives fueling sexual dominance and submission, there's no question that, as a young male, you will have more sexual "success"—defined the way biologists watching monkeys in the jungle would define it. In fact, that sort of sexual success requires behavior of just that type from you—except you wear stylish clothes and cologne when you do it.

But the emotional effects of acting like that are devastating and deadly—because you'll have to harden your heart if you're going to be the one doing the hurting. And that kills feelings (remember Māra's name in English, "Killer"). Among the murdered feelings are the ones in your genitals associated with the profound intimacy of wholesome sexual arousal. There's a significant body of psychiatric research showing that fear of such intimacy, and the emotional vulnerability that accompanies it, is the reason why people perform sado-masochistic and other sexual perversions involving cruelty, dominance, and submission to get sexually aroused. These kinds of pathetic and destructive behaviors, which get passed off in some circles as trendy transgression—a daring exploration of the edge—are in reality a product of sheer cowardice and terror in the face of real intimacy. They represent an abject surrender to Māra's Sixth Army!

And then what are you? Something any zookeeper would tell you belongs locked up in a cage. (A turn-on, sadly, for many perverts.)

It is for these kinds of reasons that Gotama called *hiri* and *ottappa* the Guardians of the World. Disgust and dread at the wrongdoing you would commit by acting like an animal obviously helps to protect all women—but they help protect you as well. Specifically, they protect your capacity to fully experience the emotional intimacy of loving and being loved. For in truth that's a capacity quite vulnerable to dam-

Something that belongs locked up in a cage

age and even, God forbid, destruction. Because it requires a clear mind, unsoiled by gnawing feelings of mistrust and unworthiness.

Just reflect for a moment: How capable of love and real intimacy would you feel if you sold your Innocence—your birthright to trust and worthiness—for the crude commodities of sex and raw power?

What good is getting the girl, or "getting your rocks off," if in the process you've lost your own soul?

Māra's (like Satan's) biggest lie, of course, is that you can do what you know is wrong and get away with it—that there *is* no price. You can almost hear his soothing whisper in your ear right now: "Hey. It's OK—you had your reasons. . . ." It is a lie so seductive to the animal soul that many late twentieth-century Americans continue fervently to believe it, despite the devastating evidence of the casualties around them and even of their own obvious misery. (The latest version of this Big Lie is the poisonous notion that everyone is entitled to self-esteem, regardless of merit. I read about a 'zine for young heroin addicts, *Junkphood,* published in Santa Cruz, California, that actually promotes "junkie pride"—a vicious lie if there ever was one. The 'zine may not be around long, though; at least one of its founders has already died of an overdose.)

Ever since Nietzsche declared that "God is dead" and science gave humans so much power over the material world that they started to think, "Who needs Him?", the Judeo-Christian version of *ottappa*—the fear of God's judgment and of going to Hell—has been increasingly dismissed by the "cultural elite" as an outgrown superstition. The prevailing attitude, and not just among teenagers, has become, "Hey, nobody's watching! There's no parent around to punish us. Let's party!"

Not so fast, said that great scientist of the soul, Gotama Buddha. He demonstrated that whether you believe God is watching or not, the moral laws of this universe continue to operate flawlessly and without exception—i. e., He *is* watching! And Gotama called the greatest of those moral laws, in Pāli, *Kammassako'mhi*.

Kamma, of course, is karma—your actions, what you willfully do. *Sako* means "one's own" or "ownership." And *amhi* (or *'mhi)* means "I am." "I am the owner of this karma. These actions, I own." This is the fifth of those five things, if you

He is *watching!*

remember, that the Buddha said every person should think of every day. (The first four were: "I will grow old; I will get sick; I will die; everything I like is going to change and become separated from me. I can't get around this; it is the nature of things, and the nature of me.")

The fifth goes on: "I am the heir of these actions." At every moment I am leaving a legacy to myself, bitter or sweet. "These actions are my womb"—my actions created me in the past and will create me in the future. Or, as we can now put it, "My actions shape my brain; my brain shapes my life." "I am inextricably bound to these actions." I cannot walk away from these actions. By making them, I make my own fate. "These actions are my only refuge." If I fear and avoid evil, I need fear nothing else. "Whatever actions I will do—good, or bad—of that I will be the heir."

Does this sound strangely familiar? It could be because Saint Paul said the same thing to the Galatians, just as beautifully: "Be not deceived; God is not mocked; For whatever you may sow, that you will also reap." That is God's law. And there is no escaping it, because it is within you as a Universal Law. Saint Paul's phrasing in this line I absolutely love: "Be not deceived"—don't kid yourself—"God is not mocked." Don't even think for a moment that Hell doesn't exist. To do so is to "dis" God Himself!! Be prepared to pay the consequences!

The sixteen-year-old girl who gave birth to her baby in a bathroom stall at the prom and then killed him; the fifteen-year-old boy who had sex with a man he met on the Internet and then raped and strangled a boy of eleven; the young boys across the country who brought arsenals to school and gunned down their classmates—*they're* in Hell right now, right here on earth. And can you imagine the suffering that still awaits them when they come to face the ripening consequences of their evil acts? Every time you start down the roads of greed, hatred, and ignorance, remember, Hell is your ultimate destination! That awareness itself brings the jolt of wisdom it takes to get off such deadly roads and stay off them.

So the answer to your question, Patrick, is yes, you should try hard to be good to the next person you date. (Of course, choose her wisely!) The reason is not simply a matter of being a nice guy. And it's not a tactic to try to catch more flies with honey. There's much more at stake than that. The reason is to keep your Spirit Free—Free to Live and Free to Love.

Your friend,
Jeff

As ye sow, so shall ye reap.

A RETURN TO INNOCENCE

Dear Jeff,

You say that the Law of Karma is that your actions stay with you, they're the one thing you really own, that you can't get rid of. What if you make a really bad mistake? Does that stay with you for the rest of your life?

This may seem like a small example, but there have been instances where somebody has confronted me that I really hurt their feelings, and it made me feel really badly. And I didn't know how to make it up to them or how I could make it better or ease it a little bit.

Patrick

KARMA AND REDEMPTION

*"The fault, dear Brutus, is not in our stars,
but in ourselves . . . "*

—Shakespeare

Dear Patrick,

One of the joys of introducing you to the Buddha's great teaching on the threshold of your adult life is that you *haven't* made the really big mistakes yet! Encountering this wisdom *now,* at the start of your solo journey, gives you a priceless opportunity to program your own brain to follow the right road, and avoid spending many years wandering lost down the wrong ones.

That's not to say you won't make mistakes. Māra has so much seductive power in this world and in our animal brains that you are bound to fall into his clutches from time to time. (It helps to recall that even Gotama himself had to struggle long and hard to get Free!) But by keeping in mind the wisdom of Buddha, Christ, and Moses, you'll be assured of escaping before the damage becomes major.

Studying the teachings of these Great Spirits prepares your mind so that you can use your own mistakes as concrete examples to learn from. At first, you may come to your senses only after damage has already been done, but then be able to look back on things with a new understanding that helps temper your chagrin. In this way mistakes themselves become brilliant illustrations of the truth of the teaching. They allow you to see and feel for yourself what happens when your actions are contaminated by the Roots of Evil— greed, ill-will, ignorance.

With practice making mental notes, though, something much better, and incredibly inspirational, starts happening: mindfulness awakens and catches you right in the act of making a mistake! Your Impartial Spectator immediately starts to guide you, enabling you to put on the brakes, change direction, and start acting instead with a clear mind and the pure motives of the Roots of Good—generosity, kindness, and wisdom. (This you can count on, because mindfulness always brings Good Roots with it.) In this way unwholesome actions, and their painful consequences, are nipped in the bud! Lessons like these are intensely vivid and deeply convincing, for they bring True Insight *(Vipassanā* in Pāli).

But, you ask, what about the legacy of your mistakes—the painful feelings which are the bitter fruit of past unwholesome karma? One way to apply Insight *(Vipassanā)* to those feelings is to use them as an occasion to reaffirm one of Gotama Buddha's core teachings: "All beings are owners of their karma (action). . . . Whatever action they do, good or bad, of that they are the heir." The very pain and regret you feel at having caused someone else pain is, in itself, faith-affirming proof that God's Universe is just and that we are given the moral senses to perceive it truthfully. And it is a wake-up call to act mindfully from now on.

What, then, would I say to someone your age who, completely unprotected from the assaults and entrapments of this culture, had already made seriously harmful mistakes—gotten addicted to drugs, used or been used by others sexually, committed a crime, conceived an illegitimate child? To someone in that sad position the great Law of *Kammassako'mhi* (I am the owner of my karma) might seem harsh and unforgiving. Indeed, the suffering such young people have already undergone confirms the truth of that Law. Reality, Gotama taught, is just. But is it punitive? Does the harm you do when you're in a state of greed, ill-will, and ignorance—what Christians call a state of sin—inevitably sentence you to a living Hell?

The New Testament teaches that if you allow Jesus Christ into your heart, at that very moment He will lift the burden of past sin and error from you, and you can start afresh, with new understanding and strength to avoid sin. Christianity's promise that *in this very moment* you can find redemption—by opening your own mind and heart—was a revolutionary change from the iron Law and seemingly harsh justice of the Old Testament Jehovah. It's quite fascinating to realize that Gotama Buddha brought a somewhat similar revolution to the fixed and ritualistic Hindu concept of karma—though there are significant differences.

Gotama (teaching five hundred years before Jesus) was stern and clear in his insistence that no force in the cosmos could separate you from the karma you create when you willfully act ("All beings are bound up with their karma"), or from the results of your actions ("There is no place found in the world where one may escape from the results of evil deeds"). And yet—to this extent like Jesus—Gotama also emphasized the tremendous importance of faith, and the ever-present potential to redeem yourself *this very moment* by the wholesome exercise of free choice.

While you never entirely uproot the seeds you have already planted by your actions, Gotama taught, you definitely can affect *how*, and even *whether*, they will grow and ripen. And you can do this *right now* by the way you maintain and care for the soil they grow in—your mind. Unlike Jesus, Gotama said he couldn't weed your spiritual garden for you. But he taught that just as he had used Mindfulness to purify himself, all beings could purify their own minds in that way, too.

Committing greedy, cruel, and stupid actions, Gotama said, is just like planting bad seeds: in the natural course of things you're going to harvest the fruit, which is suffering. But to grow to their full size and bitterness, bad seeds need *dirt*. And that dirt is an unwholesome state of mind, with the Three Roots of Evil squirming around like maggots in it. If your mind is a mess, not only will it create a perfect environment for your past mistakes to ripen into nasty consequences, you'll also be laying the groundwork for lots of new problems by sowing *more* rotten seeds. I'm sure you've watched people dig themselves deeper and deeper into a black hole in exactly this way.

A lack of remorse, due to stubborn hypocritical denial (Māra's Eighth Army!) or poor insight into the harm you've done, is certainly one kind of unclean mind. But—this may surprise you—Gotama said that *too much* remorse is another! He recommended a Middle Path not only for the body, but for the mind—avoiding the extremes of self-indulgence and lacerating penitence. Self-hatred, beating up on yourself for your innumerable human flaws, is nothing other than *dosa*—ill-will toward yourself. Like all ill-will, it is an unwholesome state of mind in which more bad things just grow and flourish. (Think of all the dieters and alcoholics who hate themselves so much for a slip that they go on a binge!) So when you've made mistakes—and you will—just look, and see how they sprang from greed, ill-will, and ignorance. And then get to work making your mind the kind of clean place where bad things don't like to grow. In this way you can surely lessen and perhaps even avoid (by attaining Nirvāna!) the sentence imposed by your own past misdeeds.

But how do you do it? Well, the essence of Gotama's whole teaching can be boiled down to one simple sentence.

"Mindfulness," he said, "is ALWAYS good."

Like a Jewish mother with her chicken soup, the Buddha prescribed mindfulness as the best medicine for everything that ails you: "Mindfulness, I declare, is *always* helpful." This is Gotama's message of Freedom. Why? Because in a moment when you are mindful, bad things cannot gain any foothold: the Evil Roots simply cannot arise in your mind. Look sharp, and you can see this for yourself: when you really observe your own anger, for example, with the eye of your Impartial Spectator, the anger deflates and shrivels. Since mindfulness is a mental state free of the Roots of Evil, it provides no nutrients to help the Seeds of Past Wrongdoing grow. The moment mindfulness drops away, however—whoosh! Those bad seeds can sprout like supercharged weeds.

Of course, when you give the Roots of Good—generosity, loving kindness, and wisdom—the rich, fertile soil of mindfulness to flourish in, they can bloom into a Garden of Delight! No weeds sprouting there, that's for sure. Here's a nice Spiritual Gardening tip—the ultimate weed-killer? WISDOM! Apply enough of it and . . . no more weeds. What's that pure Garden called? Nirvāna—and Gotama guaranteed that "just" seven days of (continuous) mindfulness would ensure the attainment of it.

But before you think that sounds easy, remember how nearly impossible it was in your meditation exercise to stay mindful for more than a few *seconds!* Now does Gotama's guarantee sound a lot more challenging? Here's one reason why the challenge is so great: the human mind moves so lightning fast that you can slip in and out of mindfulness *many* times in the space of *one* second! In particular, the moment you feel pleased and impressed with your own mindfulness—when you say to yourself, like Little Jack Horner, "What a mindful boy am I!"— you're already out of it, and Māra's got his foot in the door (via his Tenth Army, the sin of Pride). Oh, sure, that's not the worst kind of greed in the world. Far from it! But it's greed nonetheless. Do you *see* it as such? Bingo!—you're mindful again!

No, Patrick, mindfulness is anything but easy—though, like everything, it gets easier with determined repetition. No doubt that's partly because it makes your brain work better— as well as your heart, lungs, liver, kidneys, and guts! (There are numerous well-documented reports of people recovering from serious illnesses with the help of mindfulness.) Indeed, as your body and mind grow healthier and work better through the regular exercise of mindfulness, you'll find that *everything* you do gets easier.

But since mindfulness is hard work, and Māra is so intent on sabotaging it, the Buddha knew that if the state of the world depended solely on humans always being mindful, we'd be damned to eternal Hell on Earth indeed. So this great physician gave out other prescriptions for a healthy mind and a healthy world that are somewhat more elementary to follow—because they're instructions as simple, clear, and strong as (and in fact almost the same as) the Ten Commandments. These instructions—such as the precepts not to kill, steal, get high, or have transgressive sex, and not to engage in false, malicious, harsh, or frivolous talk—are guaranteed to work synergistically with mindfulness. That is, following them will help you to be mindful, and when you are mindful, you cannot help but follow them—which is highly conducive to *staying* mindful. As the ancient texts explain it, if you keep your bodily actions and your speech clean, your thoughts will tend to follow.

What's more, the discipline of acting and speaking kindly and wisely—even when your inner world still boils with fantasy, anger, and craving—will not only help you cool down your inner world, it also helps create an *outer* world less ravaged by conflict and suffering, less amped with bad excitement, and therefore less apt to inflame the animal brain. As I wrote to you many months ago, the state of the world depends on the state of your mind—but the reverse is also true. For maximum effectiveness, the Buddha's method intervenes in both, working simultaneously from the inside out and from the outside in.

The commandments and precepts are profoundly eloquent in their approach to telling us what *not* to do. And of course the Third and Fourth Commandments remind us to Keep the Sabbath and Honor our Parents. Gotama also spoke about things that are *good* to do, and the next time I write—perhaps my last long letter to you for a while—I'll share those "accustomed, ceremonious" instructions with you.

Your friend,
Jeff

A BLESSING FOR THE JOURNEY

Dear Patrick,

One of the loveliest and most complete prescriptions Gotama left us, one that spells out in brief and pithy words what it is good to do as well as to avoid, is the road map and traveler's blessing I want to leave you with. It's called the *Mahā Mangala Sutta,* or "Great Blessings Discourse."

First, a quick note on that word *"Mangala."* As we have already noted, it translates as "something that brings good fortune." Traditionally, that could be the performance of a charitable act, a religious ceremony, or a rite of passage (like coming-of-age ceremonies, weddings, and funerals). But, on the more mundane level it could also be a superstitious charm, omen, or ritual, things like a lucky rabbit's foot, an astrological transit, or throwing a pinch of spilled salt over your left shoulder. The Buddha's time—rather like our own, with its 1–800-Psychics and *TV Guide* horoscopes—was obsessed with these magical ways of divining and influencing fate. But there was much disagreement about which *Mangala* worked best, so it came to pass that the Buddha, who was reputed to be very wise, was asked to settle the issue.

"Glorious one," he was respectfully addressed: Could you please expound upon the best things to do to insure "Supreme Good Fortune for Humans and Celestial Beings?" Most likely, what was expected was an answer like, "Make an offering to the elephant-headed god Ganesh at the new moon, and don't wear green under the sign of the Rat." But do you know what was the first thing the Buddha said?

"Don't associate with fools."

Gotama, in other words, instantly made it clear that mere rituals and superstitions are not the key to life's highest blessings. Instead he gave this advice: You want to have a good life? Don't do stupid things. Reflect on this every day:

Don't associate with fools.

Kammassako'mhi. Your fate is in your own hands; it has nothing to do with luck or magic. It has everything to do with refraining from harm and doing what's right. Anyone who tells you differently is a fool, and if you hang out with fools, they'll talk you into bringing yourself bad fortune.

True. Honest. Direct. The essence of Gotama.

Of course, Gotama knew that a big part of every human being is a social primate, with a large component of "monkey see, monkey do." Until you're quite advanced in mindfulness, it's almost impossible not to be influenced by the company you keep. Fortunately, you can turn this to your advantage. And so Gotama immediately stated as the second of life's great blessings and good-fortune-bringers, *"Associate with the wise."*

That means hanging out with true friends, people who are in tune with your inner friend, who know that they are making their own fate and so try to act kindly, speak graciously, and live thoughtfully. It also means seeking out wise people as teachers—not just people with a lot of book knowledge and big ideas, but people whose way of living you admire, who can *show* you, not just tell you, how it's done. (A good example would be your friend Hal, the retired Bell

Associate with the wise.

Labs engineer who taught you how to build model boats. The patience and concentration *he* modeled for you are still very much with you.) Gotama urges you to hear and discuss his teaching at appropriate times—especially when you're most in need of it and most receptive to it. And it's always inspiring to see holy people, those courageous "martial artists" who have dedicated their whole lives to the fight for Innocence.

"Honor those who deserve to be honored" is the third great blessing Gotama named. He considered it so important that he elaborated on it later in the *Sutta* in another blessing: "Reverence, humility, . . . grateful bearing—this too is Supreme Good Fortune." When you meet people in any walk of life who have worked hard and attained self-mastery, wisdom, and skill, it's important to respond with respect and gratitude, and—another of Gotama's Great Blessings—to accept their constructive criticism with good grace. Respect for true merit is an antidote against both Envy and cheap and easy Pride. The Pāli word for humility literally means "not-wind"; Māra's flattery falsely puffs up your self-esteem, so that you slack off on your efforts at self-improvement, but respect for others' attainments deflates your vanity and spurs you to try harder. We desperately need this blessing in our democracy, where the idea that everyone is already as good as everyone else has metastasized into a noxious excuse for mediocrity—or worse.

"One's self well-directed" is a Great Blessing Gotama names in the very next stanza, summing up in four words everything I have been saying to you in these letters. Gotama means precisely being the driver, and an alert, cool-headed, and skillful one at that. Later in the *Sutta,* he counts as separate blessings some of the specific skills you've been working on: the moral reflexes to swerve quickly away from evil, vigilance, discipline, wise attention to the road, avoidance of wrong turns, energetic restraint of the animal brain.

Much of the *Mahā Mangala Sutta* is a commonsense road map to a fulfilling, decent life. "Treasure and take good care of your whole family—parents, wife, children, and relatives," Gotama counsels. (His advice on the loving care of a wife goes for a girlfriend, too, and only a fool would laugh at it: cherish her, don't look down on her, be faithful to her, give her authority in her own domain of work—and give her romantic presents!!) He says it's a great blessing to apply yourself, get a good education, and become skilled, well-trained, and disciplined in all things you do, both with your hands and with your brain. He cautions you to choose a line of work that doesn't harm living things or embroil you in conflict. He pointedly recommends using pleasant, beneficial speech—for trash talk, or animal talk as the Buddha called it, poisons the ethosphere and inflames the passions of craving, hatred, and pride. And he repeats his warning to "just say

Fare forward, voyager.

no" to all intoxicants. He advises you to cultivate generosity (the antidote to greed), contentment (the antidote to craving), patience (to conquer restlessness), and vigorous effort in the quest for mindfulness and virtue (the antidote to Sloth and Torpor, Māra's Fifth Army).

But Gotama Buddha never loses sight of the journey's destination, shining through and beyond the good things of this life. That goal is Innocence, the place free from harm that we all have the potential to reach. The *Sutta* ends with a stirring vision of arrival:

> *One whose mind is not shaken*
> *when touched by worldly things,*
> *free from sorrow, unpolluted, secure—*
> *this is supreme good fortune.*
>
> *Those who have done these things*
> *are everywhere unconquered,*
> *safe wherever they go.*
> *This is supreme good fortune.*

To be Unconquerable, Safe, and Free—these, the Buddha said, are Life's Highest Blessings. Take these messages into your heart and mind, live them, and you too will go safely and undefeated, my young friend. I'm very sure we'll keep in touch.

Fare forward, voyager. May you be well.

Your friend,
Jeff

GLOSSARY

Bar/Bat Mitzvah (Hebrew) Literally, "Son/Daughter of the Commandments." The traditional Jewish coming-of-age **ceremony**, performed at age thirteen, that marks that a person is now responsible for the results of his or her own actions.

Bare Attention "The clear and single-minded awareness of what actually happens *to* us and *in* us . . . called 'bare,' because it attends just to the bare facts . . . observed, without reacting to them." (Nyanaponika Thera, *The Heart of Buddhist Meditation*)

basal ganglia The brain's habit system; like an automatic transmission or gearbox that enables one to program in and automatically perform habitual actions.

bhikkhu, bhikkhuni (Pāli) A Buddhist monk; a Buddhist nun. Also: any man or woman who strives to develop wholesomeness and abandon unwholesomeness in order to gain liberation and true happiness.

caudate nucleus Automatic transmission or gearbox for the front of the brain; part of the **basal ganglia** (see Figures 1 and 2).

ceremony The act of marking life's great transitions and commitments, and dignifying its biological necessities, with "a formal act or set of acts performed as prescribed by ritual or custom" (American Heritage Dictionary). Also, "a conventional social gesture or act of courtesy."

cingulate gyrus Brain structure linked to the physiological changes and accompanying sensations (pounding heart, churning stomach) associated with fear; a part of the **limbic system** (see Figure 2).

compassion The sincere wish for the relief of others' suffering. One of the **Sublime Modes of Living**.

Confirmation Christian coming-of-age **ceremony**, admitting a baptized young person to full adult membership in the church.

custom "A common tradition or usage so long established that it has the force or validity of [unwritten] law" (American Heritage

Dictionary). Tacitly agreed-upon rules of conduct, with the purpose of promoting harmony and reducing conflict, traditionally based upon spiritual precepts and religious teachings. The related word morality ("The quality of being in accord with standards of right or good conduct") comes from *mores*, Latin for customs.

dosa (Pāli) Ill-will or aversion, one of the **Three Roots of Evil** which keep the minds of beings enslaved in darkness.

dukkha (Pāli) Suffering or unsatisfactoriness, a basic characteristic of existence: the First of Gotama Buddha's **Four Noble Truths**. *Dukkha* arises due to craving.

ecosphere The shared realm of earth, air, and water.

Enlightenment In Buddhist philosophy, the achievement of full and complete wisdom, resulting in liberation from suffering.

Enlightenment Factors Mindfulness, investigation of Truth, energy, joy, tranquility, concentration, and equanimity. Seven qualities of mind that lead to mental purification and **Innocence**.

equanimity Mental balance regarding all things, both agreeable and disagreeable. One of the **Sublime Modes of Living**.

ethosphere The shared realm of attitudes, behavior, and ethics.

Five Precepts The Buddha's basic rules of behavior for living a spiritual life: abstaining from killing, stealing, lying, sexual misconduct, and intoxicants.

five things to meditate on daily (1) I will grow old, (2) I will become ill, (3) I will die, (4) everything I like and cherish will change and become separated from me, (5) *Kammassako'mhi*—"These actions, I own." The Buddha advised all people to reflect on or contemplate these five facts every day. Doing so helps decrease clinging and attachment to one's self and possessions, and helps increase your awareness of the responsibility you have for your own actions.

Four Noble Truths In the first sermon delivered after his **Enlightenment**, the Buddha described the Truths of Suffering, the Cause of the Arising of Suffering, the Cessation of Suffering, and the Path to the Cessation of Suffering. (See *The First Discourse of the Buddha* on the reading list for more details.)

Guardians of the World: *hiri* and *ottappa* (see below).

hiri (Pāli) Appropriate shame, or disgust at wrongdoing. One of the "two bright states" that Gotama Buddha called "Guardians of the World."

hormone (from Greek, "to rouse or set in motion") A chemical substance formed in one part of the body and carried in the blood to another part, where it often has a stimulating effect on cellular activity.

hypothalamus A small region deep inside the brain that serves as the master switch for many of the body's survival drives (see Figure 1).

Impartial Spectator A term coined by the great Scottish Enlightenment philosopher Adam Smith for what he called the "man within"—the part of you that can stand apart and objectively observe your own thoughts, feelings, and actions.

innocence (from Latin *in-*, not, + *nocere*, to harm) Literally, "not harming": a state of mind present in all truly nonharmful actions.

kāma (Pāli and Sanskrit) Sensual desire; eros. The First Army of Māra.

Kammassako'mhi (Pāli) The Law of **Karma**. "These actions, I own."

karma (Sanskrit) What one does; one's actions.

karma-vipāka (Sanskrit) Literally, "the ripening of action," the results of prior actions; pleasant consequences arise from wholesome actions, unpleasant consequences from unwholesome actions.

limbic system A group of brain structures (including the amygdala, orbital cortex, and cingulate gyrus) that process and regulate emotion (see figure 2).

lobha (Pāli and Sanskrit) Greed, one of the **Three Roots of Evil.**

loving-kindness *(mettā* in Pāli) Wishing others to be safe and happy; one of the **Sublime Modes of Living.**

mangala (Pāli and Sanskrit) Something that brings good fortune; a ceremony, a blessing.

Māra (Pāli) Literally, "Killer." (Related to the French *mort* and English "mortal" and "murder.") Master of the sensory world, and the implacable foe of enlightenment and liberation; our false friend and mortal enemy within. The Buddhist equivalent of Satan, he marshaled his **Ten Armies** (see below) to try to prevent the Buddha from attaining **Enlightenment**.

mental notes A simple but powerful technique in which you gently alert yourself with a simple word or two to whatever you're doing or feeling or thinking at the present moment, e.g., "walking, walking" or "hungry, hungry," etc. This process helps you pay **wise attention** to what's actually going on in your mind, and helps prevent the mind from wandering into traps set by **Māra** and his **Ten Armies**.

mindfulness The mental state of being fully present, clear, and undistracted. An alert, attentive state in which the mind can observe whatever it focuses on in detail, without wobbling or drifting away.

mitzvah (Hebrew) Literally, a commandment; a good deed or commendable action that brings good fortune. The performance of Jewish customs and ceremonies are important examples of *mitzvot* (plural).

moha (Pāli and Sanskrit) Ignorance, one of the Three Roots of Evil.

Namuci (Pāli) "Enemy of Freedom" or "Enslaver." One of the names of **Māra**.

obsessive-compulsive disorder (OCD) A brain-related condition, affecting about one person in fifty, in which there are bothersome, repetitive, intrusive thoughts, called obsessions, and urges to do compulsive behaviors like washing and checking.

orbital cortex The underside of the front of the brain; a part of the **limbic system**, which alerts us with the sense that "something is wrong."

ottappa (Pāli) Wholesome dread of the consequences of wrongdoing; one of the "two bright states" which Gotama Buddha called "Guardians of the World."

PET scanner (acronym for Positron Emission Tomography) A medical device that can be used to make images of the brain that show how it uses energy and other aspects of its activity.

pituitary gland The control center for much of the body's hormonal activity (see Figure 1).

prefrontal cortex The front part of the brain's outer surface, or cortex. Considered the most evolutionarily advanced part of the brain, involved in functions like thinking, planning, and imagining (see Figure 1).

Seven Deadly Sins Pride, Envy, Wrath, Sloth, Avarice, Gluttony, and Lust. In the Christian tradition, these are, in the words of Reverend G. Bradford Hall, the "seven basic universal tendencies to sin against oneself, against one's neighbor, and against God. . . . Along with their own gravity, the seven deadly sins are distinguished by their power to generate other sins. They are in essence 'evil states of mind' that tempt us into a variety of evil acts. . . . Also note, these sins are not just confined to the individual, for each deadly sin fuels harmful social phenomena as well." See also their Buddhist equivalent, the **Ten Armies of Māra**.

Sublime Modes of Living The four virtues of **loving-kindness, compassion, sympathetic joy,** and **equanimity.** These four states are called illimitable in Buddhist psychology because they can have as their objects the infinite number of living beings.

sympathetic joy Rejoicing in another's happiness; one of the **Sublime Modes of Living.**

Ten Armies of Māra The ten mental defilements which **Māra** used to try to overcome the Buddha on the night of his **Enlightenment,** and which he still uses all the time to sabotage people's mindfulness and lure them off the path to **Innocence:**

1. Sensual Desire
2. Boredom and Dissatisfaction
3. Hunger and Thirst
4. Craving
5. Sloth and Torpor
6. Cowardice and Fearfulness
7. Excessive Doubt and Uncertainty
8. Hypocrisy and Stubbornness
9. Ill-won Gain, Honor, Renown, and Fame
10. Praising Yourself and Denigrating Others

See also the equivalent in the Western tradition, the **Seven Deadly Sins.**

Ten Commandments Given by God to Moses and the Children of Israel on Mount Sinai, as described in the Book of Exodus, Chapter 20, the Ten Commandments are as follows:

I AM THE LORD THY GOD.

1. Thou shalt have no other gods before me.
2. Thou shalt not take the Name of the Lord thy God in vain.
3. Remember the Sabbath day, to keep it holy.
4. Honor thy father and thy mother . . .
5. Thou shalt not kill.
6. Thou shalt not commit adultery.
7. Thou shalt not steal.
8. Thou shalt not bear false witness against thy neighbor.
9. Thou shalt not covet thy neighbor's house.
10. Thou shalt not covet thy neighbor's wife, nor his manservant, nor his maidservant, nor his cattle, nor anything that is thy neighbor's.

thalamus The brain's switchboard for regulating sensory information (see Figure 1 and 2).

Three Roots of Evil In the Buddha's teaching, **lobha** (greed), **dosa** (ill-will), and **moha** (ignorance). All suffering is caused by actions done when the mind is under the sway of one or more of these three.

Three Roots of Good Generosity, goodwill or benevolence, and wisdom. The opposite of the Roots of Evil, these wholesome roots form the basis for all true happiness.

unwise attention The opposite of **wise attention;** a state of mind that resists seeing the true nature of things. The Buddha taught that unwise attention causes the **Roots of Evil** to intensify in the mind.

Vipassanā (Pāli) Insight, especially as it relates to attaining wisdom; seeing clearly and directly the true nature of reality. The term is also used for the method of meditation to achieve such insight, based on closely observing how all things change and are impermanent. Watching the nature of the breath as it moves in and out was one of the main ways in which the Buddha taught this type of observation.

virtue (from Latin and Sanskrit for "manliness," implying courage and heroism) Moral excellence.

wise attention A state of mind which is open to receiving the Truth. In essence, seeing what's really there, as opposed to what you imagine or wish were there. The Buddha taught that wise attention strengthens the **Enlightenment Factors**, or purifying qualities of mind.

SOURCES AND
FURTHER READING

Many of the best books on Buddhist philosophy and meditation, including several that I quote in this book and recommend below, are published by Wisdom Publications, "a nonprofit publisher . . . dedicated to the publication of fine Dharma books for the benefit of all sentient beings." Wisdom Publications books I list here (as well as a free catalog) can be ordered directly from:

Wisdom Publications
199 Elm Street
Somerville, MA 02144 USA
(617) 776–7416
fax (617) 776–7841
Website: http://www.wisdompubs.org

Another important source of Buddhist (particularly Theravāda) writings you will see mentioned repeatedly in the following list is the nonprofit Buddhist Publication Society in Sri Lanka. "Its publications include accurate annotated translations of the Buddha's discourses, standard reference works, as well as original contemporary expositions of Buddhist thought and practice." While BPS books are often difficult to find in U.S. bookstores, they can be ordered from the BPS's U.S. distributor or you can write directly to BPS:

Buddhist Publication
  Society (BPS)
P.O. Box 61
54, Sangharaja Mawatha
Kandy, Sri Lanka
email: bps@mail.lanka.net

Vipassana Research Publications
  of America
P.O. Box 15926
Seattle, WA 99115-0926
(206) 522-8175

Finally, the nonprofit Pāli Text Society (PTS), founded in England in 1881 "to foster and promote the study of Pāli Texts," is the best source for the study of this ancient language of Buddhism by English-speaking people, and provides English translations of the complete Pāli scriptures and many other Pāli Buddhist texts. For a catalog, contact:

Pāli Text Society
73 Lime Walk
Headington
Oxford OX3 7AD
U.K.

The people at Wisdom Publications can also help you get the publications of BPS and PTS.

For the best introduction to the original teachings of the Buddha:

A. Two textbooks:

The Buddha and His Teachings. By Nārada Mahāthera (2nd revised edition, BPS, 1988). Awesome in its insight and scope, yet quite readable.

Buddhist Dictionary. By Nyanatiloka Mahāthera (4th revised edition, BPS, 1980). Authentic, clear explanations of all key Pāli Buddhist terms. An indispensable aid for all those seriously interested in learning about Buddhist philosophy, by the German-born teacher of Nyanaponika Thera.

B. Scriptural texts:

The Dhammapada, the best-known collection of inspiring statements made by the Buddha, exists in many English translations. Among the best, in my opinion, are:

The Dhammapada/The Buddha's Path of Wisdom. (2nd edition, BPS, 1997.) Translated by Acharya Buddharakkhita, with a very helpful introduction by the American scholar/monk Bhikkhu Bodhi.

The Dhammapada (A Translation). Nārada Mahāthera (2nd edition, State Printing Corp., Sri Lanka, 1977. Available from BPS.) Includes summaries of the ancient stories which explain the context in which the Buddha uttered the verse.

The Word of the Doctrine (Dhammapada). Translated by K. R. Norman (PTS, 1997). A very literal translation of the text by one of the most respected native English-speaking Pāli scholars.

The Rhinoceros Horn and Other Early Buddhist Poems (Sutta Nipāta). Translated by K. R. Norman (PTS, 1985). A collection of poems and sermons by Gotama Buddha, including the texts in which he described his battle with the Ten Armies of Mâra *(Padhāna-Sutta/*Striving) and the complete list of *mangalas (Mahāmangala-Sutta/*Great Good Fortune).

Life's Highest Blessings (The Mahāmangala-Sutta). Translation and Commentary by R. L. Soni (The Wheel Publication No. 254/256, BPS, 1978). The Pāli text, a word-for-word translation, and detailed discussion of the Buddha's sermon on the *mangalas,* or sources of good fortune.

The First Discourse of the Buddha. Translated by the Venerable Dr. Rewata Dhamma (Wisdom Publications, 1997). Two months after his Enlightenment the Buddha gave a discourse presenting the Four Noble Truths, which forms the foundation and essence of all of his teachings. It contains all the necessary information and instruction to become free from suffering and gain insight into the truth of Enlightenment. This is an excellent contemporary translation of and commentary on the Four Noble Truths, including a history of the Buddha's life and background information on Buddhism.

Meditation Instruction and Buddhist Wisdom

Mindfulness in Plain English. By the Venerable Henepola Gunaratana (Wisdom Publications, 1992). The best introduction to mindfulness meditation in English, by a very senior Sri Lankan *bhikkhu* who now teaches meditation in the United States at the Bhavana Society, Rte. 1, Box 218, Highview, West Virginia 26808 (304-856-3241).

In This Very Life: The Liberation Teachings of the Buddha. By Sayadaw U Pandita (Wisdom Publications, 1992). And: *The Four Foundations of Mindfulness.* By the Venerable U Silananda (Wisdom Publications, 1990). Two excellent series of lectures on mindfulness meditation by two great Burmese Buddhist masters and former students of the Venerable Mahāsi Sayadaw.

Thoughts on the Dhamma. By the Venerable Mahāsi Sayadaw (The Wheel Publication No. 298/299/300, Buddhist Publication Society, 1983.) Short selections on the Buddha's teachings from the works of the great Burmese meditation master Mahāsi Sayadaw (1904–1982).

Satipatthāna Vipassanā: Insight through Mindfulness. By the Venerable Mahāsi Sayadaw (The Wheel Publication No 370/371, Buddhist Publication Society, 1990.) A transcription of a lecture on how to do mindfulness meditation by one of the greatest masters of this century. In it he describes in detail his method of making "mental notes" as a path to developing Insight *(Vipassanā).* Of course, he assumes his students are profoundly motivated.

Buddhism and Sex. By M. O'C. Walshe (The Wheel Publication No. 225, BPS, 1986). *A Buddhist View of Abortion.* By Bhikkhu Nyanasobhano. (Bodhi Leaves No. 117, Buddhist Publication Society, 1989.) Two brief essays which are also very good practical summaries of Buddhist ethics, especially as they apply to sexual behavior.

Works of Nyanaponika Thera

The Venerable Nyanaponika Thera (1901–1994) was a major figure in the transmission of the Buddha's teachings to the modern world. Born Jewish (né Siegmund Feniger) near Frankfurt, Germany, in 1936 he left Europe for Sri Lanka, where he was ordained as a monk in the Buddhist tradition. A prolific translator of Pāli texts into both English and German, he cofounded and acted as the spiritual leader of the Buddhist Publication Society (BPS) for almost three decades.

The Power of Mindfulness. An Inquiry into the Scope of Bare Attention and the Principal Sources of its Strength. (The Wheel

Publication No. 121/122, BPS, 1968.) The best introductory essay on the subject: brief, authoritative, easy to understand.

The Roots of Good and Evil: Buddhist Texts Translated from the Pāli, with Comments and Introduction by Nyanaponika Thera. (The Wheel Publication No. 251/253, BPS, 1978.) A wonderful selection of the Buddha's actual words on the Roots of all wholesome and unwholesome karma.

The Heart of Buddhist Meditation. (Samuel Weiser, Inc., 1973.) A classic. The book that awakened the Western world to the power of mindfulness. Still in print in paperback for $11. May be ordered from:

Samuel Weiser, Inc.
Box 612
York Beach, Maine 03910–0612
Toll Free: 800–423–7087

The Vision of Dhamma. Buddhist Writings of Nyanaponika Thera. Edited, with an introduction by Bhikkhu Bodhi, foreword by Erich Fromm. (Samuel Weiser, Inc., 1986.) A collection of essays by the great monk/scholar on a wide range of Buddhist subjects. Includes *The Roots of Good and Evil* and *The Power of Mindfulness.* Unfortunately now out of print, but some copies may still be available from Samuel Weiser at the address above.

SOURCES IN THE WESTERN TRADITION

Poetry and Art

When I was in my early twenties, reading Yeats and Eliot totally opened up the world for me.

The Collected Poems of W. B. Yeats. Edited by Richard J. Finneran (Collier Books, Macmillan Publishing Company, 1983, 1989).
Collected Poems 1909–1962. By T. S. Eliot (Harcourt Brace & World, 1963).

The long set of poems called "Four Quartets" has been a major foundation of my own spiritual development.

William Blake. By Kathleen Raine (Thames and Hudson Ltd., 1970.) A beautiful book of art by the great visionary artist and poet (1757–1827), an important influence on Yeats.

Philosophy

Heraclitus

Ancilla to the Pre-Socratic Philosophers. By Kathleen Freeman (Harvard University Press, 1948, 1983 [paper]). Everything written by Heraclitus that still exists is contained in ten pages of this book (available within twenty-four hours from the on-line bookseller **amazon.com**). For more information on Heraclitus, consult:

The Presocratic Philosophers. By G. S. Kirk and J. E. Raven (Cambridge University Press, 2nd edition, 1988).

Adam Smith (1723–1790)

The Theory of Moral Sentiments. This classic work, which originally was presented as a series of lectures on moral philosophy to the young men of the University of Glasgow, is where the term "Impartial Spectator" was originally coined and explained. The best edition is the Glasgow Edition, edited by D. D. Raphael and A. L. Macfie, available from The Liberty Fund in Indianapolis, IN, at 800–955–8335.

Edmund Burke (1729–1797)

The quote in the frontispiece of this book is from *A Letter to a Member of the National Assembly* (1791) by this Irish statesman, who was one of the greatest British political philosophers. The best introduction to Burke is probably:

Edmund Burke: A Genius Reconsidered. By Russell Kirk (Intercollegiate Studies Institute, revised and updated edition, 1997).

David Hume (1711–1776)

The easiest way to get an introduction to the philosophy of Hume, Adam Smith's best friend and mentor in the Scottish Enlightenment, is to read the article about him in *The Encyclopedia of Philosophy*, edited by Paul Edwards (Macmillan, 1967). A beautiful edition of his essays is available:

Essays, Moral, Political, and Literary. (The Liberty Fund, see above).

Morality

The Moral Sense. By James Q. Wilson (The Free Press, 1993). A very readable demonstration that there really is such a thing as a "moral sense," by one of the most eminent of American social scientists.

The Judeo-Christian Tradition

"The Seven Deadly Sins." By the Rev. G. Bradford Hall. An inspiring sermon explaining the origins and discussing the meaning of the Seven Deadly Sins. On the Web at http://www.stmargarets.org
Lessons in Tanya: The Tanya of Rabbi Shneur Zalman. Elucidated by Rabbi Yosef Wineberg (Kehot Publication Society, 1987; 770 Eastern Parkway, Brooklyn, NY 11213). A classic text of Jewish philosophy.
Wrestling With Angels: What Genesis Teaches Us About Our Spiritual Identity, Sexuality, and Personal Relationships. By Naomi H. Rosenblatt and Joshua Horwitz (Dell, 1995). A lively, accessible guide to the Old Testament Book of Genesis and its relevance for modern life.

History of Science and Religion

Two nuanced, myth-busting accounts of the Galileo story:

"The Galileo Affair." By George Sim Johnston. In pamphlet form: Scepter Press, P.O. Box 1270, Princeton, NJ 08542.

"Galileo Galilei." By John Gerard, transcribed by Carl H. Horst. From the *Catholic Encyclopedia*, copyright © 1913 by the Encyclopedia Press, Inc. Electronic version copyright © 1996 by New Advent, Inc. On the Web at

http://www.knight.org/advent/cathen/06342b.htm

The Brain

Friday's Footprint: How Society Shapes the Human Mind. By Leslie Brothers, M.D. (Oxford University Press, 1997). A very readable and useful explanation of how the brain's basic function is deeply related to everyday social interactions.

Brain Lock: Free Yourself from Obsessive-Compulsive Behavior. By Jeffrey M. Schwartz, M.D., with Beverly Beyette (ReganBooks/HarperCollins, 1996). How to use the Impartial Spectator to work on obsessions and compulsions. Chapter 2 explains the role played by the brain in easy-to-understand terms.

ILLUSTRATIONS

A NOTE ON SOURCES

Sources drawn on more than once for illustrations by William Blake (1757–1827), Gustave Doré (1832–83), and others are listed below. In the following List of Illustrations, these sources will be referred to by the abbreviated titles noted here.

William Blake by K. Raine:
William Blake. By Kathleen Raine. World of Art Series. Thames and Hudson, London, 1970.

The Human Form Divine:
The Human Form Divine. William Blake from the Paul Mellon Collection. Text by Patrick Noon. Yale Center for British Art. Yale University Press, New Haven and London, 1997.

Dante's Inferno/Doré:
Dante's Inferno. Translated by the Reverend Henry Francis Cary, M.A. From the original of Dante Alighieri, and illustrated with the designs of M. Gustave Doré. New edition with critical and explanatory notes, life of Dante, and chronology. Cassell, Petter, Galpin & Co. New York, London and Paris, approx. 1880.

Doré Bible:
The Doré Bible Illustrations. 241 Plates by Gustave Doré, with a new introduction by Millicent Rose. Dover Pictorial Archive Series. Dover Publications, New York, 1974.

Doré Spot Illustrations:
Doré Spot Illustrations. Gustave Doré. A treasury from his masterworks. Selected and arranged by Carol Belanger Grafton. Dover Pictorial Archive Series. Dover Publications, New York, 1987.

Doré Ariosto:
Doré's Illustrations for Ariosto's "Orlando Furioso." A selection of 208 illustrations by Gustave Doré. Dover Pictorial Archive Series. Dover Publications, New York, 1980.

The Illustrator and the Book:
The Illustrator and the Book in England from 1790 to 1914. Gordon N. Ray. The Pierpont Morgan Library in association with Dover Publications, Inc., New York.1976.

LIST OF ILLUSTRATIONS

"The Keepsake for 1828." London: Hurst, Chance & Co., 1827. Steel engraving for an eastern tale. The Pierpont Morgan Library, New York. *The Illustrator and the Book*, p. 41. Reprinted with the permission of The Pierpont Morgan Library/Art Resource, NY.

p. 97 **Like riding a horse—but with millions of "horse"power**
"We to those beasts, that rapid strode along, Drew near." *Canto XII., lines 73, 74. Dante's Inferno/Doré*, facing p. 63

p. 117 **Acting like a "runaway" train**
[Train pileup] *Doré Spot Illustrations* p. 95, middle right

p. 119 **It will require a whole lot of taming from *you*.**
Samson Slaying a Lion, Doré Bible p. 62

p. 147 **The cesspool of a bad brain life**
"Then seizing on his hinder scalp I cried: 'Name thee, or not a hair shall tarry here.'" *Canto XXXII., lines 97, 98. Dante's Inferno/Doré*, facing p. 171

p. 157 **Their passions forge their fetters.**
William Blake. *Jerusalem* (1804–1820). Plate 51: Three figures in flames. *The Human Form Divine*, p. 52. Reprinted from a b/w photograph with the permission of the Yale Center for British Art, Paul Mellon collection.

p. 160 **Figure 1: The location of some key structures of the brain.** Drawing by Will Weston.

p. 164 **Figure 2: The location of three gray matter structures of the brain.** Drawing by Will Weston.

p. 170 **The cosmic battle for your brainpower**
The Destruction of Leviathan, Doré Bible, p. 128

p. 181 **Three Roots of Evil that grow in every untamed human mind**
"And straight the trunk exclaimed, 'Why pluck'st thou me?'" *Canto XIII., line 34. Dante's Inferno/Doré*, facing p. 67

p. 183 **Every kind of negative emotion**
"That sprite of air is Schicchi; in like mood/Of random mischief vents he still his spite." *Canto XXX., lines 33, 34. Dante's Inferno/Doré*, following p. 58

p. 189 **Greed, ill-will and ignorance cannot coexist with mindfulness.**
"Then my guide, his palms/ Expanding on the ground, thence fill'd with earth/ Raised them, and cast it in his ravenous maw." Canto VI., lines 24–26. *Dante's Inferno/Doré*, following p. 30

p. 200 **Where people sit down to meals together**
Simeon Solomon (1840–1905). A Seder. Wood-engraved proof from "Illustrations of Jewish Customs," after Simeon Solomon. The Pierpont Morgan Library, New York. *The Illustrator and the Book* p. 114. Reprinted with the permission of The Pierpont Morgan Library/Art Resource, NY.

p. 208 **How Mara treats his prisoners once he's ensnared them**
"'Lo!' he exclaimed, 'lo! Dis; and lo! the place,/ Where thou hast need to arm thy heart with strength." *Canto XXXIV., lines 20, 21. Dante's Inferno/Doré*, facing p. 179

p. 216 **A multitude of ways to tempt and trick you**
"Scarcely had his feet/ Reach'd to the lowest of the bed beneath,/ When over us the steep they reach'd." *Canto XXIII., lines 52–54. Dante's Inferno/Doré*, facing p. 121

p. 228 **Mara's forces of destruction—his Ten Armies** "Be none of you outrageous." *Canto XXI., line 70. Dante's Inferno/Doré*, facing p. 113

p. 230 **Boredom and Dissatisfaction is an evil state of mind.**
"Tuscan, who visitest/The college of the mourning hypocrites,/Disdain not to

instruct us who thou art." *Canto XXIII., lines 92–94. Dante's Inferno/Doré*, following p. 122

p. 233 **Bloating himself up to as much as 400 pounds**
Dore's Illustrations for Rabelais. A Selection of 252 Illustrations by Gustave Doré. Dover Pictorial Archive Series. Dover Publications, New York, 1978. p. 12

p. 235 **Mara's first — and most seductive—Army**
The Whirlwind of Lovers, Plate 10, *Divine, Comedy*, 1824–7. *William Blake* by K. Raine. Plate 146, p. 199

p. 238 **Sabotage by sleepiness, procrastination and lethargy**
Honoré Daumier (1808–1879). *Paysagistes au Travail* . . . [Aug. 17, 1862]. Landscapists at Work. *Daumier: 120 Great Lithographs*. Edited by Charles F. Ramus. Dover Pictorial Archive Series. Dover Publications, New York, 1978. Plate 103

p. 240 **Canny selectivity and regal reserve**
Bradamante pines for the absent Ruggiero. *Doré Ariosto*, p. 146 bottom

p. 242 **Envy is an animal-brain response.**
"Curst wolf! Thy fury inward on thyself/ Prey, and consume thee!" *Canto VII., lines 8, 9. Dante's Inferno/Doré*, facing p. 35

p. 249 **Back and forth you go with that gnawing anxiety.**
Air: 'On Cloudy Doubts of Reasoning Cares.' *The Gates of Paradise*, 1793. *William Blake* by K. Raine. Plate 43, p. 22

p. 251 **The dark inner recesses of the animal brain**
"The guide, who mark'd/ How I did gaze attentive, thus began: 'Within these ardours are the spirits, each/ Swathed in confining fire." *Canto XXVI., lines 46–49. Dante's Inferno/Doré*, facing p. 137

p. 252 **That tangled thicket fed by the Three Roots of Evil**
"'Haste now,' the foremost cried, 'now haste thee, death.'" *Canto XIII., line 20. Dante's Inferno/Doré*, facing p. 71

p. 258 **Making physical touching an expression of loving kindness**
Angelica and Medoro escape happily to India (30:16). *Doré Ariosto*, p. 95

p. 263 **Something that belongs locked up in a cage**
Proteus ravishes the king's daughter (8:52). *Doré Ariosto*, p. 24

p. 264 **He *is* watching!**
The Lord Answers Job out of the Whirlwind, c. 1799. *William Blake* by K. Raine. Plate 88, p. 121

p. 267 **As ye sow so shall ye reap.**
William Blake. The Poems of Thomas Gray. London, 1797–8. "Elegy Written in a Country Church-Yard." 'Oft did the Harvest to their sickle yield.' *The Human Form Divine*, p. 67. Reprinted from a b/w photograph with the permission of the Yale Center for British Art, Paul Mellon Collection.

p. 276 **Don't associate with fools.**
[Card players] *Doré Spot Illustrations*, p. 107 bottom

p. 277 **Associate with the wise.**
"So I beheld united the bright school/ Of him the monarch of sublimest song,/ That o'er the others like an eagle soars." *Canto IV., lines 89–91. Dante's Inferno/ Doré*, facing p. 20

p. 279 **Fare forward, voyager.**
"By that hidden way/ My guide and I did enter, to return/ To the fair world." *Canto XXXIV., lines 127–129. Dante's Inferno/Doré*. following p. 182